Mr Prescott.

Ferry

Point.

RTMOUTH

Personal regards,
Daniel Brownlow,
Mayor, City of Dartmouth

April 14th 1982

Jacquie Guzette

Noel L. Knockwood (MICMAC)

Sharleen Irvin

W. P. Olivier

Like a Weaver's Shuttle

A HISTORY OF THE HALIFAX-DARTMOUTH FERRIES

Joan M. and Lewis J. Payzant

NIMBUS PUBLISHING

Grateful acknowledgement is made to those who have given
permission for the use of previously copyrighted material in
this book. Every reasonable care has been taken to correctly
acknowledge copyright ownership. The authors and publisher
would welcome information that will enable them to rectify
any errors or omissions in succeeding printings.

ISBN 0-920852-00-9 (Regular Edition)
ISBN 0-920852-01-7 (Presentation binding)

Library of Congress Catalog No. (Application made)

Payzant, Joan M. and Lewis J.

LIKE A WEAVER'S SHUTTLE

Published by:

NIMBUS PUBLISHING LIMITED
P.O. Box 1590,
Halifax, N.S., B3P 2G6

Design: Cam Mustard

Printed and bound in Nova Scotia, Canada.

Contents

Introduction

"Here is the utilitarian ferry boat,
like a weaver's shuttle,
plying incessantly between the shores;
and there, flying across her track,
is the bark canoe of the lonely Indian."

"Thoughts in the Steamboat. November 1850."
Ex Halifax Sun, December 1850

Since you have picked this book up, and opened it to this page, it seems likely that you are interested in one or more of these: history of ships and shipping; technology of transportation; industrial archaeology; the commuter and those who get him to and from his daily work; or the history of the Halifax-Dartmouth Ferries.

All of these topics are lightly woven throughout the pages of this book. Before you put it down now, a bit more about its contents may interest you.

The role of the small harbour ferry has not received much attention by maritime historians. Within the last decade or so, a very large number of works on ships and the sea have been published, presumably in response to a growing public interest in such subjects. However, except for one or two examples, ferries have not appeared.

Even without going back to aboriginal man and his log, it will be remembered that all of the great early civilizations had their beginnings on river deltas, rivers or coastal areas. Major ones were the Egyptians on the Nile, the Sumerians on the confluence of the Tigris and Euphrates rivers, the Grecians on the Greek archipelago and the Romans on the Tiber. Historians, having pointed out the fact that travel on water was easier than across the desert or through forests, did not dwell on man's need just to get to "the other side", but rather spoke only of trade and commerce, or of expeditions of war and conquest.

In this book, we talk about how the need arose to get to "the other side", from the beginnings of a settlement in a North American harbour, centuries later. The story would closely parallel those of other settlements taking place in other harbours or river mouths in North America and elsewhere around the middle of the 18th century.

The parallel includes the development of maritime transportation technology; the progression from oars, sail, several stages of steam and then the internal combustion engine. A final stage is the traumatic effect on the ferries made by the construction of bridges across their harbours.

This is not entirely a parochial history. The names of Samuel Cunard, successors of James Watt and those of ship and engine builders of Scotland, Wales, England and the United States will appear.

We hope that you will get as much pleasure out of your reading of this account as we did in putting it together.

Dartmouth
Nova Scotia
1979

J. M. P. & L. J. P.

I.

The Earliest Ferries

On June 21, 1749, Governor Edward Cornwallis sailed into the harbour known as Chebucto, on the ship **Sphinx**, to establish a British settlement and fortress on the Atlantic coast of Nova Scotia. Other ships arrived soon after, bringing 1,400 settlers in all. Immediately preparations were begun to clear land and to lay out the town of Halifax. Since the new arrivals knew nothing about wood frame construction, at first building materials were brought by ship from Massachusetts. Soon, however, sawmills were constructed to utilize the native trees and by autumn suitable accommodations had been built for many of the soldiers and settlers. Those who still had no shelter stayed on the transports which remained in the harbour for the first winter.

One of the sawmills was built on the opposite side of the harbour, and the lumber produced there was ferried across to Halifax. Indians raided this mill in September and four soldiers were killed and a fifth carried off. The sixth soldier escaped to tell the gruesome story and rangers were sent off in an attempt to retaliate. They caught up with the Indians and killed three of them.

Late in the following summer 353 additional settlers arrived on the ship **Alderney**. Cornwallis wrote to the Board of Trade that "their coming so late distresses me much. But I shall do everything in my Power to make them as easy as possible and useful to the Settlement." What he did was to locate them on the land cleared for the sawmill, and there the village of Dartmouth was laid out in blocks, each block having 16 or 18 lots.

Thus it was that Halifax and Dartmouth had their beginnings on the opposite shores of Halifax Harbour. From the start the two settlements were interdependent—Halifax, the military, economic and political capital of British Nova Scotia; Dartmouth, the supplier of raw materials—lumber, water, agricultural produce, fresh water and, later on, manufactured goods such as rope, grain, beer and sugar. For 200 years Dartmouth remained a small community "where it was possible for most people to walk to work and to find recreation within a short distance of the edge of the town, and the needs of social life within the close knit pattern of the built-up area."

With the construction of the sawmill in 1749, even before the settlement of Dartmouth, there was the need for transportation by water, to get the soldiers and the lumber they produced to the Halifax side. Apparently the owners of small boats occasionally tried to take advantage of this need by charging exorbitant fees for carrying passengers back and forth, and then only at their own convenience.

Before long a delegation of citizens petitioned Governor Cornwallis and Council for a regular ferry service with some effective regulation.

Accordingly, at a Council meeting on February 3, 1752, it was decided that a ferry would be established between Halifax and Dartmouth. Rules were drawn up governing its operation, and one John Connor was given a charter for three years. This was the first sanctioned and regulated ferry service in the harbour.

The regulations required Connor to run the boats from sunrise to sunset through weekdays and with a fare of threepence. If a boat was needed beyond these hours, the fare was to be sixpence. Two boats had to be operated and hand baggage was to be transported free. "A reasonable price" was to be paid for larger goods. If Connor or his employees attempted to charge more than these fares, a passenger so charged had the right to swear an oath before a Justice of the Peace, who would then fine Connor 40 shillings. Twenty of these were to be given to the wronged passenger and 20 to the poor.

On Sundays the boats were permitted to run only twice; once to take Dartmouthians to church services in Halifax and then to bring them back.

The regulations which protected the public from unreasonable fares also protected Connor from competition. Any person attempting to set up a similar ferry service was to be severely dealt with—fined ten shillings for each person carried, or imprisoned for two months.

At the time he was running the ferry, Connor was about 24. He either became disenchanted with this activity or found better opportunites elsewhere, because in December 1752, he applied to the Council for permission to abandon the service. It is recorded that he sailed from Halifax the following February and returned by canoe in April with six Indian scalps. At this time there was a bounty of ten gold guineas for every Indian taken alive or killed and since Connor had a family to support (his wife and children came out to Nova Scotia in the ship **Merry Jacks**) 60 guineas must have been welcome income. Although he appears to have been an active and adventurous man (his wooden leg is thought to have been the result of a sea battle), John Connor died when he was only 29. His tombstone, in St. Paul's cemetery, Halifax, bears the following inscription:

Here lies buried
The body of Mr. John Connor
Who departed this life
December 16, 1757
Aged 29 years

His descendants still live in Nova Scotia. In Dartmouth a short street running from Summit Street to Maynard's Lake bears the name Connor, a reminder of the large tract of land once owned by the family in that area.

The Ferry Charter was transferred in December 1752, to Henry Wynne and William Manthorne on the guarantee of the sum of 30 pounds which was a form of performance bond. Very little is known about these men. The name of William Manthorne appears as owner of Lot 4, Block "B" on the 1750 list of original land grants in Dartmouth.

After little more than two months of operating the ferry, Wynne and Manthorne petitioned that the boats be permitted to cross the harbour at stated times. A resolution was passed accordingly. A schedule was to be posted, and would have appeared somewhat as follows:

1. *Dartmouth, as seen from Halifax, 1759, showing windmill. Drawing by Richard Short.*

2. *Dartmouth shore as sketched in the log book of* HMS Pegasus, *1786. Sketched by the Duke of Clarence (William IV).*

THE TIMES OF CROSSINGS

25th March to 29th September
5 TRIPS: Sunrise
8 a.m.
12 noon
4 p.m.
Sunset

29th September to 25th March
4 TRIPS: Sunrise
10 a.m.
2 p.m.
Sunset

SUNDAYS: Two trips only to accommodate persons attending divine service.

In January 1756, three years after Wynne and Manthorne were granted their charter, a new petitioner, John Rock, addressed the Council at Halifax. Since Wynne and Manthorne's charter had expired and they were no longer running the ferry, he wanted to take it over. He was granted the charter under the same terms as those of his predecessors.

There is no record of where the terminals of this early ferry were, nor of how long John Rock operated it.

By 1766 there were 39 people living in Dartmouth, according to the Census. By 1776 Loyalists began arriving in the harbour in British ships. A number of them settled on the eastern side of the harbour, and farms were established in Cole Harbour, Lawrencetown, Preston and along the Eastern Passage Road.

3. *Halifax Harbour, 1759. Warships of the period and small boat with lugsails (middleground), a likely form of early ferry. Drawing by R. Short.*

When the Nantucket Whaling Company moved from Nantucket to Dartmouth in 1785, many of the original grants of land were assigned to the newcomers. There was some bitterness over this move as Lieutenant-Governor John Wentworth was himself a Loyalist. The Whaling Company was heavily subsidized by the Nova Scotia Legislature but only remained in Dartmouth for seven years. In 1792 it moved on again, this time to Milford Haven in Wales. Some of the Whalers stayed in Dartmouth, and their industry and foresight contributed to the beginnings of progress and development for the little town.

This development was evidenced by the fact that there were soon two ferry charters granted to meet the demands for harbour passage. These ferries were to run from the northern and southern extremities of the settled portion of the Dartmouth shoreline.

5

II.
Upper and Lower Ferries

An early chart of Halifax Harbour, by Thomas Backhouse from an original survey done by James Cook, and published in 1798, was discovered recently in the library of the National Maritime Museum, Greenwich. On the chart are marked landmarks prominent enough to be used as harbour pilotage guides. One of these is "Ferryhouse," believed to be the earliest graphic reference on chart or map to the ferry.

This "Ferryhouse" could be part of the earliest ferry service, but it is more likely the Inn built by James Creighton on his property in the Dartmouth Cove, being part of the Lower Ferry or Creighton's Ferry. Today there is a street named "Old Ferry Road," at the bottom of which Creighton's Ferry was located. This street ends at the waterfront near the southern end of Dartmouth Cove. The land involved was granted to William Clapham, Samuel Blackdon and John Salisbury in 1752, and was, in the 1780s, purchased by James Creighton, who was among the earliest settlers of Halifax.

In 1754, the first road along the Eastern Shore to Cole Harbour, Eastern Passage, Cow Bay and Lawrencetown was begun. It started at a place where troops were landed on the Dartmouth shore to obtain fresh water and timber. Farmers who lived along this road came to the Lower Ferry to take their produce to the Market Slip in Halifax,

having stabled their horses at the Creighton establishment.

A bill introduced in the Legislature in 1785 by Hon. Michael Wallace for the establishment of a "Public Ferry" is thought to be the first mention of the Lower or Creighton's Ferry, which began operation in 1786.

Whereas the Settlement of Lands at Dartmouth, Preston and other places on the Eastern side of the Harbour of Halifax, promises to be of great public Utility, and whereas a Number of Loyalists with their familys and disbanded Soldiers have already taken up their lands there, and are frequently obliged to come to Halifax on necessary Occasions and with vegetables to exchange for other necessaries of life, which their Lands do not as yet furnish them with, and have not the means of paying their ferriage

For remedy whereof, and encouraging the Settlement of the aforesaid Lands—

1st. Be it enacted by the Governor Council and Assembly, That from and after the 1st day of January 1786—His Majesty's Justices in their general or Special Sessions of the peace for the County of Halifax, shall be, and they are hereby authorized and impowered to establish a ferry between Halifax and Dartmouth, and to contract with a fit person or persons to undertake the management of the same.

2nd. Be it also enacted, That such Undertaker shall

6

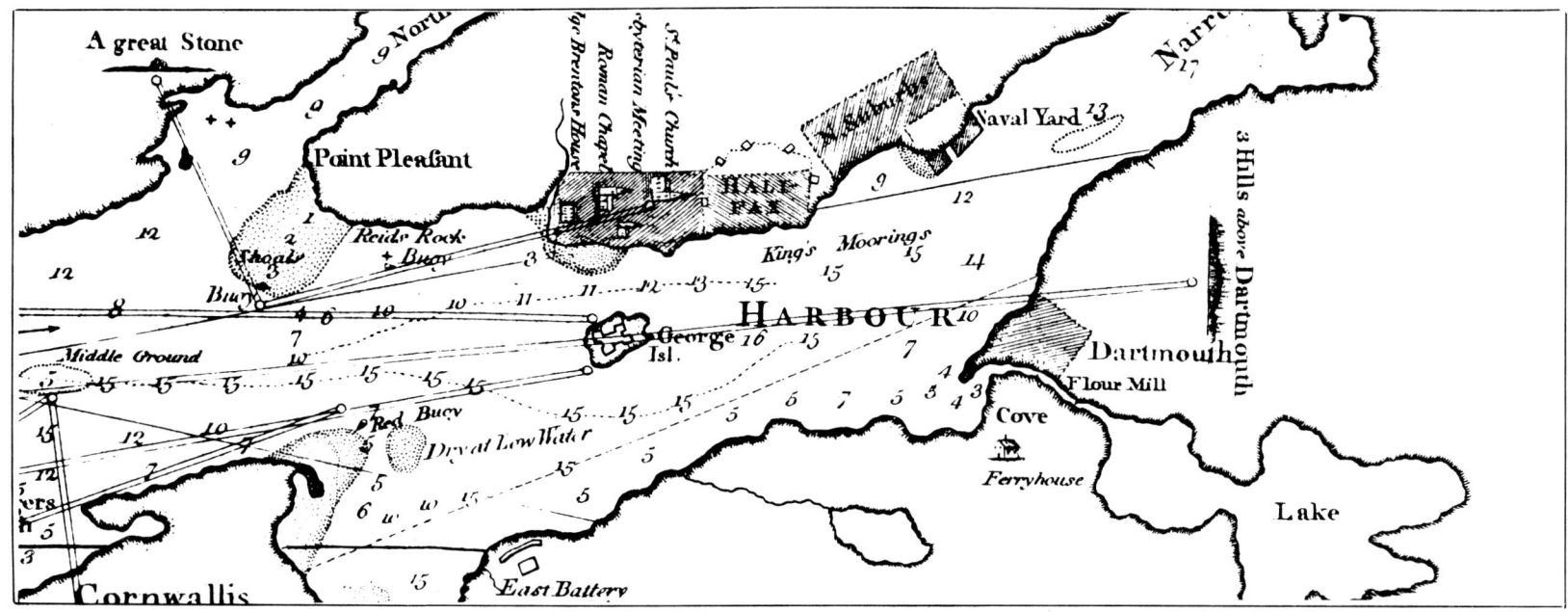

4. Early harbour chart, 1798, showing "Ferryhouse" drawing by Backhouse, after Captain James Cook.

5. James Creighton Jr., 1762-1828, and Creighton's Inn. Inn sketch by Nina Purcell.

6. Skerry's Inn. John Skerry—d. 1838.

provide two or more Staunch and Sufficient Boats capable of carrying 12 persons including the ferrymen and that two carefull able men shall attend each Boat, which Boats shall constantly ply between the Kings Slip in Halifax and Creighton's Wharf or such other convenient place on the Dartmouth side as the Justices of the Sessions may see fit to order at Dartmouth from sunrise to sunset each and every day in the week.

3rdly. Be it further enacted that two days in the week viz Wednesdays and Saturdays the ferry shall be free to all such persons coming or going with Vegetables and provisions to and from the Market, who shall have obtained from the Justices of the Quarter Sessions a Certificate or Certificates that he, she, or they are entitled to such privilege.

And be it further enacted that the expence incurred by this Act for making the ferriage free two days in the Week, shall be paid out of the Public Treasury, and Lieutenant Governor or Commander in Chief of the Province is hereby for an Sum or Sums empowered to grant a Warrant for the same not exceeding Sixty Pounds upon certificate being produced from His Majesty's Justices in Sessions, that the person undertaking has faithfully discharged his Duty as a ferryman.

5. And be it further enacted that this Act shall continue and be in force for One Year and no longer.

An illustration of Creighton's Inn gives an impression of charming surroundings. It was described as the "snug little inn or ferry-house. Behind this building was a verdant hillock, and before it a stream went babbling beneath the old willow trees and flowed into the sea near the ferry wharf." The boats were large and awkward, with heavy oars in thole pins. Lug or square sails were used when the wind was favourable. If the weather was bad the trip might be very lengthy. In such circumstances the passengers might help with the rowing or with the chopping of a path in the ice.

While the Lower Ferry was serving the southern reaches of the Dartmouth side of the harbour, another ferry was operating at the upper or northern end of the Dartmouth shoreline. This was Skerry's Ferry, for which a charter had been granted in 1797. Unlike Creighton's Ferry, which was operated by a succession of lessees, John Skerry owned and operated his own establishment and was very successful. Not only was he an astute businessman, but he was popular and highly regarded by friends and patrons alike.

The Upper Ferry was located at the foot of Ochterloney Street, with an accompanying inn at the corner of Ochterloney Street and Alderney Drive, where the big Queen's Square building stands today. From this location John Skerry operated ferry boats and rafts for over 30 years. His property became the market square of Dartmouth, and he himself grew prosperous enough to be thought of as the banker of the town. In the early years he kept three boats, similar to ships' longboats, plus his rafts or scows for larger loads. Ordinarily, the boats would cross from Skerry's wharf in 30 minutes, and if the wind was favourable, in even shorter time. If the wind was unfavourable it was not uncommon for passengers to find themselves on McNab's Island.

Both Upper and Lower ferries charged fourpence and landed at the Market Slip on the Halifax side. Before leaving either side, the operators would shout, "Over! Over!" and blow a conch shell, similar to those used by farmers to call the field hands to their meals.

At this time sail, oars and sole proprietorship were about to disappear, marking the end of one ferry history period and the beginning of another. Cross-harbour transportation was soon to become big business, owned and operated by groups of businessmen, with whom the profit motive was combined with slight knowledge of advances in technology as applied to maritime transportation. The inception of the steam age and the attendant growing pains highlight the next and longest period of the ferry story.

III.
Hopes
and
Expectations

7. *Judge Charles R. Fairbanks, d. 1841. Secretary of the Halifax Steam Boat Company.*

8. *William Lawson, Jr., 1772-1848. First president of the Bank of Nova Scotia. Painting by Robert Field.*

After World War II, technically oriented minds of the major developed nations became preoccupied with space travel, and what has since become known as the "space race" had its practical beginnings. In similar manner in the early 1800s, steam power, the progenitor of the Industrial Revolution, seized the imaginations of engineers and businessmen, who quickly saw its possibilities in the field of transportation. One of the Halifax businessmen was Samuel Cunard, who later became a world-renowned pioneer of steamboat navigation.

In 1802, Alexander Symington, an engineer in Scotland, supervised the construction of a small vessel named **Charlotte Dundas** for use on the Forth and Clyde Canal. This little ship was steam-powered, and had a single centre-line paddle wheel. Under ordinary conditions she could travel at six miles per hour. Two intensely interested young men inspected her and independently developed steamboats of their own in widely separated parts of the world. The first was Robert Fulton and his **Clermont**, which ran on the Hudson River, New York, in 1807. The other was Henry Bell with his **Comet**, which operated on the River Clyde in 1812.

Just three years later, a group of wealthy and intelligent Halifax men met at the Exchange Coffee House (later to become City Hall) to take the first steps towards the incorporation of the Halifax Steamboat Company. The following names are listed in the minutes of the first meeting of the company in December 1815:

The Hon. Michael Wallace, Chairman
The Chief Justice (Sampson Salter Blowers) by his proxy, Thomas Boggs
John Tremain
Lawrence Hartshorne Jr.
John Albro
Michael Tobin
Charles R. Fairbanks

9

Charles Morris
Thomas Boggs
William Lawson
Frederick Major
Jonathan Tremain

Richard Tremain
Samuel Cunard
Robert Hartshorne
H. H. Cogswell
William Bowie

These men were the elite of Halifax—merchants, lawyers, legislators. At this time the city was governed not by aldermen, but by the powerful magistrates, against whom Joseph Howe was soon to write in his newspaper, "The Novascotian." In the Steamboat Company were three of these Halifax magistrates—Hon. Michael Wallace, Charles Morris and Jonathan Tremain. A fourth, Robert Hartshorne, was a Dartmouth magistrate.

The province of Nova Scotia was governed by a Governor and Council. The Governor recommended appointees to the British Privy Council, and for the most part the recommendations were approved, and the appointments conferred by the King. These men controlled the government, but were not elected representatives, as is our Cabinet today. Hon. Michael Wallace, the treasurer of the province, Chief Justice Blowers and Charles R. Fairbanks were members of the Council.

The House of Assembly, on the other hand, was made up of elected representatives, but this body was not as powerful as the Council. Steamboat Company directors who were also members of the House of Assembly were Charles Morris, William Lawson, Lawrence Hartshorne Jr., John Albro and H. H. Cogswell.

Many of the directors of the Steamboat Company were from Loyalist families, and leaders in the American townships from whence they came. In Halifax and Dartmouth they had become active in community affairs such as the militia, judging agricultural shows, acting as firewards, commissioners of the streets and administering funds for the relief of destitute European immigrants.

For the main part, these men lived in well-built homes in Halifax, near Government House and the centre of the city. A few of their homes still stand today—such as H. H. Cogswell's home, the present Carleton Hotel, built originally for Hon. Richard Bulkeley. Both Michael Tobin

and the Hon. Michael Wallace owned summer homes in the Ellenvale area of Dartmouth. Brookhouse School commemorates the name of Tobin's residence. Wallace and Boggs owned large tracts of land in Dartmouth, but lived in Halifax. Charles Morris had a summer home on Lake Loon. These men would have had close contact with the existing ferry service, and thus would be aware of its limitations.

Jonathan Tremain and Lawrence Hartshorne's father, also Lawrence Hartshorne, owned a large and prosperous gristmill at the inlet to Dartmouth Cove (later to be the starting point of the Shubenacadie Canal). Lawrence Hartshorne Jr. and Thomas Boggs ran a hardware business at the corner of Hollis and Prince streets, close to the harbour. John Albro's business was the Halifax Marine Insurance Company of Water Street. Michael Tobin was in business with his brother at Tobin's Wharf. William Bowie was a merchant in partnership with Stephen W. DeBlois, and they also acted as auctioneers. Jonathan and John Tremain, like other directors owned merchant sailing ships. One of their ships, the **Three Sisters**, became well known in a famous piracy case in 1810. Charles R. Fairbanks, a young law student at the time, reported the story of the trial in a short-lived newspaper called the "Novator." John Tremain's house was further from the centre of the town than most, on the south side of the road leading up from Freshwater Bridge (Inglis Street). Adjoining his house was a rope-making plant, another profitable sideline in the shipping business. Samuel Cunard, although still in his twenties, was well established with his father in the firm, A. Cunard and Son. Like the Tobins, they owned a wharf on the Halifax waterfront.

Obviously, the directors of the Halifax Steamboat Company were a group of men with a vast sum of business knowledge which related to maritime trading as well as local commerce. Aware of the pressures of population growth and the growth of agricultural and commercial activities on the eastern side of the harbour, these men, with high hopes and expectations, set out to improve the ferry service. They looked to the steam engine as a means of achieving this end.

10

IV.
The Team Boat

Considerable correspondence was carried on during 1815 by a committee of the Halifax Steam Boat Company and various builders of steam engines. Richard Tremain travelled to New York to see at first hand ferries operating there and to report back to the other company directors at Halifax. The following letters were written by Tremain and three engine builders:

New York, May 4, 1815
Messrs. Robert Hartshorne
Thomas Boggs &
Others

Gentlemen:

Your letter of the 7 April was handed me on my arrival in this place. I have since continued to make every enquiry & procure what information I could on the subject of them as follows.

I am induced to think our Boat should be sixty feet long—the proper proportion of width is about 10 feet broad each boat, leaving a centre space of ten for the wheel to play and to give room on deck for passengers. They extend about 4 feet over the outside of each boat. Such a one would carry 4 or 6 Horses and Carts at a time and as many passengers as will ever want to cross at a time—say 150 or 200. Whether you use the Steam Engine, or work it by Horses the size of the Boat should be the same. In either case a round House is built in the Centre of the Boat for Steam or for Horses. The probable expence of such a boat will be from two to three thousand Dollars.

I enclose a Copy of a Letter from Robert McQueen & Co. /72 Duane Street /giving the price of a Steam Engine Complete except the Boiler. This he tells me will cost here nearly as much money. If from England he thinks it might be less. This is getting it to Halifax. He will bind himself to send a man to Halifax to put it together and to set the boat a going until he can instruct another person.

The expence of machinery for a Horse Boat will not complete exceed two to three thousand dollars. I am

9. *Ink sketch of team boat*, Sherbrooke.

offered a Set for three thousand but do not think it can be worth two.

I have taken pains to consult with the different persons interested in both Boats. They have each constantly crossing these Ferrys—and I am of opinion that a Boat worked by Horses (or perhaps oxen) would answer every purpose at Halifax. Horse Boats are found to answer well here where the Tide is 4 Knots and upward. Their principal draft seems to be to stem the Tide. The expence of working them is much less here—and would probably be less with us. The first cost is much less. The machinery so simple that if out of order any Millwright or Carpenter could repair them with ease. At Halifax there is little Tide and the Horses would not find the labour hard. The Boat I allude to is an Eight Horse power. They have a larger one crossing to Brooklyn which brought me across in 7 Minutes with Nine Horses. The Steam Boat crosses in about equal time. The Horses walk quick—which turns a large wheel which carries the shaft that has the Fan or paddles. A person can be had to go there, to build either the Boat, or to put the Machinery together—the expence 3 or 4 dollars a day. Mr. Brown who built the Steam Frigate says he thinks his foreman would go, he now pays him 3 doll. a Day but he will require something more. I must refer to my Letter to Mr. Robert Hartshorne for any further information.

> Your Obt. Servant
> Richd. Tremain

The enclosed letter from Robert McQueen & Co. reads:

> Columbian Foundry
> New York, May 3rd 1815

Sir:

In answer to your inquiries this day, we inform you

12

that a Steam Engine capable of driving a Boat of Sixty feet long, should possess the power of about eight Horses. We can make such an Engine for about Four Thousand dollars—exclusive of the Boiler—a workman could be procured who would proceed to Halifax to put up the same in the Boat at about three dollars per day from the time he left this place until his return. The Engine we could finish in about Three months after receiving the order.

Very Respectfully
Your obt. Sevts
Robt McQueen & Co.

Another engine builder writes:

City Foundry
Philadelphia, 25 May 1815

Mr. Tremain
Sir:

I will put you a Steam Engine of 14 Horses Power on board of a Boat at Halifax for the Sum of Six Thousand Dollars you paying the Freight of the Engine, my own passage to and from Halifax. I will run the Engine for Ten Days before I leave her, if you wish me to stay any longer the Charge will be four Dollars per Day. I will undertake to have the Engine ready for Delivery at Philadelphia One Hundred Days after the Contract is made. The Terms of Payment will be as follows:

$1500 When the Contract is made
 1500 Sixty Days after
 1500 When the Engine is Shipped
 1500 Ten Days after the Boat has run
$6000

William Somervile

The lack of descriptive detail of these engines and their boilers and auxiliaries will frustrate the technically minded historian and reader alike. Still, a third engine builder writes:

Wilmington, Del. June 22nd 1815

Sir:

Yours of the 7th inst. has been forwarded to this place, and came to hand yesterday.

I can furnish the Steam engine and machinery for the boat which you describe.

With respect to the building of the boat, I would recommend you to confer personally with Col. Ogden. I have written to him this day on the subject.

The whole of the machinery ready to put up in the boat, exclusive of the boilers, can be furnished for 4000 dollars. The boilers (copper) will cost 3000 dollars. The difference of expense between copper, and wooden boilers would not, perhaps, exceed 1000 dollars—as there must of necessity be a very considerable quantity of copper employed, if wood is substituted as far as is practicable.

I would not, by any means, recommend wooden boilers—as I have in two or three instances, seen the experiment tried, and the result has been unfavorable.

I am now engaged in fitting up a Steam Boat at this place, which will detain me about two weeks. Immediately on my return to Elizabeth town, I can commence the engine for you, which may be ready to ship in about three months.

I am Sir
yours etc
Daniel Dod

It must be assumed that considerable discussion and contemplation of the options took place among the directors during the latter half of 1815. The prices they had received for steam engines coupled with their probable ignorance of the economics of the operation of this mode of propulsion undoubtedly added to the difficulties of their decision-making. Another complication was that their Act, as it stood, only permitted them to operate "Steam Boats."

So, along parallel paths, they took another look at horses, and sought an amendment to their Act.

The following transcription of an unsigned manuscript letter indicates their anxiety and need for further detailed advice:

Sir:

The Committee for the Steam Boat Company are

authorized and requested to address you again on the Subject of a Boat for this Harbour—which they do, in the hope that you will excuse the trouble they are about to give you—and under the impression that no one in that Country is so well qualified and will feel an equal interest in serving them.

The prevailing opinion now seems to be in favor of a Horse Boat which it is Contended will cost less, and be worked at a Cheaper rate than that carried by Steam and less liable to accidents and expensive repairs. The Committee have therefore to request that you will endeavor to learn from impartial persons Competent to judge, which is the best and most approved boats crossing the east river that are worked by an 8 or 9 Horsepower—and that you will have the goodness to obtain every information you can on the subject of Such Boats—more particularly to obtain answers from Competent persons to the several inquiries attached to this.

They have also to beg you will procure from the builder or Owner of such Boat or Boats as are considered most approved a wooden model & Cause it to be put up Carefully in a Case and forwarded to Halifax. They of Course expect that you will pay the person from whom you procure it any reasonable price which must be left to your judgement. Most of the parties interested are so totally ignorant of the nature of Horse Boats that you will oblige them by having the Model as Complete as possible.

For any expences or Cost in procuring the information & model please call on Boggs & Thompson who are authorized to pay you.

It should be accompanied with a written description of the Boat giving the exact dimensions of each part so that the builder if necessary may work by it.
N.B. They have to beg you will inquire and let them know how much fuel the Steam Ferry on the East River consumes between Sunrise and Sunset in summer.
The Harbour of Halifax is about a mile & quarter wide—the tide runs perhaps two miles an hour subject occasionally to considerable swell from the Sea. The parties interested are inclined to think a Boat of about

60 feet long and 24 or 30 ft. Wide will be quite sufficient. The Timber & Ship Carpenters may be had here unless it may be for the Cogs which had better be imported from the United States. With this general information they submit the following questions and request the opinion and answers from some person competent to judge for them—viz.
What will be the expence of Building a Boat for a Ferry to Carry Carriages Cattle & passengers? What the proper dimensions & power? Note the parties interested are under an impression that 8 or 9 Horses will be necessary—but wish to know if a Smaller Boat & with what number of Horses will Answer:
What will the necessary machinery cost for such a Boat as may be recommended Complete?
What number of men will it require to attend such a Boat?
What number of Horses will be required to keep such a Boat running from Sunrise until Sunset?
Can One or more mechanics be had to come to Halifax to build the Boat? & what will their terms be?

Can one or more men be had to come to Halifax to make & put up the Machinery, and what will be their terms?
When can such persons come if required?
Will a Boat built for Horses answer for a Steam Boat, provided the parties may think proper to Change the Works?
How long will such a Boat be going a mile?
Of what wood is it considered best to build the dif. parts of such a Boat?
Would it not be advisable to build with Composition Bolts?

In the above we have confined our enquires to the Horse Boat, we have not however decided whether we shall give a preference to such a Boat or one moved by Steam, and the information we want you to obtain for us is to enable us to make our election. We must therefore request you will give us the best information you can on the following points.

1st What will be the probable cost of a Boat to be driven by Steam 60 feet long & 27 or 30 feet wide—or

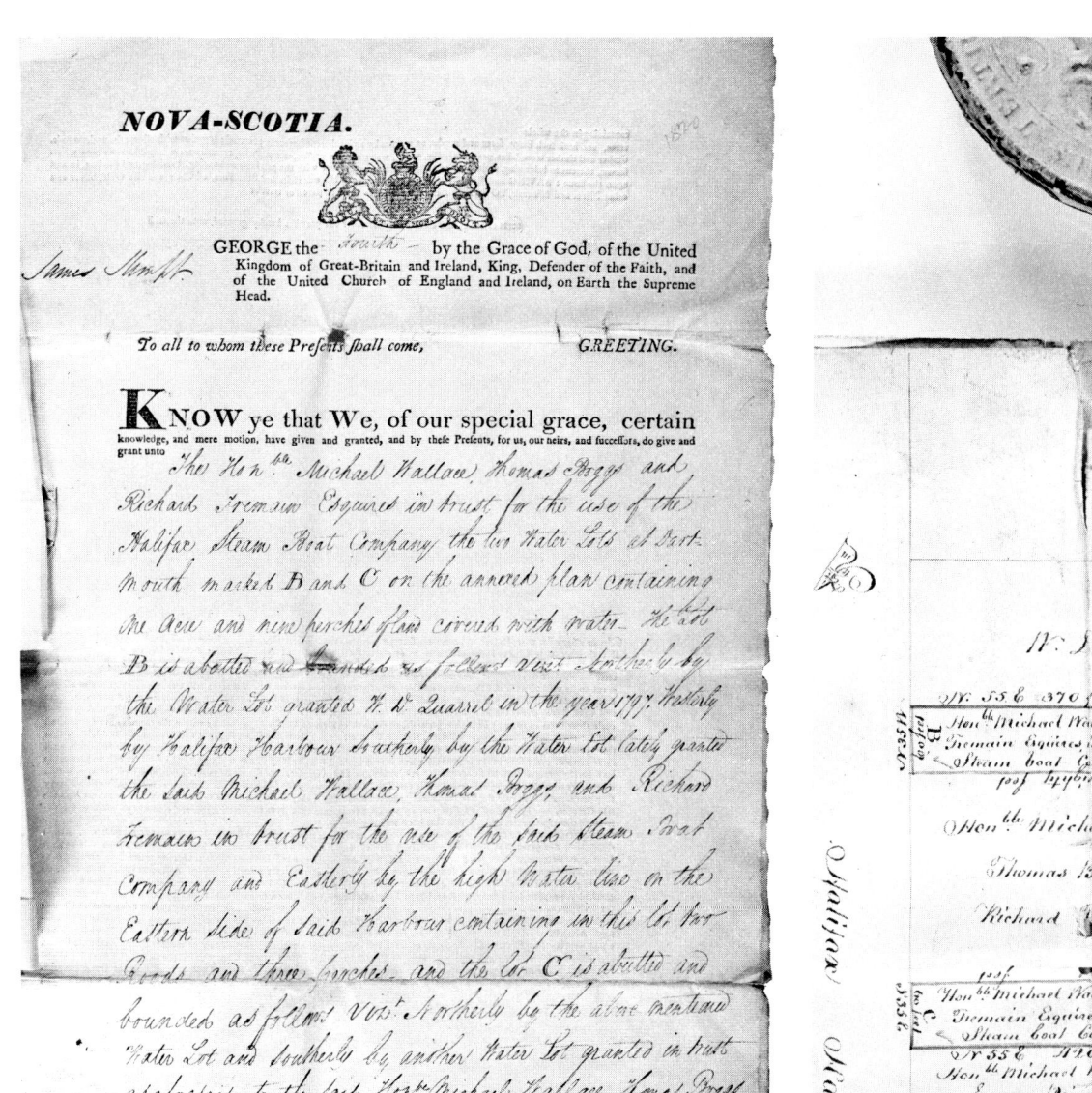

NOVA-SCOTIA.

James Munsft

GEORGE the *fourth* — by the Grace of God, of the United Kingdom of Great-Britain and Ireland, King, Defender of the Faith, and of the United Church of England and Ireland, on Earth the Supreme Head.

To all to whom these Presents shall come, GREETING.

KNOW ye that We, of our special grace, certain knowledge, and mere motion, have given and granted, and by these Presents, for us, our heirs, and successors, do give and grant unto

The Honble Michael Wallace, Thomas Boggs and Richard Tremain Esquires in trust for the use of the Halifax Steam Boat Company the two Water Lots at Dartmouth marked B and C on the annexed plan containing one Acre and nine perches of land covered with water. The Lot B is abutted and bounded as follows vizt. Northerly by the Water Lot granted W. D. Quarrel in the year 1777, Westerly by Halifax Harbour Southerly by the Water Lot lately granted the said Michael Wallace, Thomas Boggs and Richard Tremain in trust for the use of the said Steam Boat Company and Easterly by the high Water line on the Eastern side of said Harbour containing in this Lot two Roods and three perches, and the Lot C is abutted and bounded as follows vizt. Northerly by the above mentioned Water Lot and Southerly by another Water Lot granted in trust as aforesaid to the said Honble Michael Wallace Thomas Boggs and Richard Tremain, Esquires Westerly by Halifax Harbor and Easterly by the high Water line aforesaid containing in

10. *Deed and plan of Halifax Steam Boat Company's waterfront lands in Dartmouth.*

rather we should say, two Boats connected in the usual manner?

2nd What will be the cost of the Steam Engine Copper Boiler, and Machinery Complete, delivered at New York—and at what rate of Hour will such Boat move?

3rd What quantity of fuel will such a Boat consume p. day, either Wood or Coal & which is preferred?

4th How many men will she require to work & constantly attend upon her?

5th Will she be liable to be frequently out of repair and will such repairs be expensive & difficult?

6th Can we obtain in America such information as will enable us to order the Engine Boiler & Machinery, or any part of them from Britain? Shall we be likely to get such as will answer our purpose equally well and what will be the probable cost and quality compared with those made in the United States?

It is in contemplation to Run the Boat from the upperside of Collins & Allisons (late Prescott & Lawsons) Wharf directly across to Dartmouth.

All we have said on the subject of the two Boats may be nearly reduced to this—

That we are desirous of Establishing one of them without delay—and as either will probably be sufficient, at least for some years to come to do all our work, and probably may not be very profitable—we wish to adopt that which shall be deemed best for our purpose & at the same time least expensive to keep up.

As you are well acquainted with our Harbour and must also have good information of the Estimation the two Boats are held in, we must beg you will do us the favour to give us your own opinion, under all circumstances which you think best suited to our purpose.

This communication to Barclay has undertones of anxiety, if not desperation, containing as it does questions already asked and answered earlier. It was likely that the directors were under considerable pressure. Not only did they have their Act with its fixed term of years, but there must have been some clamor from the cross-harbour

travelling public. It is possible also that there was some pressure from those wishing to subscribe in the venture.

Apparently not being willing to await a reply to their letter to Henry Barclay, a further letter to Daniel Dod, a thinly veiled attempt to negotiate price and other details, was written for the directors by Richard Tremain:

Halifax, Dec. 23, 1815
Mr. Daniel Dod

Sir:

Your letter to me of the 22nd June last, has been laid before the Gentlemen who are authorized to procure a Steam Ferry boat for this Harbour—and after considering the different proposals handed in seem disposed to favor yours—they have therefore requested I would write to you again to know if any alteration in price has taken place in the hope that it may be now made Cheaper.

They have also to beg you will let them know what quantity of Fuel such a Boat as described to you (like those that Cross the east River) will Consume between sunrise & Sett.

You were aware that they want a Boat for a Ferry to Carry Passengers Etc. Those on the east River of 60 feet long and two Boats of ten feet wide each with the wheel & works in the centre has been recommended—but if a Smaller boat would answer their purposes, in your opinion and there would be any Material difference in the price have the goodness to write me & sent a model & proposals. If the Machinery is made by you, the Gentlemen will expect that you should give such directions for the Coppers or boilers as will insure their being made to suit the machinery. If they get them at New York they may be made under your own Eye, but if they get them from England it will be necessary to be more particular. What will be the speed of such a Boat—say how many minutes to a Mile. I have understood there was some difference in the Construction of your boilers from those of Mr. Fulton's Boats—What is it?

In haste
Your Obt Servant
Richd Tremain

11. *Sir John Sherbrooke, Lieutenant Governor of Nova Scotia—1811-1816, by Robert Field.*

The directors had still not had a reply to their long letter to Barclay, when they received the following from Dod:

Elizabethtown, N.J. Feb. 17th 1816

Sir:

Yours of Dec. 23d has been recd. An unusual absence from home, must be my apology for not giving you an earlier answer.

No abatement in the price of materials for Steam engines has taken place since the date of my letter to you in June last. On the contrary copper has experienced a trifling rise since that time.

The quantity of pine wood requisite for a Steam Boat of the size proposed (with boilers of my construction) would be about one cord per day. As we have no boats in which coal is used, I am not able to say what quantity of that kind of fuel would be necessary.

It is my opinion that two boats connected together, with the wheel in the centre would be best calculated to answer your purpose. Perhaps 60 feet long, and 10 feet wide each, would be the size most advisable.

If you employ me to make the machinery I would prefer making the boiler also. At the present price of copper I can furnish the boiler at 50 cents per pound. If however, you prefer getting them made in England, I will give the necessary directions respecting the form and dimensions.

There is a difference between my boilers and those used in Mr. Fulton's boats, which I consider very important.

Mr. Fulton's boilers are made in such a manner that it is necessary to fit them in furnaces of mason work—in consequence of which the boat is incumbered with a considerable weight—and part of the fuel is expended in heating the furnace. I have dispensed with the mason work by making the boilers in such a manner that the water they contain surrounds the fire—thereby saving fuel and dispensing with weight.

As I am now under no engagements abroad, your communications hereafter shall receive immediate attention.

Your most obt.

Daniel Dod.

17

Shortly after receiving the letter from Dod, the directors had a reply to their lengthy letter to Henry Barclay:

New York, 28 Feby. 1816
Thos Boggs and Richard Tremain Esqrs.

Gentlemen:

On the 19th Ulto. I received your letter of the 12th Decr. last, requesting me to procure answers to questions proposed, and other general information on the subject of horse and steam ferry boats, and I have now to give the result.

There is not the least doubt but that a horse boat will answer your purpose infinitely better than a Steam boat—both the original expence and the management being very small in the former when compared with the latter. It is believed that horse boats will get into general use for ferries & the steamboats be used for long passages up rivers etc. As the steam engine alone will cost nearly as much as the complete boat for horses.

You cannot require a boat of more than fifty feet long by 35 to 40 feet wide, such a boat in moderate weather will go at least six mile an hour & six or seven horses will be fully sufficient, she will require three men viz. one for the horses, one at the helm & one to assist in getting fast to the dock, one man will be required to attend on each side of the harbour also to make the boat fast when she arrives. Such a boat with all the necessary machinery may be built here for $4500—and there will be no difficulty in making a Steam boat of it at any future period. She will draw 12 to 14 inches water. Besides the expence of the boat however, the necessary docks or floating wharves will be a heavy expence. As your harbour is much infested with worms, composition nails or bolts & a copper bottom will be very advisable. The machinery (here) complete will cost from $800 to $1000. The horses and machinery will occupy a circular space of 25 feet diameter on the deck of the boat, knowing this you can easily calculate the size you will want, if you have any idea how many passengers & carriages may require to cross at any one time. It appears very immaterial of what wood the boats are built, but pine for the decks & large beams which run entirely across both boats & extend beyond their sides, & on which the deck is laid is best, in consequence of the lightness. There will be no difficulty in getting mechanics to go to Halifax to build the boats (if necessary) but that is a very simple business, and all the machinery can be made here of the most approved materials and cheaper than with you.

The expence of sending men to Halifax will depend entirely on the demand for workmen at the time.

Mr. Moses Rogers who brought the horse boats into use has been trying several experiments in a few months past, and has made some great improvements; from him I have obtained most of my information. He engaged some time since to have a complete model made for me with such descriptions as would enable any mechanic to build the boat etc. I called yesterday to inquire how it was getting on, then for the first time he told me he should require remuneration for the use of his inventions for which he is about taking out a patent. I pressed him to fix on a specific sum he would require, but he proposed to furnish every information gratis, the committee to pay for the model & every other expence, to carry the boats into operation, and whenever the income shall exceed 12½ per cent on the capital he to be allowed one half of the excess from that time to the end of 14 years from the present time, when his patent right will expire.

This proposition I think you may safely accede to without much chance of paying him anything.

He is now building a fine boat for the North River with all his recent improvements—and a workman is now engaged in making an exact model, which I am to have for you in case you accede to his proposition, it will cost from $75 to $100—made principally of mahogany; the whole is so simple that the most ignorant mind can at once perceive all its merits.

It is composed of two wall sided boats, with flat bottoms sharp at both ends 10 feet wide by 35 ft. long, these are placed parallel at 10 ft. asunder & a deck laid entirely over them & extending 1, 2 or 3 feet, at pleasure, beyond the sides and bow and stern; in the

18

centre is a wheel with eight paddles, on its axletree are coggs which are operated on by the coggs of a large horizontal wheel above it, to this the horses are harnessed & put the whole in motion—it goes either end foremost, & the wheel is so contrived that it can be made to turn either way without stopping the horses which gives great facility to bringing the boat to the wharf. The wharves are so contrived as always to float on the level with the boats gunnel or deck.

> Very respectfully I am Gentlemen
> Your obedient Servant
> Henry Barclay

It is not known when the directors received this letter from Barclay but it, along with previous correspondence, must have provided them with as much information as was felt needed. The next recorded meeting was August 26, 1816, at which time a resolution was passed to have a horse boat built. A committee was appointed and instructed to send to New York for the services of a master builder and to place an order for suitable horse boat machinery. The committee was also charged with the responsibility of making arrangements for "landing places." Permission was obtained to use the north side of the Market Slip at Halifax, and to build "such erections as necessary." The Dartmouth landing place was to be at the site of the present ferry terminal. Original deeds with plot plans under the Great Seal of Nova Scotia are still intact.

It is incredible that the committee's decision to have this boat built, being made near the end of August, resulted in her launching just over one month later on September 30, 1816.

A contemporary account states:

> Mr. Holland—I have been present at many launches but never witnessed one, take it "all in all," with so much pleasure as that on Monday last. Dartmouth Cove is in itself picturesque, the assemblage of beauty on the shore, the boats plying in the Cove and the novelty of the teamboat, formed a scene worthy of the pencil of the first masters in painting; the public spirit and disinterestedness of the gentlemen who have so promptly come forward—the pen of the poet—that both may be found is the earnest wish of . . .K.I.

Completion of fitting-out and adjustments to machinery appear to have taken at least one month, because she made her first trip to Messrs. Fairbanks' wharf at Halifax on November 8.

The directors may have been conscious of the expectations of the travelling public, in view of the undoubted publicity generated by them for the **Steam** Boat Co. It seems that the new ferry being called the **Team** Boat may have been an early example of clever public relations.

While no reference to her christening at the time of launching can be found, a note on her name may be of interest.

Three months previously, the Lieutenant Governor, Sir John Cope Sherbrooke, had left Halifax to take up the post of Governor General of Canada. Two of the Halifax Steam Boat Company directors had taken prominent parts in a farewell dinner for him. Chief Justice Blowers as chairman, and Hon. Michael Wallace as vice-chairman. Thus when a name was to be picked for the new team boat, **Sherbrooke** seemed to fit. Apparently Sir John approved.

Temporary Dartmouth stabling arrangements were provided by Hartshorne, who offered a building owned by him, "where the spermaceti works had been carried on [the Nantucket Whalers' wharf was on the site of the present Dartmouth Shipyards] for twelve months or until the stables of the association shall be prepared."

An early historian writes, "It required about twenty minutes for this boat to reach Dartmouth from Halifax. It was considered an immense improvement on the old ferry boat arrangement, and the additional accommodation for cattle, carriages and horses was a great boon to the country people as well as to the citizens of Halifax, who heretofore had been compelled to employ Skerry's scow when it was found necessary to carry cattle or carriages from one side of the harbour to the other."

So began the operational history of the Halifax Steam Boat Company.

V.
Early Problems

The **Sherbrooke** began its regular trips on November 8, 1816. However, ice in the harbour or difficulties with the boat itself must have put it out of operation that first winter. "The Royal Gazette" of May 28, 1817, reports that it commenced its operation on the morning of that day—a clear implication that it had been out of service. This was late for ice to be the cause of the trouble, but whatever the cause, the minute book of the Halifax Steamboat Company confirms that the boat would commence employment on May 28.

Earlier, in February, the committee in charge of the boat had been given instructions by the directors to obtain two smaller boats "to ply as Ferry Boats with the Horse Boat." By May, the Halifax Magistrates had ruled that the Steam Boat Company's license was for the Horse Boat only. Then, on May 20, 1817, the shareholders voted to purchase nine horses, and on June 19, three more horses. There is no mention of what had happened to the original set of horses, but it might be assumed that they were sold in order to save the cost of fodder while the boat was out of service. At that same June meeting, a committee was appointed to consider the building of an inn on the Dartmouth side. This was done with great dispatch. An advertisement in the newspapers of September 17 proclaims the presence of the "Dartmouth Coffee House . . . head of the team boat wharf . . . Mary Scott."

A further advertisement in the Nova Scotia "Royal Gazette" of August 27, 1817, informed the travelling public of the services offered by the company:

HALIFAX TEAM-BOAT COMPANY
Sherbrooke Team-Boat
The Committee appointed to conduct the business of
the Halifax Team Boat Company, beg leave to inform

the Public, that the Sherbrooke continues to ply between their wharf at Dartmouth and the Market Slip, from sunrise until one hour after sunset, remaining fifteen minutes on each side the harbour. The Committee also inform the Public, that they have reduced the Rates of Fares for Cattle, and Carriages of every description; and that they are proceeding to prepare a comfortable Ferry House at Dartmouth, and more extensive stabling for Horses, &c.

Every exertion will be made to accommodate Passengers, and to give satisfaction.

The stable, which had been provided by Lawrence Hartshorne Sr. was promoted to "Ferry House," and he offered new accommodation for the horses. This was a condemned ship's hull which he bought at auction. The company bought it, and it housed the horses for some years.

Not the least among the company's problems was one act of gross vandalism and cruelty. An earlier historian wrote:

The following year [1817] an outrage was committed which caused much excitement and feeling in the town. All the eight horses in the boat were stabbed by a young man named Hurst. No motive for this cruel act could be assigned, drunkenness alone appearing to be the cause. The culprit was tried for the offense and suffered a lengthy imprisonment.

(This event was not recorded in the company minutes.)

Their confrontation with, and reluctant eventual acceptance of, the burgeoning Age of Steam, seems to have proceeded slowly.

Early in the New Year of 1818, Dr. Almon, in charge of the committee for procuring an additional boat, reported that a steam engine would cost 500 pounds, plus 500 or 600 pounds per year to operate it. The committee felt that this was beyond the finances of the company and recommended that a small boat with hand-cranked paddlewheels should be built, to supplement the **Sherbrooke** service.

This proposal caused great consternation to James Creighton and John Skerry, who immediately sent a petition to the House of Assembly which was presented on February 26, 1818 by one Mr. Archibald. He read that "each of the petitioners has been in the possession of a Ferry at Dartmouth for a number of years, which have been kept up and maintained at a considerable expense, that the petitioners are likely to be much injured in consequence of the Steam Boat Company being about to employ boats of a small description in conveying passengers etc . . . and praying relief in the premises . . ."

The Creighton and Skerry prayers were not answered. It can safely be assumed that the fact that many members of the House of Assembly were also shareholders of the Steam Boat Company had something to do with this. So, by the end of 1818, two small boats were operating along with the **Sherbrooke**. John Skerry took his grievance to court. The story of the litigation and negotiation is outlined later.

At this point, an historical note on paddlewheels may interest the reader, remembering that the **Sherbrooke** had one, and that the then proposed "small boats" were to have two.

The paddlewheel was used in Roman times, and a Chinese picture of the 16th Century shows a paddlewheel boat being propelled by slaves on a treadmill.

In "Curious Boating Inventions," Joachim Schult states that "the simplest of manual propulsion devices was invented by Franz Xaver Resch of Wanettee, Oklahoma, in 1912, and consisted of no more than two wheels with six slim paddles each, which were turned by means of handles. They were mounted on the gunwales. Although paddlewheels had been in use for about a century and paddle steamers had made their appearance and vanished from the scene again, this form of propulsion had never been used on boats, and Resch was granted a patent for his original idea."

This patent was granted almost a century after the Steam Boat Company had been using hand-cranked paddlewheel boats as ferry boats. Unfortunately, no pictures or sketches of these boats could be found. They

12. *Hand-cranked paddlewheels.*

were known locally as "Grinders."

During the winter of 1818, all boats were forced to stop running when the harbour froze over "a considerable way below George's Island."

The first recorded complaints against a boat's crew for incivility to passengers was heard in September, at the Team Boat Company meeting. This was the same meeting where it was announced that Wallace had agreed to advance 150 pounds to make the road passable from the Dartmouth Ferry Terminal to Fletcher's (Waverley), "on receiving a guarantee from the Company against any loss he may sustain thereby."

This road was an important one to the business of the company, since it enabled farmers and travellers to use the ferry rather than take the longer route, driving around Bedford to Halifax.

Regardless of whatever improvements the expenditure

13. William John Bowie, 1782-1819. Oil painting by Robert Field.

of 150 pounds could achieve on some 12 miles of roadway (even in the early 1800s), the company felt the need to take further measures.

Ten horses were sold at ten pounds each. The number of trips per day for the **Sherbrooke** was reduced, since there was only one set of horses to work it. In order to facilitate improvements to the Dartmouth terminal, the company voted to buy two more Dartmouth water lots. There was also a motion passed to petition the General Assembly for financial assistance.

In several newspaper stories and Dartmouth Natal Day brochures, published in the last 60 years, it was stated that the ferries have never been subsidized. This was true only for a number of relatively short periods. Throughout the minute books of the various ferry administrations are records of petitions to the government for aid, usually with the justification that the ferry boat served as a highway link, a claim which has a startlingly modern ring.

During this period, the minutes of the Team Boat Company were kept in a serious and most correct manner by Charles R. Fairbanks. They are an impersonal record of the company's business.

For example, no mention was made of the sudden disappearance from the scene of one of the directors, William Bowie, treasurer. In July of 1819, Richard J. Uniacke Jr. (whose father of the same name was Attorney General) angered Bowie with a remark he made while addressing the jury during a trial in the Supreme Court. Bowie challenged Uniacke, a young lawyer, to a duel, which took place near the present Lady Hammond Road. Bowie was shot and died shortly afterward. Not surprisingly, this event caused a great deal of talk throughout the community, but there was no mention of Bowie's death in the Steam Boat Company minutes.

Uniacke and the two seconds were tried for murder but were acquitted. Richard J. Uniacke Jr. later became a Judge of the pre-Confederation Supreme Court of Canada. Although the event and the trial did not affect his legal career, it has been recorded that concern about what he had done shortened his life, for he died at the age of 45.

Bowie was buried in St. Paul's cemetery. The inscription on his tombstone reads:

WILLIAM BOWIE
Died 21st July, 1819
aged 37 years
Strict integrity and a high sense of
honour rendered him respected as a
merchant, a warm, benevolent social
disposition made him beloved as a man.
This stone was erected by his friends
in testimony of their esteem for his virtues
and regret for their loss.

Still not satisfied with the **Sherbrooke's** performance, Lawrence Hartshorne Jr., in January of 1820, presented the latest information on improvements to team boat mechanisms, details of which had been sent to him by Mr. Eddy of New York. The improvements were the invention of a Mr. Watts, and worked on the principle of the inclined plane (like an escalator moving downwards due to the weight of people on it). The Steam Boat Company passed a resolution in favour of obtaining such a boat, and petitioned the Assembly for the necessary funds.

This improvement in horse-powered paddlewheel boats is described in an earlier work in which it is stated that "the latest improvement was on the direct self-acting treadmill principle, the power being regulated by the weight of the horses and the pitch of elevation given to the revolving platform on which the unfortunate animals were perched."

At the March meeting it was announced that the company had sent two copies of a "Memorial" (petition), one to His Majesty's Council, and the other to the House of Assembly, asking for "advances between Two and Four thousand Pounds" for "building another large Boat . . . to increase the facilities of the communication with the Capital." Included with the memorial was a "Statement of the Expenditure since the Establishment of the Halifax Steam Boat Company." It is reproduced in pounds, shillings and pence:

24

14. *Richard John Uniacke, Jr., 1789-1834. Oil painting by Robert Field.*

Team Boat Cost	4053	4	2
Small Boat No. 1	49	5	2
—Ditto— No. 2	70	8	11
Horses	368	2	7
Halifax Wharf	321	7	3
Dartmouth Do	1706	15	8
Stables	503	10	6
Ship used for Stables	130	16	1
Ferry House	176	10	1
Floats	46	12	1
Well at Dartmouth	21	5	4
Dockyard Grant	12	2	10
	7460	8	8

The result of this petition was disappointingly meager, and the company was granted only 250 pounds. The minutes do not record this fact, but in an effort to cut costs, a committee composed of Starr, Major and Stayner was instructed to buy oxen (presumably to determine if the fodder/performance ratio was better than that of horses) and to fit the boat with sail if practical. A Mr. Tapper recalled in the early 1900s that he was the "driver" of the oxen used in this experiment.

Akins "History of Halifax City" states that "the teamboat after a year or two received an addition to her speed by the erection of a mast in the centre of the round house on which was hoisted a square sail when the wind was fair, and afterwards a topsail above, which gave her a most picturesque [or, it might be speculated, ludicrous] appearance on the water. This addition considerably facilitated her motion and relieved the horses from their hard labour."

Perhaps these "improvements" were the work of yet another committee consisting of Dr. Almon, Cunard and Fairbanks. These gentlemen were to "see what alterations to the machinery in the Horse Boat could be made for diminishing the labors of the horses."

This is the first mention in the minutes of an active interest on the part of Samuel Cunard. Apparently the experiment with the oxen was not a success.

An abbreviated financial report for the year 1820 was included in the minutes of March, 1821:

Revenues:		Expenditures:	
Large Boat	569	Forage	190
Small Boat	290	Wages	632
Other sources	327	Contingencies	327
	1108		1150

Sharp-eyed readers will observe something wrong with the addition. While some of the apparent errors may be due to the carrying of the shillings and pence, this does not account for the larger error in the revenue total.

In a further effort to reduce expenses, the company decided to reduce the wages paid to the men in the small boats to "six shillings per day for both men employed in each." Company employees at the time were recorded as Findlay, Bussey and Avery.

A resolution with important consequences was passed at this same March meeting: "Resolved that Major Bazalgette be requested to communicate with John Skerry on the subject of the opposition now supported by him against the Company, and to ascertain if any arrangement can be made for terminating the same."

This resolution marked the beginnings of the keen negotiations between the astute John Skerry and the powerful Steam Boat Company and not the end of their early problems.

VI.
The Competition Disappears

In spite of the operation of the comparatively large Team Boat, John Skerry was still doing a prosperous business from his wharf at the end of Ochterloney Street. The Steam Boat Company directors, in March 1821, heard Major Bazalgette's report on his failure to talk Skerry into giving up his own boats and joining the company as a shareholder. He reported that the only condition under which Skerry would accept a share in the company would be if he continued to run his own boats from his own wharf, and managed his own financial affairs—hardly a compromise.

A hint of desperation creeps into the company's minutes. The harbour iced up again, and the Team Boat was laid up during the winter. When the spring thaw permitted operations again, the Creighton and Skerry ferries also started up, still competing with the Steam Boat Company. The Legislature granted the company 250 pounds. This short-term remedy could not solve their serious problems.

The harbour froze again the following winter, and again the company received a grant, this time only 150 pounds. The Legislature still refused to allow the company monopoly rights. By the fall of 1822, the company apparently decided to take more serious measures to solve its problems. The Team Boat was laid up for the winter, the horses sold and once again a director approached John Skerry, Richard Tremain being chosen to talk to him this time. Skerry replied:

To the Members of the Team Boat Company, Halifax
Halifax, 4 December 1822
Gentlemen:
    I have received your letter enclosing the terms on which the members of the Team Boat company propose I should retire from the Ferry, which I have conducted between Halifax and Dartmouth during the

15. *John Skerry letter, 1822.*

last twenty-four years and am sorry that I cannot comply therewith.

I enclose a proposal for joining the Team Boat Company which should it be approved of, I am prepared to ratify by an interchange of the legal documents requisite.

> I have the honour to be
> Gentlemen Your
> Most Obdt. Servt.
> John Skerry

The proposal:

John Skerry to receive a proprietor's share in the Team Boat, and all her appurtenances of every description both on shore and on board without paying for the same.

John Skerry will deliver over for the use of the Company all his boats, and will retire from conducting his present ferry, provided all Rowboats-Wheelboats, or any kind of small boat now used or hereafter to be used by the Team Boat Company, ply between the Market Slip in Halifax and John Skerry's Wharf in Dartmouth, which is to be kept in repair at the expense of the Company, the profits to go to the Company, and John Skerry to share as a proprietor, John Skerry to have the privilege of boarding all the men, and to have the superintendence of all the boats, and to have the power of hiring the men, and dismissing them when they act incorrectly—John Skerry to receive compensation for his services as superintendent—The rate to be hereafter agreed on.

> John Skerry

To these he added further conditions:

Gentlemen Sir:
I request that 3 Roe Boats will run from my warf and kept there for the use of the Publick from the first day of May Until the last day of October.

27

Gentlemen I Request of you half Cord of wood
fromm Every member or allow the price of it Every
fall for the good of the Publick in the Wintertime,
License free in Dartmouth & ferriage free for meself.

John Skerry

This addition was obviously written in John Skerry's own hand, for the signature on both letters was the same, and this matched the writing of the afterthought.

The directors did not react favourably to Skerry's proposals and presumably turned them down.

Skerry wrote again:

Halifax 9th December 1822
Gentlemen,
   I have received your answer to my proposal to unite with the Team Boat Company, and am sorry they do not think it will be for their interest to make me an allowance for my services as the superintendent of the small boats, consequently I consider my proposal as rejected.
   As the first offer was made to me by Mr. Richard Tremain on the part of the Teamboat Company viz. of allowing me 100 pounds a year for ten years provided the other members were willing, I was in hopes that an union would have taken place, but finding that the majority were not of the same opinion as Mr. Tremain, I made my own proposal which I hoped would have been considered reasonable. And that as the superintendent I would have received some allowance, adequate to my services.

I have the honor to be Gentlemen
your obedt. Servt.
John Skerry

After this letter was delivered, Skerry was invited to attend a meeting of the shareholders on December 11. Skerry stood his ground firmly, but when the President H. H. Cogswell, pointed out that one of the directors had been superintending the ferries for no fee at all, Skerry then suggested that he would settle for five per cent of the profits from the small boats which were to ply from his wharf.

That meeting ended the opposition from the Upper or Skerry's Ferry. John Skerry became a conscientious director of the Steam Boat Company and served on many committees until his death in 1838. By that time he was a wealthy man, leaving large parcels of land to his wife and various relatives. In spite of his long association with the directors of the Steam Boat Company, Skerry's will requested that his executors "not seek for pall bearers among the rich and great men of the Town [Halifax], but call upon such friends as may be in Dartmouth or its vicinity to help me to my last home."

Meanwhile, Creighton's (Lower) Ferry and Inn were still being leased to a succession of tenant operators. Documents exist which show accounts paid to James Creighton by one William Bell who managed the property from at least 1801 until 1811, when he moved to a farm near Windsor.

Bell was mentioned in Lawson's History as being an employee of the Lower Ferry in 1798. At that time he had innocently escorted a young lady, Mary Russell, to her home on the Cole Harbour Road, unaware of the fact that she had recently broken her engagement to a violently jealous neighbour. Hearing of Mary's new companion, the ex-suitor borrowed a knife from a neighbour, went to the Russell home where he demanded to see his ex-fiancee, and stabbed her fatally. He was later hanged for the crime, and Mary Russell was buried in the Woodlawn Cemetery.

For a few years after William Bell had given up the Creighton Ferry it was managed by a man named Ryan. In 1817, when the business was advertised for sale, Peter McCallum was the lessee. The property was advertised again in 1821, but was not sold. At a Steam Boat Company's meeting in March, four years later, Tremain reported that James Creighton was willing to lease the Lower Ferry property to the company for 60 pounds. The company agreed to this proposition, and sublet the operation to Thomas Davie. Subsequent receipts show that the Lower Ferry was leased in 1826 and 1827, again to William Bell.

However, in 1828, a resolution was passed by the company to abandon this operation. The returns indicated that it was not as profitable a venture as Skerry's had been, partially a consequence of being located farther from the town centre.

James Creighton's lands were again offered for sale that year, 1828, and much of the property was bought by Halifax barrister James W. Johnston, whose son was later to become active in the Steam Boat Company.

The **Sherbrooke** was still operating. Her captain at this time was Joseph Findlay, a neighbour of John Skerry's. Findlay seems to have had his problems as well. The following letter, published in the "Acadian Recorder" of October 20, 1827, points up one of them:

> Sir:
> It has fallen to my lot to cross the ferry from Dartmouth to Halifax in the Team Boat during the fall run of mackerel. I have frequently seen the deck covered with fish, and splitting and salting carried on with as much facility as at any fishing establishments along the shore.
> From the "delicate" manner this complaint was canvassed by the Magistrates last Spring, I am disposed to think the public will be compelled at last to take other steps to regain their rights on the above ferry.

As noted earlier, several of the Halifax Magistrates were directors of the Steam Boat Company.

In the next issue, another reader replied, saying that Captain Findlay "always renders the voyage as commodious as possible. If he has sometimes permitted passengers to amuse and exercise themselves with hauling in a mackerel, it is more proof of his desire to accommodate."

Later, at the March 26, 1828, meeting of the Steam Boat Company it was reported that in regard to the complaint of one Peter Manning against Joseph Findlay, the resulting investigation had been favourable to Findlay.

It is not clear whether these controversies made Findlay wish for a quieter life as manager of the Lower Ferry.

However, he did manage it, and was the last ferryman to use large 40-passenger boats with oars and lug sails. They crossed the harbour in 30 to 40 minutes.

On May 5, 1828, James Creighton Jr. died. His funeral procession crossed the harbour not on the Lower Ferry, but on the Team Boat. He was buried in Halifax.

There must have been a conflict on account of overlapping routes between the Halifax Steam Boat Company and Creighton's Ferry. On September 21, 1829, it was reported that a meeting of the Magistrates had resulted in a notice to the effect that "Creighton's Ferry may operate from Old Ferry Road in Dartmouth Cove (but not Northwards of Cooper's shop which is near the first Cove to the Northward of the Dartmouth Point). The Boats of the T.B.C. are not to operate southward of Cooper's shop."

There was a tragedy at the Lower Ferry in September of 1839. During a severe southeasterly gale and torrents of rain "a Ferry Boat with two men, in attempting to cross from this side [Halifax], to the lower ferry was unfortunately upset, and before any assistance could reach them, they were both drowned. Their names were James Purvis and Patrick Riley."

The following summer a worse accident occurred to one of Skerry's ferries. Liquor outlets in Halifax were closed on Sundays, so many people came to Dartmouth where they could still buy alcoholic beverages. Here is an account of the accident in the newspaper language of the day:

On Sunday evening last (Aug. 14, 1831) between eight and nine o'clock, about thirty persons took passage in a Ferry Boat at Dartmouth, intending to cross to Halifax, when at a short distance from Skerry's wharf she grounded on the shoal, and another Boat was sent to take out some of the passengers. Ten persons succeeded in getting into her, and others, (as Costley, the Ferryman, and some of the persons in the first Boat were intoxicated) were desirous of following their example but were prevented by Costley—the two boats separated, and when about half way across, a heavy squall of wind and rain overset that which had the greatest number of passengers, plunging them into the harbour and producing a scene which must have been as horrible as it was destructive. Out of twenty only six were saved—prompt assistance was given, but the night being dark, and the rain falling in torrents, the whole must have perished had not some few had good fortune and presence of mind sufficient to grasp the gunwale of the Boat. A woman named Murphy was seen to sink with Costley the Ferryman, to whom she was clinging for assistance. She had endeavoured to get into the other Boat, and in doing so, her child fell over, but was caught up by some friendly hand, and thus escaped the sad fate of the mother, to whose bosom it was folded but a few moments before. Nearly all the persons who perished belonged to the labouring class, and we have not been able to procure any correct list of the names.

Little more than a month after this accident, on September 23, 1831, a new schedule of "Rules, Regulations, Fares and Rates" were established for the ferries.

In 1833, the Lower Ferry was leased by Thomas Brewer. He kept on with the business until about 1836. By way of modernizing the large cumbersome boats, he changed them from Findlay's lug sails to sloop rigging, with fore and aft sails.

A newspaper advertisement of October, 1833, stated:

Thomas Brewer informs his friends
that he has taken over the establishment
recently conducted by Joseph Findlay
and will carry on the House of Entertainment
at the South Ferry where his larder
will always be well supplied and his liquors
will be of the best quality.

The Ferry boats will touch at
Dartmouth Point when requested.

Despite this attractive advertisement, the days of the Lower Ferry must have been numbered, for by 1848 the following nostalgic description appeared:

In the days of team and ferry boats, before steam bridged the harbour the sonorous note of the conch came hourly during the day from the ferry slip, inviting passengers bound for the lower ferry, to improve the opportunity. Similar notes came from the lower ferry wharf, at the Dartmouth side, where the ferry house, and garden, and groves, and picturesque road had many animated features. Now however, the traffic and transit are all on one line; the town of Dartmouth has perhaps doubled its population and importance; places of worship—a Mechanics Institute Hall, and other matters, denote the progress of improvement in that direction, but the lower ferry has correspondingly declined; the spacious house is deserted, fields and gardens are lonely as if many miles in the interior, grass and weeds encroach on the road way, the wharf crumbles, and the once neat, busy position is an emblem of forgetfulness and solitude. The scene is one of picturesque sadness.

The Lower Ferry finally ceased operation and the Old Ferry Inn was burned in 1858. For years afterward there were traces of the wharf, and great willow trees marked the place where farmers from Eastern Passage, Cole Harbour, Cow Bay and Lawrencetown had embarked with their produce on the long and sometimes precarious trip to Halifax.

The Halifax Steam Boat Company finally achieved its monopoly, in fact if not in law.

VII.
Steam Gets Closer

Although there were mutterings of discontent about the Team Boat, both from the directors of the company and the public at large, the **Sherbrooke** was busy. She even participated in special occasions.

The official sod turning of the Shubenacadie Canal was performed by the Governor General of Canada, Lord Dalhousie, in July 1826. At an impressive ceremony near a lock site betwen Lake MicMac and Lake Charles, Hon. Michael Wallace, one of the Steam Boat Company directors, presided. Like several other directors, he had invested heavily in both ventures. The **Sherbrooke** had brought bands and spectators across the harbour to attend the festivities, as did Skerry's Ferry.

The **Sherbrooke** also hired out as a tow craft. This same year when Samuel Cunard's 400-ton sailing ship **Pacific** was launched from Lowden's Shipyard in Dartmouth, she was towed across the harbour to Cunard's wharf on the Halifax waterfront by the **Sherbrooke**.

On another occasion she assisted in fighting a downtown Halifax fire by carrying Dartmouth firemen to Halifax after lay up time.

Employed by the Shubenacadie Canal Company was an engineer from Montreal, Francis Hall. He was invited to a meeting of the Steam Boat Company directors early in January 1827, to speak to them on the subject of steam navigation. His talk fired their enthusiasm once more, to the extent that two committees were appointed. The first was to apply to the Legislature for a capital assistance grant, and the other was to continue, or renew, efforts to procure a new steam boat.

At this same meeting, perhaps by way of showing both need for, and capability to manage the burden of a new boat, the following summary of receipts (in pounds) from the various routes was presented:

Year	Creighton	Skerry	Team Boat	Total
1823		467	302	769
1824		476	249	726
1825	189	424	609	1223
1826	265	457	768	1491

The figures show a doubling of revenue in four years, and suggest that any improvement in facilities would probably be justified.

The next few monthly meetings were occupied with schemes for the implementation of such improvements. A Mr. Leppert prepared a tender for a single (hull) steam boat. John L. Stairs explained the construction of a double (hull) steam boat at New York. Mr. Starr's memorandum from New York told how the **Sherbrooke** could be converted from horse power to steam power.

Francis Hall, the Canal Company engineer, was invited to attend another meeting and was asked to write to Quebec and Montreal. In the minutes is a copy of a letter to a Mr. Ward of Montreal asking for "information respecting an Engine fitted to propel the boat [**Sherbrooke**] 10 miles per hour, and the cost of such Engine, also the model and cost of a suitable Steam Boat with a bill of Scantling therefor and the expense of a superintendent per day to build the boat at Dartmouth." The paddle was to be in the centre. Hall begged Ward to reply as soon as possible by way of Boston and New York.

James Boggs, who had been so obliging in obtaining information in respect to team boats 11 years earlier, was also contacted in New York, and requested to supply information similar to that asked of Ward.

Two months later, at the April 1827 meeting, the directors were shown a model of a steam boat sent to them by James Boggs (what a treasure it would have been today). However, the directors were more favourably impressed with the proposals received from Ward of Montreal, who had submitted a price just for a steam engine. This engine would be suitable for installation in the existing Team Boat. Further communications with Ward resulted in a contract with the firm of Bennett and Henderson in Montreal for the supply of an engine and boiler for the **Sherbrooke.**

Almost a year passed. Clark and Cunard on March 13, 1828, were appointed as the committee to ascertain whether the **Sherbrooke** was in sound enough condition to accept the new machinery. At the same time they were to obtain an estimate of the cost of building a new boat of the same dimensions.

Then, once again, the hopes of the company for a steam boat were rocked. A letter from Bennett and Henderson advised that the steam engine parts had been dispatched on the schooner **St. Ann**, which had since gone aground. Temporarily, the parts had been safe, but then the **St. Ann** had parted from her new mooring, began drifting down river, and had been abandoned. Fairbanks, the company secretary, informed their underwriters with whom the engine was insured, and on motion of the directors it was resolved to abandon it to them.

Towards the end of the month a bill came from Bennett and Henderson for 300 pounds which the company refused to pay. In May it was learned that the boiler of the engine was at Crane Island in the St. Lawrence. The remainder of the engine parts were still on board the **St. Ann** which had been "taken up, floating in the Gulph" (of St. Lawrence) and taken into one of the harbours of P.E.I.

Negotiations took place between the company, the underwriters and Henderson who made two personal visits from Montreal. Henry Yeomans of Halifax, represented the underwriters, Nova Scotia Marine Insurance Company. He advised the Steam Boat Company to advance 660 pounds to Bennett and Henderson "on account of what may be received on the Policy of Steam Machinery." Henderson, present at this meeting, was satisfied, but it was six months later before the Steam Boat Company received its settlement from the underwriters.

Fate may have dealt the company a kindly blow. Even

Mr Thomas Boggs
Hallifax.————

Darth mauth June 11 1829.

Mr Boggs Dr Sir

Mrs T & L Pearn is willin
for me to Gow on to New yorke to
Gite the Infformation required
in regarde of the Steem Boat &
the floats & docks for the Steem
Boat to enter

If the Company will allow the
time that I am Gon on the Contrackts
to Gite him & and it will be to your
Benefit to Gite her Beter seasoned thin
for me to Gow right on with hir

Plese to Gite all your letters made
out for me and I will Gite all inform
tion that may be nesesry for all Partys

and how much that you will allow
me to Gow on Plese to lett me know
this Evening and you will oblige your
Humble Servante Alexander Lyle

16. *Alexander Lyle letter, 1829.*

33

without detailed drawings of the **Sherbrooke**, today's reader may well believe that the technical problems in installing such machinery in her at that time would have been horrendous.

The company continued its search. The directors looked again to the model of the steam boat sent to them by James Boggs of New York. While contemplating this, they received a proposal, again from Henderson of Montreal. This time he offered to construct a new steam boat and engine, an offer promptly turned down. It seems that the directors had no desire to deal further with Henderson.

As an interesting aside, Samuel Cunard had a further and separate business connection with Bennett and Henderson in 1831. This firm fitted the 200 H.P. engines of the **Royal William**, which was built for the Quebec and Halifax Steam Navigation Company. Among the directors of this company were Samuel, Henry and Joseph Cunard.

By now, the Team Boat had been in operation for 13 years. The company's charter for sole rights to operate a paddlewheel boat had been originally granted for 25 years. With 12 years to go and with the "steam age" beginning and well on its way, they were rightly concerned that others might procure a steam boat which would provide better service, and thus be in a position to contest their charter. The company passed a resolution to petition the Legislature for a further extension of time, and for financial aid to build a steam boat.

Accordingly, an Act was passed in 1829, "Whereas, although the said Company have hitherto received no returns whatsoever, for the large capital vested in the undertaking, the said Company have now made arrangements for establishing a sufficient Steam Boat on the said Ferry . . . it is deemed reasonable to extend the term of years . . . Therefore the Halifax Steam Boat Company . . . shall remain . . . as if the term of fifty years had been originally mentioned in the said Act . . ."

In February 1829, tenders for the new boat were read at a directors' meeting. These were from Alexander Lyle of Dartmouth, a Mr. Leppert of the North West Arm, and a Mr. Pope. Lyle and Leppert offered to "combine forces"

and to begin work on the new boat immediately, using James Boggs' model, sent from New York two years previously. The directors thought it advisable for them to go to New York to observe the latest improvements in boats and docks in that city. The company's request elicited the following replies from Leppert and Lyle:

(From Mr. Leppert)

North West Arm—May 25th, 1829
To The Committee of the Steam Boat Company

Gentlemen:
    As you are desirous for me to Superintend the Steam Boat now building at Dartmouth by Mr. Lyle and with his admission and both Parties agreeing that I will be a Competent and impartial Judge of the workmanship and materials, agreeable to a Copy of Contract, and specification of the same to be furnished me by the Committee—I will agree to Superintend on the following terms—viz.—To Attend at the place where the Steam boat is building Twice every week and to make a report of the progress of this work, to the Committee each time—at the rate of Ten Shillings for each time free of ferriage.
    As going to the United States will put a stop to all my other business during the time I may be away—I would request the Company to furnish me with a passage to and from the States and also to pay all expenses incurred by Travelling during the time I am away. And for my Services to pay me at the rate of Ten Shillings per day. The Committee to provide me with Letters of introduction to persons there, which will enable me to get every information requisite for the purpose intended and for the interest of the Company—particularly the fastening of the Deck works and inboard work for the reception of the Machinery, as well as the Slip and Dock for Landing.

I remain Gentlemen
Your humbl Servt.
William Leppert

(Mr. Lyle then wrote to Thomas Boggs)

Dart Mouth June 11 1829

Mr. Boggs Dear Sir
Messrs T. & L. Piers is willin for me to gow to New York to gite the Information required in regarde for the Steam Boate & the floats & docks for the Steam Boate to Enter.
If the Company will allow that Time that I am Gon on the Contracke to Gite her of and it will be to your Benifit to Gite her Beter Seasoned then for me to Gow right on with hir. Plese to Gite all your letters made oute for me and I will Gite all information that me be neserry for all Partys and how much that you will allow me to Gow on. Plese to lett me know This Evening and you will oblige your Humble Sarvent

Alexander Lyle

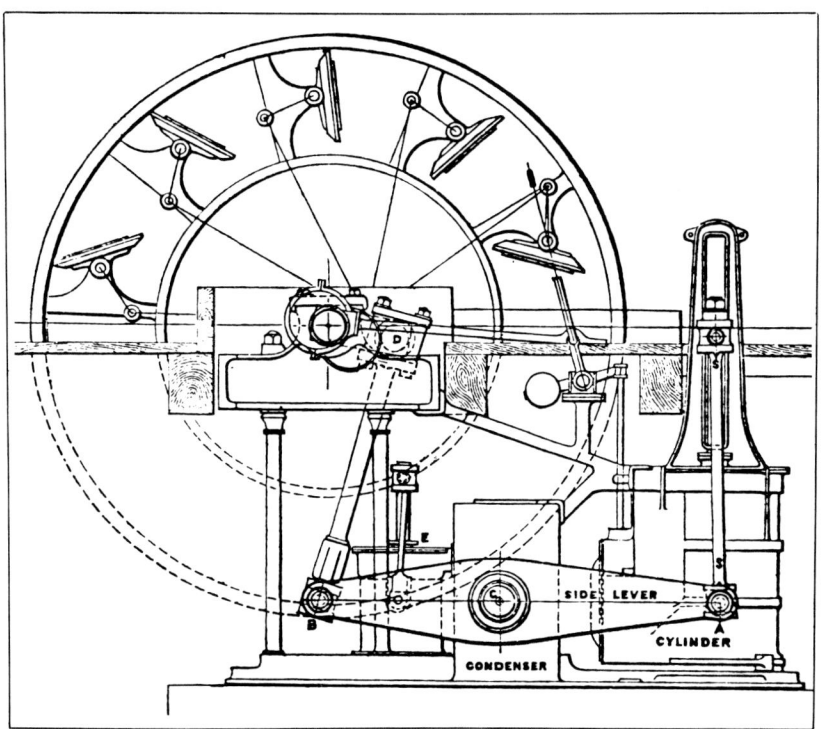

17. Drawing of side lever engine with paddlewheel.

The company satisfied these requests of Leppert and Lyle, and they went to New York to seek the required information. On their return they attended a meeting of the company on July 9, bringing a letter from James Boggs. This was read to the directors. Lyle and Leppert then exhibited the deck plan of a New York steam boat which was somewhat different from the boat under construction at Lyle's yard. The two men were asked to prepare a statement showing alterations needed to make it conform to the newer plan.

The specification for the alterations and the agreement are most explicit, and will be of considerable interest to readers interested in such aspects of maritime history.

It appears that these alterations did not change the contract price and a resolution was passed to accept the alterations and amendments.

The minutes for this July 1829 meeting were written for Charles Fairbanks by Alexander Primrose who was acting as secretary in Fairbank's absence. The latter had left for Liverpool, England, earlier on June 4, as a passenger in the Brig **Corsair**. He was on a dual mission: to raise capital for the the Shubenacadie Canal Company (another story), and to arrange for the purchase of a steam engine for the Steam Boat Company.

The engine was ordered from Edward Bury of Liverpool through the agency of one Fairclough, also of Liverpool. Fairbanks had the sanction of the company to consult an engineer if necessary in regard to the best type of engine, and with respect to the material of which the boiler was to be constructed—iron or copper (copper might well have done in view of the low temperatures and pressures involved at this time).

At the August meeting, the Steam Boat Company received a letter from Fairbanks, written on June 28. Edward Bury had agreed to deliver the engine to Liverpool by September 10. It would cost 1,250 pounds, one-half payable on delivery at Liverpool, and the balance to be paid when the boat was in full operation. There were not sufficient funds to cover this expense, so money was borrowed from a Halifax bank.

The 1829 Bury engine, a side-lever type, arrived on the sailing ship **Halifax**, along with a letter from Fairclough, Liverpool agent for the Steam Boat Company. The letter, dated October 3, 1829, was read at the November directors' meeting, and presumably provided information respecting installation and fitting of the engine and boiler.

It was just ten months since tenders had been awarded for the building of the new steam boat. As this was the first to be built in Nova Scotia, it was a notable achievement. The weather had cooperated to allow the work to proceed quickly. At the December 28 meeting of the Steam Boat Company it was announced that the construction of the hull and the fitting of the boiler and engine were nearly completed.

At the same meeting a resolution was passed to

18. *Model of side lever engine.*

name the boat in honour of "A person endeared to the Community by repeated acts of kindness, and a vigilant attention to the interests of the Navigation and Commerce of this part of His Majesty's Dominions."

The person the Steam Boat Company directors had in mind was Rear Admiral Sir Charles Ogle, Baronet, Commander of His Majesty's Ships and Vessels on the North American Station. Accordingly, a letter was sent to Sir Charles Ogle:

> The Halifax Steam Boat Corporation have recently built a valuable Steam Vessel, to be employed in the Harbour of Halifax.
>
> As the building of the first Steam Vessel in Nova Scotia has been performed during the period of your command upon the North American Station—the Company avail themselves of the opportunity of expressing an opinion, which they, in common with the people of the Province, entertain of the zealous, unremitting, and effectual aid which you have ever afforded to the Navigation and Commerce of this part of His Majesty's Dominions, during the period in which it has been confided to your care. '
>
> As a memorial of such opinion, they request permission to call their Vessel "The Sir Charles Ogle," a name which will be long gratefully remembered and respected in this Province.
>
> > Henry H. Cogswell
> > Thos. N. Jeffery
> > Lawrence Hartshorne

The Rear Admiral replied the same day with the following:

> Gentlemen;
>
> I feel highly flattered by the honour you have conferred upon me, in proposing to name the first Steam Vessel built in the Province of Nova Scotia, after me, which I shall with much pleasure accept.
>
> The opinion which you are pleased to entertain, in common with the People of the Province, that my endeavours to render every aid in my power to the Navigation and Commerce of this valuable part of His Majesty's Dominions, have been effectual, affords me the most heartfelt satisfaction, and the kindly sentiments which pervade your Address, I shall cherish with gratitude as long as I live.
>
> Be assured Gentlemen, that your patriotic undertaking has my best wishes for its success. I have the honour to be, Gentlemen,
>
> > Your most obedient
> > humble Servant,
> > Charles Ogle.

Sir Charles' command on the station appears to have been a successful one in all respects. Two other ships were named for him and Lady Ogle. There were many entertainments for him that same year when he left the command to return to England. One of these was a dinner at Medley's Hotel in Dartmouth. This dinner followed a tour of the Shubenacadie Canal works, with Hon. Michael Wallace, the Lord Bishop and other Canal Company directors.

The **Ogle**, named although not yet christened, almost finished but not yet launched, was eagerly awaited by the cross-harbour travellers. Of these there would be many who were aware of the technological achievement, and who would share the excitement of entering the steam age.

VIII.
Early Days of the
SIR CHARLES OGLE

The keel of the new steam ferry boat was laid at Alexander Lyle's yard in Dartmouth, on April 18, 1829. Eight months later she was ready for launching, the first steam boat built in Nova Scotia. It was an amazing feat to have been accomplished in such a short period of time, by people with no previous experience with steam engines of any kind. There appeared to have been a notable lack of coordination, or experienced supervision over the total project. This makes the subsequent spectacular success of the vessel most remarkable.

Consider also the following:

1. Company secretary Charles Fairbanks was a lawyer with no technical training. On June 4, 1829, he set out for Liverpool, England, with the responsibility for the procurement of a suitable engine for a vessel already under construction.

2. Alexander Lyle and William Leppert travelled to New York to observe steam boats and their docks there, and returned with plans leading to modifications of the existing construction, already based on a hull model obtained two years earlier from New York.

3. Thus, built in Dartmouth from a model made in New York and equipped with an engine from England which did not arrive until November 1829, the **Sir Charles Ogle** was ready for launching by the year end.

Senior naval personnel on the station were intensely interested in this first regional venture into the world of steam propulsion. When the **Sir Charles Ogle** was launched on New Year's Day 1830, Captain Boxer of **H.M.S.Hussar**, and Captain Travers of **H.M.S.Rose** were in attendance.

After the usual preliminary ceremonies, the **Sir Charles Ogle**, "owing to some defect in the ways, stuck after going nearly her length." There she stopped, to the great disappointment of the spectators. That evening, when the

19. Sir Charles Ogle (*glass negative*).

tide was high again, Captain Boxer and Travers returned with some of their men to Lyle's shipyard. With their assistance the launching was completed, and, as an enthusiastic spectator said, "she now sits the water gracefully as a swan, an honour and an advantage to the community."

The very next day, Saturday, January 2, Alexander Lyle had a "card" in the paid advertisements of the "Gazette:"

20. *John Howe cheers the* Sir C. Ogle *on the North West Arm. Drawing by Robert W. Chambers.*

The Subscriber is desirous thus publicly
to express his gratitude and thanks to
Captains Boxer and Travers of the Royal Navy,
and the Officers and Men
acting under their orders,
for the ready, generous and effectual aid
afforded him, under the unexpected difficulties
he encountered in launching the
Sir Charles Ogle,
Steamer, on Friday last.
Similar acknowledgements are also due
to all who were present on the occasion
for their kind assistance.

A few days later, at a meeting of the directors, it was decided to write the following letter of thanks to Captain Boxer:

Halifax, 5th January, 1830

Sir:

At a meeting of the Steam Boat Company held yesterday, it was unanimously resolved, that the Thanks of the Company be given to the Officers and Seamen of H.M. Ships, who voluntarily and successfully rendered their assistance on the night of the first instant, to rescue the new Steam Vessel from a very exposed and dangerous situation.

It has therefore, become my duty, and it affords me much pleasure on behalf of the Company, to convey their best Thanks to yourself, to Captain Travers and the Officers and Seamen under your command, for the prompt and effectual aid voluntarily rendered on that occasion.

I am aware that British Seamen are more delighted to earn their honours in the face of an enemy, and to draw their praises from the lips of the vanquished in time of War than in time of Peace to receive thanks for services rendered to their fellow subjects by their noble daring on the dangerous element, on which they exercise their vocation; yet the Company cannot omit the present occasion, to bear testimony to the fearless intrepidity, and utter contempt of danger, which characterize British Seamen, when opportunities of distinguishing themselves give occasion for their exercise of their exertions.

I have the honor to be, Sir,
Your most obedient Servant,
Henry H. Cogswell,
President

Captain Boxer replied in equally contemporary style:

Although it is characteristic of the service I have the honor to belong to, to be foremost in rendering assistance when their services are required, yet, on the present occasion, I have been most highly gratified in having it in my power to return in some measure the very marked attention which myself and officers have received from the kind People of Halifax . . .

We sincerely hope that an undertaking which the Community at large will derive so much benefit from, may be crowned with complete success.

Like Rear Admiral Ogle, Captain Boxer appears to have taken an active part in community affairs, including harbour regattas. In addition, he was married to James Creighton's grandniece. Thus he may have had more than passing interest in the ferries of Halifax Harbour.

Joseph Howe reported favourably on the new steam boat, contrasting its performance with that of the old Team Boat: "The former Boat seldom crossed, we believe, in less than 20 minutes, and was often near an hour in making the passage—the present will glide over the Harbour in seven minutes, making four passages within the hour. Her length of deck is 108 feet, width of beam 20 feet, width of deck 35 feet; she measures 176 tons, and her engine is 30 horse power."

On January 21, the **Ogle** made two excursion trips—one in the morning up to the Basin, and to the North West Arm in the afternoon. The weather was beautiful for the time of year, the "placidness of the waters of the Arm, never before disturbed by the paddles of a steam engine . . . Mr. Howe, (Joseph's father) suddenly beholding in front of his retired habitation that, perhaps, which he had indulged

little expectation of seeing effected in his day, and hearing the solitude of his retirement unexpectedly broken in upon by three hearty cheers from the passengers on the deck of the first steamboat that ever glided along the shores of that pretty inlet—which was no less heartily returned by the good old gentleman—added in no small degree to the pleasure of the trip."

Another newspaper account reads, "On Wednesday in three trips of the Steam Boat from Dartmouth she conveyed 53 teams loaded with produce to our market. The scene was "exhilarating, and it was scarcely less so to observe on the next morning, that instead of a glut being in the market, the articles had nearly all disappeared."

Newspaper reporting was even more contradictory in those days. A rival report states that "35 teams" were carried across in three trips. This seems more realistic for the **Ogle** was able to carry about ten teams in her carriage lane.

The Steam Boat Company directors invited "Members of Council and the House of Assembly, the Naval Commander-in-Chief, Colonel Norcott, Captains Boxer, Gosselin, and Dewar, R.N., and the Staff and Field Officers of the Garrison and the Gentlemen in charge of the Public Departments" to go for a trip on the **Sir Charles Ogle**. They left from the Market Slip at noon on Monday, February 17. Maintaining a speed of eight knots, she went first, "north, past the Dock Yard and into the Basin as far as the ice would allow her. She then returned, went around Point Pleasant Buoy, and at three o'clock landed the Party at the Slip.

"A Table was laid in the Cabin, and covered with a plentiful supply of Provisions of which the Company partook, and all the Guests appeared highly gratified with the kind attention paid to them."

A further newspaper report mentioned that "on this occasion the **Ogle** proceeded up and down the harbour, breaking the thin ice which impeded her progress into morsels, and exhibiting all the advantages of an aquatic locomotive."

The company minutes recorded that the **Ogle's** first crew

included Captain Hunter (100 pounds per year), Engineer William Guthrie, Steersman Patrick Tierney and Fireman Jack Wicke.

Guthrie had come from England at the same time as the engine, recommended by the engine builder, Edward Bury. Guthrie was reprimanded for some misdemeanour at the February meeting and the following May, the company moved to pay his back wages of 7/6p per day, double on Sundays, plus his passage back to Liverpool on the ship **Atlantic**. Soon after, James Simmonds of Prince Edward Island was hired for the Engineer's position.

Simmonds' career as Engineer on the first steam ferry was brief. The following newspaper account explains: "Drowned—On Tues. A.M. an inquest was held on the body of James Simmonds who had been employed on board the Steam Boat, and was left on the previous evening when the boat made her last trip, standing on the slip in a state of intoxication. Shortly afterwards he was heard to fall into the water, and assistance being immediately procured, he was taken on shore, but although he had only been about five minutes in the water, he was completely extinct. Verdict—accidentally drowned."

Guthrie, however, was still around. The company minutes recorded that he was once again the Engineer on the **Ogle**, and that he had asked that his claim against the company for further services should be readjusted. With Simmonds' unfortunate demise, it may be assumed that Guthrie was in a good position to reoffer his services as Engineer on the first and only steam boat in the harbour.

As in the earlier (1753) days of Wynne and Manthorne, two schedules were in effect—winter and summer.

From April 25 until September 20, the boat was to leave Dartmouth at 5:30 a.m. From September 20 until April 25, the first trip began at sunrise.

The boat was to ply continually, not stopping longer than eight minutes in the dock except for the crew's breakfast and lunch breaks—half an hour for breakfast, and 45 minutes for lunch.

These recesses for meals frequently coincided with the arrival of the stage coach from Truro at the Steam Boat Wharf. The ensuing delay for the stage passengers, at this point so close to their destination, must have been annoying. In addition, these coaches carried the Royal Mail, some of which was for overseas and destined for a specific ship about to depart. These things did not impress the crews. The steam boat did not leave the dock until the crew had breakfasted.

After two years of this, the stage coach owners refused to pay their fare on the grounds that they were the carriers of the Royal Mail. The dispute went on for some time until June, 1833. At this time the stage coaches were given a reduced rate of ten shillings per week.

The stage coach from Pictou on August 24, 1833, carried among its passengers a man whose name is still familiar to thousands of bird-lovers throughout North America. He was John James Audubon, famous ornithologist and artist.

We learn from his diary that the distinguished naturalist spent at least forty-five minutes at or near the ferry in Dartmouth, because the stagecoach seems to have arrived there just at the time when Captain Hunter and the crew of the **Sir Charles Ogle** were off to their midday meal.

Audubon was making his first visit to Nova Scotia. He had been in Labrador, and afterwards went to Pictou where he was presented with several specimens of stuffed birds and sea shells from the collection of Dr. Thomas McCulloch. The latter had accompanied his guest as far as Truro.

We append the portion of the diary dealing with his impressions of Dartmouth. The party had left Truro at 11:00 p.m., and breakfasted at Grand Lake (about 50 miles).

The road from that tavern to Halifax is level and good, though rather narrow, and a very fine drive for private carriages. We saw the flag of the garrison at Halifax, two miles before we reached the place, when we suddenly turned short, and brought up at a gate fronting a wharf, at which lay a small steam ferry boat. The gate was shut, and the mail was detained nearly an hour waiting for it to be opened.

While the novelty of steam propulsion may have been thinning out for her regular commuters, novelty and utility occurred in other forms of service.

In a contemporary newspaper account it was reported that one ship, the Brig **Kate**, returning in bad shape after a year's voyages "could not work up [the harbour], the weather was intensely cold and beside the risk of property, the state of her hands was a matter of serious consideration. The **Sir Charles Ogle** offered her services. She proceeded gallantly amid the gathering ice, took the **Kate** in tow and in a short time had her alongside her owner's wharf. This is one specimen on the vast importance of Steamers as tow boats. Three months before the present time, and by what method could the **Kate** have been directly reached from her unpleasant situation; she might have been for days at her unsafe anchorage, or be wrecked on the beach, for want of effective assistance. Halifax is less destitute in such matters than it was. If we wish to get on we should keep advancing—is a truism worthy of recollection."

In the advertisements of another newspaper was this card: "A thank you from the Owners of the Brig **Kate** to the proprietors of the Steam Boat **Sir C. Ogle** for towing the **Kate** up from her anchorage at the Beach through the ice."

Although the "proprietors of the Steam Boat" were enjoying the novelty of the new mode of transportation, and using her for excursions and good causes, there was criticism in the press. Grumbled one editorial, "Owners receive public grants of money with exclusive rights to operate the ferry, and it is much to be regretted that the public are so easily imposed on."

Joseph Howe was concerned about the extension of time granted to the company to have "the exclusive right to navigate Steam Boats. We have no doubt," he wrote, "before the expiration of the original charter [1842], the company will not only have reimbursed themselves for their outlays, but have realized a handsome profit upon their investment and we trust that long before the close of 37 years [the extension of the charter] they will have pocketed a pretty round sum. So long as the public are well served, of course they will have no reason to complain, but there is nothing like a little competition to ensure them the greatest measure of accommodation that circumstances will afford."

Joseph Howe could know little of the tribulations still to be experienced by the directors of the company. Recall that in 1815, before the Team Boat, **Sherbrooke**, had been acquired, the directors had written to Henry Barclay of New York: "we are desirous of establishing one of them [either Team or Steam Boat] without delay—and as either will probably be sufficient, at least for some years to come to do all our work, and probably may not be very profitable we wish to adopt that which should be deemed best for our purpose and at the same time least expensive to keep up."

At that time they decided on the Team Boat, and it subsequently proved to be an expensive, troublesome and altogether disappointing venture. Although the **Sir Charles Ogle**, at the close of her career had given over 60 years' service, her infancy and childhood did not prove to be the profitable undertaking envisioned by Joseph Howe.

IX.
More Problems

With the **Sir Charles Ogle** now operating on the harbour, she was soon to become a familiar sight also in sketches, engravings and paintings of Halifax Harbour done during the mid-1800s. In spite of occasional artistic license, such as the addition of a bowsprit, her two rounded ends and high black funnel with its trail of even blacker smoke, are a highly identifiable detail, however small, of reproductions of the harbour of the period.

The directors of the Steam Boat Company resolved to dispose of the **Sherbrooke.** The crew was discharged and the horses sold at auction. Captain Oakes was allowed to stay on in one of the houses belonging to the company. Avery was to be employed about the property.

On January 21, 1830, Joseph Howe's newspaper, "The Novascotian," printed a witty article by "the Club" about the retirement of the Team Boat horses. It was filled with puns based on such words as "mare" and the French word

"mer," "neigh" and "nay," "docked" and so on.

The old upside down schooner hulk, sold to the company by Lawrence Hartshorne Sr. and which had been used as a stable for the Team Boat horses, was now put to use as a coal shed. A new floor had to be laid, "the old deck having fallen down."

By April, the Team Boat had not yet been disposed of, and was used to "drive a few necessary piles." In November, an advertisement appeared for the sale of the **Sherbrooke** at auction. Among her few remaining virtues extolled in the notice were that she was copper bottomed and had machinery suitable for milling purposes. While her first cost is in doubt, she brought 85 pounds at the auction.

Expenses of the Steam Boat Company were heavy. A statement from Alexander Lyle in January 1830 noted 1,000 pounds received, and 800 pounds still owing. Dr.

21. *Halifax from Eastern Passage, ca. 1837. Drawn by Wm. Eagar,
Halifax, engraved by J. Gellatly.*

Almon and Tobin were appointed to negotiate a loan for insurance on the **Sir Charles Ogle.**

Near the end of April, several modifications were suggested:

(1) A strip of hardwood at the water line to guard against ice.

(2) Altering the rudders, "they being too much under water and too narrow to affect the boat when she loses way."

(3) "A copper or lead pipe to connect with the one that now conveys the bilge water upon deck, which is very inconvenient and the water might...be conveyed just under the deck and led through the side of the boat, as it is at present very destructive to the boilers if there should be a leak in the deck."

(4) "Wharves should be finished as there is danger to the paddlewheels."

(5) "Devise a way of carrying waste steam to paddlewheels in winter so ice should be prevented from accumulating around paddlewheels."

In contemplating these proposed solutions to the problems being experienced, we should recall that the company had sought advice from operators of ferry boats on rivers of New York State or from those of the warmer climate of England. Thus the Steam Boat Company became faced with the joint and several problems of ice and boiler feedwater.

Present-day readers will find it unbelievable that sea water was fed to the **Ogle's** boiler. It turns out that during her early years there were no municipal water distribution systems in either Dartmouth or Halifax. Fresh water would have been available from lakes or streams, but this would have to have been brought in barrels or some such means and would have been prohibitively expensive. The use of harbour water meant that as steam was generated in the boiler to drive the engine, the salt left behind was deposited on the boiler tubes. The salinity of the boiler water would rise, increasing the boiling temperature, and the solid salt deposits would act as insulation between the fire and the water. Then in order to maintain a workable steam rate the firing would have to be higher, and resulting higher furnace temperatures could approach that which could cause catastrophic failure of the boiler.

At the May 18 meeting the directors were told of the problems with the steam engine and boiler:

> When the boat first ran, the boilers remained four weeks without cleaning. Lately from [May 3-15] they were so choked up with salt as to make it dangerous to run her an hour longer and it took all hands the whole of yesterday and last night to get the engine in order to run this morning.

One newspaper reported in early April that a young man had been instantly killed when he tried to clean the boiler before the pressure was reduced. The following day the Nova Scotia "Royal Gazette" revised this, stating "The death of a young man reported in yesterday's papers is incorrect. He was however almost lifeless when taken out of the boiler."

Troubles mounted. A Halifax resident complained that he had tried for two days to take a trip in the Steam Boat, but it was not running, and he had to "cross on one of Findlay's barges." His problems were far less costly than those of the owners of teams loaded with produce for market. These were lined up for several days awaiting the Steam Boat's repairs, and in some cases the farmers had to pay for shelter.

The Steam Boat Company meeting on August 2, 1830, directed the secretary to write to Richard Smith of the Albion Mining Company to get a competent engineer to examine the **Sir Charles Ogle.** Richard Smith was a mining engineer from England who had come to Nova Scotia to manage the General Mining Company at Stellarton having arrived three years previously in the brig **Margaret Pilkington.** He had brought with him "the knocked down components of steam hoisting and pumping engines. The natives were vastly mystified when the huge iron boilers that Richard ordered thrown overboard into Pictou Harbour did not sink, and were easily floated up river to what is now Stellarton, where the engine began puffing

22. Halifax from Dartmouth, by Wm. Henry Bartlett, 1842.

away on December 7, 1827." This stationary steam engine of the General Mining Company was the first steam engine in Nova Scotia.

Meanwhile, Charles Fairbanks had returned from England where Parliament had made a grant of 20,000 pounds for furthering the work on the Shubenacadie Canal. At his reappearance at the company meeting it was resolved that he should make inquiries regarding a new boat. The directors were beginning to suspect that there was something very wrong with the **Ogle's** engines.

Somehow they kept the boat running, if intermittently.

One Peter Donaldson presented a petition signed by a great number of citizens, requesting the right to operate a new ferry from his wharf—just to the south of the present Dartmouth City Hall. The Steam Boat Company was in a bind. The directors were well aware that the Steam Boat often presented a "severe disappointment to the travellers." Yet in spite of all the mechanical troubles, receipts from the Steam Boat, January to October, totalled 1,568 pounds. For the same period, the small boats' receipts were 513 pounds. A letter was sent to members of the Assembly offering them free passage on the Steam Boat during the Session—a gesture that may have had something to do with the Assembly turning down the Donaldson petition.

Meanwhile, the company petitioned the Assembly for further funds, setting forth its case in moving terms. Having enlarged the wharf accommodations and provided a valuable Steam Boat, they said the expenses for 1830 had been more than 4,000 pounds, making the total outlay over 12,000 pounds. Contrary to Joseph Howe's earlier prognostications, none of the shareholders had even received a dividend, let alone the "handsome profit" he thought would be forthcoming. The result of the petition was a handsome grant of 190 pounds.

To relieve the company's increasingly desperate financial situation, Fairbanks was prevailed upon to borrow 671 pounds from the Shubenacadie Canal Company, to pay off the remainder owing on the Bury engine. This paved the way for an order to be sent to Fairclough, the company's agent at Liverpool, for a new boiler, "to be somewhat larger than the present."

In February, Alex Lyle sent specifications for a new ferry boat, which were presented to the meeting, but not acted upon. By May 1831, the secretary was directed to write to Bury, the engine builder of Liverpool, to say that there was "some material defect in the engine." They still, apparently, had not realized that most of their problems were due to using sea water in the **Ogle's** boiler.

The Shubenacadie Canal Company loan soon came due, and it was agreed by the directors that a superintendent must be found, the work being too demanding for John Stayner, who had volunteered in this capacity. For his services, his grateful fellow directors granted him 100 guineas.

Richard Smith of the General Mining Company, put forward a proposal to lease the whole of the Steam Boat Company's establishment, including Skerry's ferries. The proposal was for a seven-year period, for which Smith offered to pay 100 pounds per year. The directors liked the concept, but not the terms. Smith turned down their counterproposal.

Then the company hired William H. Davies of Pictou, an engineer, to put the Steam Boat in order. This was done, but necessitated the laying up of the **Sir Charles Ogle** for a considerable time. Skerry and Stayner were called upon to serve the needs of travellers and commuters wanting to cross the harbour, and with the small boats to fill the large gap left by the now well-known **Ogle.**

Davies' bill of 68 pounds, presented and paid the following month, was accompanied by an offer to stay and work the boat for a year for the sum of 1,030 pounds. An agreement with considerable detail was signed in July.

Meanwhile, the new boiler which had been ordered in February, had not yet arrived. At the August meeting it was stated that there was "reason to hope (it) would be shipped in the brig **Atlantic** now hourly expected."

The **Ogle** had to be taken out of service August 15, in spite of Davies' efforts, and except for Captain Hunter, all the crew was discharged, pending the arrival of the new parts.

At this same August meeting, a further gloomy announcement was made to the effect that each shareholder would have to be assessed at seven pounds, ten shillings per share in order to pay off the Shubenacadie Canal Company loan.

This was the month that saw the first appearance of the **Royal William** in Halifax Harbour, carrying mails between Halifax, Quebec and Boston. The **Royal William** performed this service until a cholera epidemic curtailed her sailings in 1832, and consequently her owners were faced with great financial loss. In 1833 she was sold in England, having crossed the Atlantic from Pictou. She was the first ship to cross the North Atlantic using steam propulsion exclusively.

When the "hourly expected" boiler finally arrived in November, the services of Davies were again sought. He could not make himself immediately available, so his foreman, John Baker, was sent to begin the work. Davies arrived sometime later, but even then the company felt

23. *Halifax from the Eastern Battery, 1839 (Imperial Oil refinery).*
Drawing by J. S. Clow, engraved by W. Douglas.

that it should have a permanent resident superintendent. Applicants were sought and only one, from Edward Lowe, was prepared to meet a particular requirement that the holder of the position must be a permanent resident and live near the Dartmouth ferry terminal. Lowe was appointed at a salary of 100 pounds per year. He stayed for 30 years.

Despite Davies' and Lowe's combined knowledge of steam engines and management capabilities, the financial position of the company worsened. Some shareholders refused to pay their seven pounds ten assessment, and their shares were auctioned in order to admit new shareholders to the company. This may have helped the company deal with its obligation to Fairclough of Liverpool,

on the Bury account for the new boiler. The amount outstanding was 593 pounds.

The Legislative Assembly turned down further requests for grants, so various schemes to reduce the company's indebtedness and at the same time finance a second steamboat were bandied about. One was to sell an additional 100 shares, another was to levy a further assessment of 10 pounds per share.

Lowe, the new Agent, produced the following report at the June, 1835, meeting:

Mr. Davies—for making and keeping   [pounds] 1100
the engine in order—fuel, salary of
engineers and two firemen.

Repairs	200
Salary of Agent, captains, steersmen and dock labourer	336
Insurance (Mr. Yeomans)	75
Small boat maintenance	250
[pounds]	1961

At the same meeting, a special committee of J. L. Starr, M. B. Almon and Wm. Lawson Jr. recommended a four-point plan:

(1) Do without Mr. Davies' services (presumably the engineers and firemen had learned how to deal with the corrosion problems).

(2) Abandon the small boats.

(3) Acquire a second steam ferry.

(4) Levy a 25 pound per share assessment on all shareholders.

This last recommendation seems to have put the cat amongst the pigeons. Albro, Chief Justice Blowers and Lawrence Hartshorne Sr. refused to pay their 25 pound assessments and so their shares were auctioned.

It was an indication of the seriousness of the problems that these shares were sold at five shillings each. The company's fire insurance underwriters threatened to enforce a judgement against the Steam Boat Company. Davies had not been paid, but was allowed to complete work on the boat by kind permission of Samuel Cunard, Agent for the General Mining Company which was Davies' official employer. It is noted that Cunard was also a large shareholder in the Steam Boat Company.

By January 1836, Charles R. Fairbanks and William Lawson, his father-in-law, were thoroughly disenchanted. Fairbanks had been a faithful secretary of the Steam Boat Company since its founding, 20 years previously. He had sailed to England in 1829 on a dual mission—to raise money for the Shubenacadie Canal Company and to seek a suitable engine for the **Sir Charles Ogle**. Some of the Canal Company money had briefly tided the Steam Boat Company through a difficult period, through his intercession. Up to this point, when the shareholders had been levied the latest 25 pounds, he had contributed his assessments.

It must have been with considerable disillusionment that Fairbanks wrote in his last minutes (January 5, 1836):

> Charles R. Fairbanks and Mr. William Lawson have decided not to advance any further sum of money towards this Enterprise, being satisfied that the present management of the Company is such that the undertaking will never succeed or be advantageous to the Shareholders or the Public.

It is with some sadness that the reader contemplates Fairbanks' final compensation for his expenditure of time, energy and money—he was to be allowed free passage on the ferry because of his "long and gratuitous service."

X.

The BOXER
and Samuel Cunard

The departure of Fairbanks and Lawson did nothing for the remaining directors' morale. Long-time President H. H. Cogswell and John Stayner also resigned. They too were granted free passage on the ferry in return for their long service to the company.

It has been frequently observed that when a responsible position needs to be filled, the busiest person in the vicinity is a likely candidate. Thus the directors elected Hon. Samuel Cunard to the presidency of the Steam Boat Company in 1836. Cunard at this time was heavily involved in the shipping business, S. Cunard & Co. The Cunards owned whaling ships, had mail contracts with Quebec, Boston, West Indies and Newfoundland, and were lumber dealers as well. In addition to these direct business activities, Cunard was Agent for the General Mining Company, a major shareholder in the Shubenacadie Canal Company, and active on many government committees,

such as relief for poor European immigrants and as Commissioner of Lighthouses. Possibly it was coincidental that as soon as Cunard took over the presidency of the company its situation improved. More probably this was due to his good management, business acuity and wide contacts in the world of shipping. His fellow officers were Thomas Boggs, Vice-President; M. B. Almon, Treasurer; and Lawrence Hartshorne Jr., Secretary.

With the new slate of officers, three managing directors were appointed, and these were to be elected annually. The first three were Hartshorne, W. A. Black and Edward Cunard. For several years thereafter the minutes recorded only the annual meetings held in February. Occasionally an emergency meeting was also held, but for the most part the three directors managed the affairs of the company through the capable day-to-day direction of Lowe, the Agent. This presumably left Samuel Cunard free to pursue his other interests on both sides of the Atlantic, in the knowledge that the ferry business was in good hands.

One of these emergency meetings took place in April of that same year, 1836. It was called for the purpose of considering the tender for a new steam boat, a plan of which was presented by Alexander Lyle. The boat was to be 90 tons, 20 H.P. and the price quoted was 585 pounds (without engine). Although the minutes do not reveal what, if any, decisions were made, three days later, on April 30, 1836, two of the directors sent a letter to Samuel Cunard, then in Britain, by the **Camden Packet**:

Dear Sir:
We enclose herewith a Memo of a Steam Engine of the power of 20 horses, required by the Steam Boat Company for the new Boat they are building to run on the Ferry crossing this Harbour. We request you will forward it to Mr. Fairclough, whose attention in Procuring and shipping the Engine for the **Sir Charles Ogle** in 1829 are thankfully acknowledged by the Company. A plan of the boat drawn by the builder, and contained in a Tin Case, will be forwarded by this Packet, the **Camden**, to Falmouth, and we hope it will be a sufficient guide to the Manufacturer in the construction of the Boilers and Machinery. It is of much consequence that the Engine should be shipt as early as possible that it may arrive out and be put in operation before the short days and cold weather.

And in addition to this, the Company's interest is suffering daily from the want of increased accommodation to the public. We request Mr. Fairclough will give us early advice of the engagements he may make with the Manufacturer, that the requisite remittances may be made. It may be necessary to remark that the boat is intended to convey Carriages and Cattle, as well as passengers, consequently the Shaft and other Machinery must work under deck. We have so much confidence in his judgement and experience in these matters that we do not think it necessary to add more than beg his exertions to have our order executed as soon as possible and on the very best terms, and that he will

24.   *Samuel Cunard, 1787-1865. Oil painting by Albert G. Hoit.*

effect insurance on the amount of Invoice when shipt. It will not be required, as in the former case to send out an Engineer to put the Engine in operation as we presume our own people will be competent to do it, and we trust a considerable saving will thus be made to the Company.

Mr. Fairclough will no doubt take advantage of any modern improvements in the construction of Boilers etc. to prevent their corrosion by salt water, and limit the consumption of Coals.

We are Dear Sir
Very Faithfully Yours
L. H.
E. Cunard
Directors

The Honble S. Cunard
President of the
Halifax Steam Boat Company.

The enclosure in the letter was a specification for a marine steam engine written in the 1830s. We shall never know who wrote it, for it is almost certain that the directors, being businessmen, laywers and politicians, must have sought assistance in this matter. Perhaps they had the help of the engineer from the General Mining Company.

Two years later the company's second steam boat was launched, again from Lyle's Shipyard at Dartmouth, on Monday, February 19, 1838:

She has a superior engine of 25 horse power, is well adapted to carry passengers, with carriages, cattle etc. and will be the means of keeping up a more regular and certain communication with Dartmouth. The boat is called the **Boxer** in remembrance of the gallant Officer of that name, now commanding HMS **Pique**, to whom the Company are under lasting obligations for the kind and ready assistance he afforded them when in command of **HMS Hussar,** on this station in 1830.

The **Boxer** was never as satisfactory as the **Ogle.** This

may have been due either to her design or to the materials of which she was constructed, for after 27 years her hull was sold, and her engine removed to be used in a new ferry boat, built in Dartmouth in 1865. The **Ogle** was still in service in 1890, and for this reason there are photographs

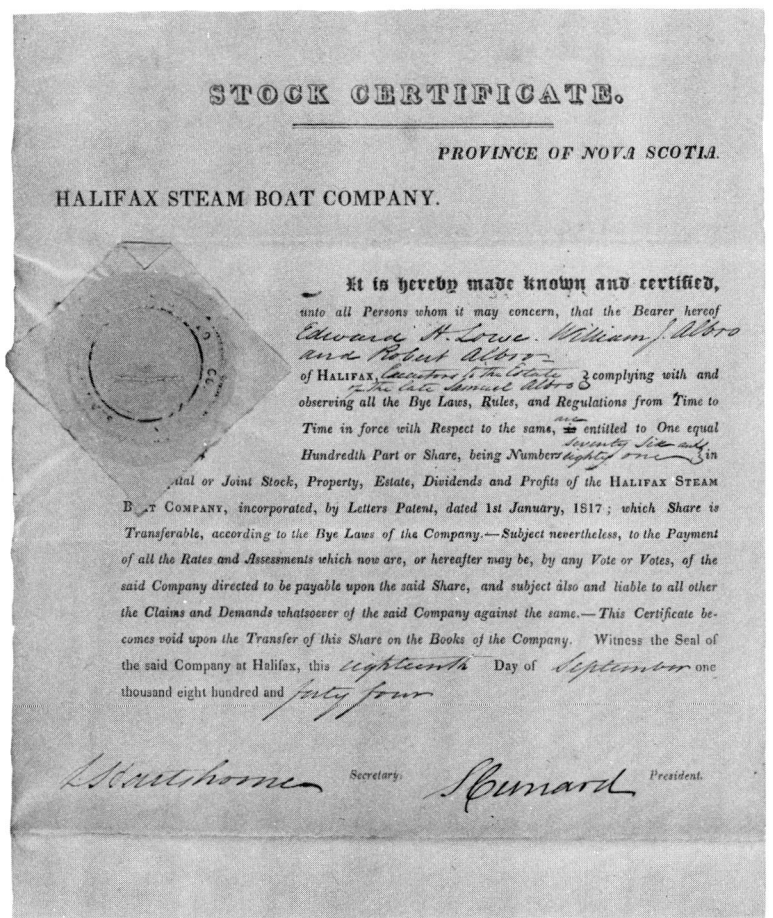

25.   *Share certificate, 1844.*

53

of her in her latter days. Unfortunately there are not even any good drawings readily identifiable as the **Boxer**. However because her engine was used in a boat of later years, there is a description of it in a Bill of Sale. The story of the authors' search and verification of the source of the **Boxer's** engine is presented in a chapter-end note.

In addition to having been so helpful at the time of the **Ogle's** launching, nine years previously, Captain Boxer took an active part in community life in Halifax and Dartmouth. In those days regattas were held on the harbour each summer, largely inspired by the naval authorities. A very special "Grand Regatta" had been held in 1829 in celebration of the Coronation of George IV, under the chairmanship of Captain Boxer. A week later the winners were announced and two forthcoming rowing matches were mentioned, "one between Captain Boxer's Gig, and the Dartmouth Whale Boat; and the other between the **Bugleman** which last year beat Capt. Fitzclarence's Gig and a new boat that has been built by and will be rowed by gentlemen of the town." The boat had been built by **Mr. Coleman** of the Nantucket whaler community in Dartmouth.

Now that two steam boats were operating "on the ferry," it might be thought that the service would run continually and smoothly. This was not so. Frequently only one boat was used for commutation purposes, while the other was used for excursions and as a tug boat when requested.

In 1838 sightseers were taken to watch the regatta on the **Ogle**, while the **Boxer** handled the regular traffic. The **Ogle** also took excursion passengers to Prince's Lodge twice a week during the summer months. These trips appeared to have generated significant revenue and undoubtedly contributed to the slow improvement of the company's financial position.

In 1902 an elderly resident of Dartmouth, Mrs. Thomas Mott, told a reporter for the "Dartmouth Patriot" that she could remember the old **Boxer** and the captain steering her by a tiller. She said that if the captain's view was obscured by a high load of hay a man would stand on top of the load to direct the steering. The engineer's job was equally primitive—in regard to signals, he merely looked out his window and "used his own judgement about when to start or stop."

The first Halifax Natal Day was celebrated in June of 1839. On this occasion the **Ogle** was used to take passengers to a picnic at Prince's Lodge. Shortly after, the Union Engine Company hired the steam boat for a dinner and cruise:

Pic Nic—A very pleasant Pic Nic Party appears to have passed off on Wednesday last. The Union Engine Company with their guests, and a large number of ladies, celebrated their annual festival, by a Pic Nic on the grounds of John Howe, Esq. Belmont. (Joseph Howe's father, on the North West Arm). The company left the steam boat wharf in the Sir Charles Ogle steamer, between 10 and 11 o'clock, forenoon. The weather was splendid, the harbour smooth as glass, and the picturesque shores and islands in all their midsummer richness. The boat proceeded up the harbour, round the Winchester, the band playing and a party dancing on deck; she then proceeded out to the Light House; in again, and up the North West Arm, where after a cruise, the company landed and dined. While gliding amid the sylvan scenes of the Arm, the deck was again occupied by a dancing party, the band supplying exquisite music. At about 8 o'clock in the evening the company walked in from Belmont. The band preceded them through the town, playing a favourite march. The ladies and gentlemen who walked in close column numbered about 200 we should think. This novel and very pleasing feature in the day's amusement attracted much notice. A large crowd followed to the Engine House, where Auld Lang Syne, and the National Anthem were played, and three times three cheers concluded the festivities.

Although Samuel Cunard made very rare appearances at the Steam Boat Company meetings after 1837, he held the office of President for many years. Thomas Boggs, the Vice President, chaired the meetings, but the name of Samuel

Cunard lent status to the company, which was beginning to prosper.

Meanwhile in Britain, Cunard had signed the "contract with the British Government for seven years to institute and maintain a steam service from Liverpool to Halifax and Boston." After signing the contract and making arrangements for the building of new paddle steamships, Cunard returned home to Halifax. Local merchants and officials celebrated his achievement with an outdoor banquet at McNab's Island, in August.

A special meeting of the Steam Boat Company was called to "consider the propriety" of offering a steamer to the entertainment committee for the transportation of guests. John Starr, a company director, was the master of ceremonies for the banquet. After some discussion at the meeting, the secretary wrote in the minutes: "to express the estimation of the Character of the President of this Company, The Honourable Samuel Cunard, and particularly their sense of the benefits they anticipate from his recent engagements with H. M. Government to establish Steam Communication between Great Britain and these Provinces, have invited him to a Public Dinner on McNab's Island on Wednesday next. Resolved unanimously that this Company, eager to mark their approbation of the merited compliment thus paid to their President Mr. Cunard, and to cooperate in carrying the same into effect, do request the Directors to tender the use of the Steam Boats for Tuesday and Wednesday next, making such arrangements as will not interfere with the Public Ferry."

The following year both Halifax and Boston greeted the arrival of the paddle steamer **Unicorn** with wild enthusiasm. She "arrived at Halifax in 14 days from Liverpool. The wharves were jammed with people cheering as if at a great victory; guns fired, flags waved, and during the ship's brief stop at Halifax no less than 3,000 Haligonians went aboard for an inspection of this marvel of the age."

The **Unicorn** did not return to Liverpool, for she was to be used on the mail service between Quebec and Pictou. Her Captain, Walter Douglass, later undertook to make

26. Britannia. *Drawing by J. S. King, 1844.*

inquiries at Quebec in regard to a third steam boat for the Halifax-Dartmouth ferry service.

Although the **Unicorn** had caused a stir when she arrived from Liverpool, even larger crowds of spectators greeted the first of Cunard's new mail ships, **Britannia**. She arrived in Halifax on July 17, 1840, having made the passage from Liverpool in a startling 12½ days. No time was lost in unloading passengers and freight, and the **Britannia** left for Boston, arriving the following evening.

"As she left Halifax, she went around **HMS Winchester**, which was decorated with flags, and cannon were fired to salute the first of Mr. Cunard's regular line of steamships. The passengers wrote a glowing letter of praise to Samuel Cunard, and he replied modestly, expressing his thanks for their kindness."

It was certainly the Age of Steam, even on this side of the Atlantic, and as each of the new Cunarders appeared in Halifax Harbour, further tributes to Samuel Cunard appeared in the press. A long gushing poem entitled "The Cunard Enterprise" appeared in the "Haligonian" and was subsequently copied in the "Novascotian." The last verse was to Cunard himself:

> Cunard, Acadia's Enterprising Son,
> Thy noble work is gallantly begun—
> And it shall prosper if a people's prayer
> For such improvement be the Almighty's care.
> Thy youthful Country's benefactor, thou,
> We bind the laurel on thine honoured brow!
> Thy name, great man! to every Patriot dear,
> Our children's children from their sires shall hear;
> And, taught by thee, in future time shall rise
> High spirits meet for equal Enterprise!

Altogether, four of these paddlewheelers were built for "The British and North American Royal Mail Steam Packet Company." They were as nearly identical as four different builders could build them, so that the passenger amenities would be of the same standard.

All four had Napier side lever engines—440 horse power, with cylinders of 72½ inches diameter and 82 inches stroke. The ships were named for the four "countries" they served—**Britannia** for England; **Caledonia** for Scotland; **Acadia** for Nova Scotia; and **Columbia** for the United States of America.

The last reference to Cunard's presence at a meeting of the Halifax Steam Boat Company was in connection with a special meeting held August 11, 1840, to consider selling a piece of company property at the end of Ochterloney Street, once owned by John Skerry. This may have been the lot mentioned in the 1837 minutes, which was under dispute between Skerry and the directors. The only other evidence found of Cunard's involvement with the company is his signature on a share certificate dated 1843.

The financial position of the company changed drastically for the better during Cunard's presidency. By January 1842, the price of the shares had risen to 105 pounds—a staggering increase when it is recalled that Fairbanks' shares went for five shillings in 1836.

The first return on the shareholders' investment was in 1843, when a dividend of 9 pounds per share was declared.

Two years later semi-annual dividends of 5 pounds per share were disbursed on March 1 and September 1.

The prosperity that had begun under Cunard's presidency continued, and from this time on the shareholders received dividends.

Cunard spent much time during his remaining years in London, but maintained his home in Halifax. In 1859 a baronetcy was conferred upon him. Six years later, in 1865, Sir Samuel Cunard died in England. His death, as reported in the press, was overshadowed by U.S. President Abraham Lincoln's assassination.

Shortly after his death, and just one year after Confederation, Halifax was dropped from the Cunard Line mail contract. New York became the western terminus, and there was a branch line to Boston. During his later years Cunard often came home, both to visit his relatives and to attend to business interests. He maintained his position as Commissioner of Lighthouses for many years. S. Cunard and Company, "Heat Merchants Since 1827," is still carrying on the fuel business in Halifax and Dartmouth. As with all ocean passenger-carrying fleets, the once-huge Cunard Line has passed its zenith, but the small ferries which claim Samuel Cunard as part of their heritage still ply their ancient route.

There was no information in the minutes or press about the *Boxer's* engine, but two clues led us on. E. H. Lowe, the Steam Boat Company's Agent, wrote in a report that the *Boxer's* engine was to be placed in a new boat, the *Chebucto*, launched in 1864. The *Chebucto's* Bill of Sale, 1886, stated that her engine had been built by Rigby of North Wales in 1835. From another source we learned that Rigby was the son-in-law of Robert Napier, colleague of Cunard in the trans-Atlantic Royal Mail contract awarded by the British government. A. G. Veysey, archivist for the Clwyd County Council, North Wales, confirmed the fact that the Rigby family did build engines at Hawarden and later, at Sandycroft.

XI.
MICMAC
Queen of the Fleet

"The Farmers' Almanac" of 1843 listed the names of three marine insurance companies in Halifax, along with the names of their directors. A number of these directors were also shareholders of the Halifax Steam Boat Company. These dual business interests did not assist the ferry company. The minutes of an April 1840 meeting record that the insurance rates on the **Ogle** and the **Boxer** were so high it was deemed "not expedient to insure the boats." In addition to the high rates, the insurance companies added difficult riders, such as "not liable for bursting of the boilers" and "warranted not to proceed beyond Meagher's Beach."

The harbour's ocean water was still causing great difficulties with the ferries' boilers. Perhaps the insurers' actuarial decisions were based on some knowledge of these problems.

Lowe, the Agent, recommended that a third boat be acquired in the event that the present two were laid up for repairs at the same time. To promote some action in this direction, he presented a report to a directors' meeting in April, 1843: "Report upon the state of the Halifax Steam Boat Company's Ferry Steamers **Sir Charles Ogle** and **Boxer** and their Engines."

The Engine in the *Sir Charles Ogle* has been in use about 13 years, during that time it has been taken down twice and the third set of Boilers were put down in the month of May of the year 1841, they are now in good working order. The Engine was last taken down in the summer of the Year 1838 and the Boat hauled up and partially repaired. At that time the Bed Plate under the Air Pump was found defective but as time would not admit of getting a new casting some lead was run into the weak parts and rivets put through to

27. *Two ferries at Harbour Regatta. Dartmouth shore in background.*

keep it in its place. This part of the Engine is always immersed in salt water the action of which upon the cast iron seems to soften it. From the time passed since it has been examined there is every reason to suppose that this part cannot hold good much longer and we have not the power of examination or remedy without taking down all the Engine.

The Breast Pipe or Steam Case is cracked in several places and is now patched and bound with straps and this part could not be put up again; if once disturbed it must be entirely new cast. If either of the parts of the Engine herein mentioned should give way the whole is useless until completely refitted, and to do this the Engine must be taken out of the Boat and new Castings made the patterns for which cannot be taken until the whole is down—for these castings we must send to England or to Pictou to get any that can be depended on.

The Engine must be taken into the shop and set up and fitted before replacing it in the Boat.

The Boat must be hauled up on account of the holding down bolts going through the bottom—it is probable that she will require some copper and some caulking. This repair will require 14 weeks of time and we suppose may cost 500 pounds as the vessel requires a new Deck and upper works, the Hull we have reason to believe is sound.

The Engine in the Steamer *Boxer* has run five years with one set of Boilers; it was taken up and repaired in the winter of the Year 1842 and we are not aware of any defect further than that the time the Boilers have run may lead us to suppose that repair will be required before any length of time passes. She works well at present.

This Vessel should have a new Deck and though eight years younger than the *Sir Charles Ogle* is not so good a Boat.

No possible answer can be given to the question asked, "How long do you think the Engine in the *Sir Charles Ogle* will run?" because the most serious part supposed defective is not open to examination, but in view of the facts above stated and with our general experience in such cases we say that we should not be surprised at its failure at any moment, and yet it may run out the summer.

In our opinion an Engine in this state should not be trusted and we should object to taking the *Sir Charles Ogle* outside the harbour in the present state of her Engine.

Dated at Dartmouth the 17th day of April AD 1843.

Edw. H. Lowe   Samuel Hunstone
Agent Manager   Chief Engineer

This charming and lucid handwritten report was found loose within the pages of the company's minute book of the 1880s.

It apparently impressed the directors with the

seriousness of the situation. They must also have been aware of boiler explosion tragedies which had occurred elsewhere and duly reported in the newspapers of the day. With over a hundred years of hindsight, and given the historical facts regarding their boiler problems, it is amazing that neither the **Ogle** nor the **Boxer** had any serious accidents due to boiler explosions.

The directors pressed on. As mentioned earlier, Captain Douglass of the **Unicorn** was asked to inquire about sources of boats in "Canada," and Almon was to do likewise at Saint John, New Brunswick. If there were no existing boats available on this side of the Atlantic the directors proposed to order an engine from Scotland and to have the hull built locally, as they had done twice before.

Apparently Douglass and Almon were unable to find any available boats. So another report was presented by Lowe:

Information respecting the cost of putting a new Steam Boat on the Ferry between Halifax and Dartmouth.

Tenders have been received for furnishing Engines of 35 and 40 Horses Power, the lowest is from Messrs.

28.   *View of Halifax from the Red Mill, Dartmouth, 1853.*

Wingate & Co. of Glasgow offering to furnish one of the largest mentioned in four months after order for the sum of 1,300 pounds sterling.

From the information gathered respecting the cost of building a Boat equal to the *Sir Charles Ogle* it would probably cost 1,259 pounds currency to which may be added for contingencies about 200 pounds. Then calculating the cost of Engine at 50 per cent advance upon sterling say 1,950 pounds currency the whole would amount to 3,400 pounds currency.

The tenders for the engine were reported as follows:

(Liverpool) Bury, Curtis & Kennedy	1,830 pounds
(Wales) Rigby & Co.	1,700 pounds
(Liverpool) Smith	1,900 pounds
(Glasgow) Wingate & Co.	1,300 pounds

They accepted the lowest bid and ordered the new engine from Wingate & Co. Like its two predecessors, it was a side lever engine, but with a 35 inch diameter cylinder, three foot stroke and 40 horsepower.

Wingate, incidentally, had achieved some fame and stature as the builder of the engine of the steamer **Sirius**. The **Sirius** in 1838 was the first ship to cross the Atlantic to New York under sustained steam power. Her side lever engine of 320 N.H.P. was assisted by a new development, a surface condenser. This device was a huge step forward in the Steam Age, both ashore and at sea. Not only was exhaust steam recovered as fresh or "distilled" water for reuse in the boilers, instead of being wasted to the atmosphere, but the vacuum at the engines' exhaust, caused by the condensing of the steam, greatly increased the efficiency of the engines.

It is not known whether the engine built by Wingate for the Halifax Steam Boat Company was fitted with a surface condenser. It seems likely that it was so equipped, however, since there were no reports of corrosion or other boiler problems.

Alexander Lyle's shipyard was once again chosen for the building of the new ferry boat. In February 1844 it was well underway. At the company meeting that month the treasurer reported that 650 pounds had been borrowed towards the cost of the engine, and that 1,000 pounds was still required. This total, 1,650 pounds, substantially exceeds Wingate's tender of 1,300 pounds, the difference probably being accounted for in "extras," contingencies, insurance, ocean freight and the like.

Long before the keel of the new boat had been laid, and all through its construction, many citizens of Dartmouth were voicing protests concerning the poor service extended by the Steam Boat Company.

Not only were both steamers occasionally used simultaneously for excursions and for observing harbour regattas, but when the Cunarder **Caledonia** went aground on George's Island, both were employed as tugboats. When three large sailing ships transported the 76th Regiment from Bermuda to Halifax, the 800 soldiers were taken ashore by the **Ogle** and the **Boxer**. It is not surprising that the commuters were upset over the company's ignoring its obligation to its regular patrons.

During a public meeting in February 1844 it was resolved to petition the Legislature to reduce fares on the steamboat. "Acron," in a letter to the editor of a Halifax newspaper said that grants from the Legislature to the Steam Boat Company were "nothing less than a premium for them to get rich." The directors, he wrote, owned the most valuable real estate in Dartmouth but gave "poor service and charge double the rates they should."

Newspapers at this time were full of the wreck of the **Saladin**, and the subsequent trial, conviction and hanging of her pirate crew. The Steam Boat Company was mildly affected by this turmoil. Alexander Lyle, builder of the new boat, volunteered to deliver the warrants for the arrest of the crew members. The warrants were previously sent to Guysborough by a naval vessel, but strong headwinds prevented landing there, where the **Saladin** was anchored. Lyle, a United Empire Loyalist, had lived at Country Harbour, and is presumed to have had local knowledge of the coastal area. His absence on this expedition caused some delay in the completion and launching of the new ferry boat.

29. Micmac *at Nova Scotia Hospital wharf, 1885.* (*Sinclair glass
negative.*)

However, on June 17, 1844, the new steam boat was launched. She was christened **Micmac** by Miss Mary Hartshorne, daughter of Secretary Lawrence Hartshorne.

Not a great deal was written in the newspapers about the launching. The novelty of steam-powered vessels may have been lessening, but one amusing story was reported in two papers, the "Morning Chronicle" and the "Novascotian." A young lawyer said that the name Micmac honoured three different parts of the British Empire: MIC for Ireland, MAC for Scotland and Micmac for the native people of Nova Scotia.

The following year, 1845, saw a reduction in the fares. Adult passengers now paid three pence instead of four. Also at this time, since there was no insurance on the boats, Lowe recommended that a night watchman be hired.

There was still restlessness and dissatisfaction with the service. Various schemes were put to the Legislature to attempt to improve the cross-harbour transportation. Arthur W. Godfrey and John E. Starr wanted to build a bridge of boats across the Narrows while John Ross of Dartmouth wanted to start a competitive ferry. These two requests were turned down by the Legislature, but surprisingly, another proposal was approved.

This new venture was an outcome of some 40 years of experimentation in Britain. Instead of paddlewheels an Archimedian screw had been designed for the propulsion of ships. **Archimedes**, a ship of 237 tons, was so fitted in 1838. Isambard Kingdom Brunel, a famous British engineer, remembered mainly for the unfortunate **Great Eastern**, was one of the earliest advocates of the screw propeller. He arranged a most dramatic demonstration. Two ships, identical in all respects except for their propulsion systems were to have a "tug-of-war." The **Rattler** was equipped with a screw propeller, while the **Alecto** had paddlewheels. Connected stern-to-stern by a suitable cable, the two ships ran at full power. **Rattler** managed to tow **Alecto** at the rate of 2.8 knots.

This Archimedian screw principle was the basis of the proposal to the Legislature put forward by Arthur Godfrey and John E. Starr of the former bridge-of-boats proposal.

The Legislature granted their request to operate a North End ferry service, on Sundays only, from Richmond in Halifax to the Windmill in Dartmouth, located near the foot of the present Jamieson Street.

This new ferry boat, also named **Archimedes**, was, like the old "Grinders," hand-cranked. Four men, sometimes helped by the passengers, turned the cranks. The **Archimedes** must have been large and commodious, for it carried 100 passengers. Adults were charged two pence and children one penny. The trip was reported to be very smooth, and took from eight to 12 minutes, the harbour being narrower here, and the route straight across, rather than the diagonal route of the Halifax Steam Boat ferry.

The Steam Boat Company directors may have felt some concern when they read in a newspaper, "We have seen the old heavy ferry boats in competition with the Teamboat; the Teamboat succeeded by the Steamboat, and who knows to what extent a competition with the Steam Boat Company may be carried by the Screw Propeller."

Apart from an advertisement—"Grand Picnic at Albro's Grove in Dartmouth, Boat **Archimedes**. Tickets, One dollar. Sports, food, drink, hodge podge"—nothing more was heard of the **Archimedes**. The Steam Boat Company continued to flourish. As for the **Micmac**, she lived a long life, and for most of it she was regarded as Queen of the Ferry Fleet. Launched in 1844, she was scrapped in 1901. The first issue of "The Dartmouth Patriot," April 20, 1901, reported that the **Micmac** "was pulled up on the beach just below Fort Clarence (Imperial Oil refinery site) last week and stripped of her upper sheathing. Most of the hull was then set on fire. The sight of the 57-year old ferry being towed down the harbour brought back recollections of the days when many an animated discussion on town affairs took place on the trips across the harbour. When Joe Howe was on board, the voyage must have been particularly enlivened because everybody knew and spoke to Howe. Being the largest of the old ferries, (with **Ogle** and **Boxer**), the **Micmac** was the queen of the fleet and was consequently always chosen for excursions and Sunday School picnics."

XII.
Gesner's Gas and Other Developments

The launching of the **Micmac** heralded a new age for the Halifax Steamboat Company. Like a hesitant unsure schoolboy who is eventually transformed into a confident and secure businessman, the Steam Boat Company matured as it prospered. Whereas only a few years before, the annual meetings were fraught with anxiety and uncertainty as all the shareholders assembled, now the meetings were brief and precise. The company affairs were capably in hand, running smoothly and efficiently under the four directors, Lawrence Hartshorne, William A. Black, Edward Cunard and William Stairs. Edward Lowe, the Agent, gave practical advice obtained from his daily observations of the ferry operations.

Indeed, the greater community was coming of age. Halifax celebrated its 100th birthday in 1849. A water system was proposed, street lighting was coal gas, and the coming of the telegraph were all tangible evidence that the provincial capital was no longer a mere outpost of western civilization.

Dartmouth had grown from the small village it had once been. The annual regatta, usually held on the harbour, was moved to the first Dartmouth lake in 1846.

In 1848 the Dartmouth Water Company was organized. This could have been a great boon to the Steam Boat Company, but the town seems not to have actually constructed a water system until 1892. However, the following clue suggests that the Steam Boat Company did not have to wait until then for fresh water for the steamers' boilers:

"The agent having reported on the trouble experienced with the water supply at the City dock in winter from the waste of water to prevent the freezing of the pipes, it was resolved to replace the present tap with a hydrant, provided it can be placed where it will be free from frost."

30. Dr. Abraham Gesner, 1797-1864.

So for many years, until Dartmouth's water system was installed, it seems that the company purchased water from the City of Halifax.

Returning to the 1840s, there remains something of a mystery concerning the utilization of the boats. At the time of the launching of the **Micmac** in 1844, the company was running **Ogle** and **Boxer**. Yet in 1848, four years after **Micmac's** launching, the local press held forth in wordy paeans of praise regarding the advent of a second steamer on the ferry.

> On Monday morning at an early hour a salute of cannon reported the circumstances of a second steamer being put into regular employment for the first time, in crossing the harbour. Many were at a loss, until a later hour to know the reason of such a celebration, as they imagined it must have been the arrival of the new Admiral of the Station, or a French man-of-war from St. Pierre, that was so announced rather than the fact of the meeting of two ferry steamers in command of new Captains (Allen and Coleman). To the public this addition to ferry accommodation is so highly agreeable and advantageous that the enterprise cannot miss being profitable to the Steam Boat Company, as well as favourable to the interests of Dartmouth.

Further, in the same paper this account appeared:

> Not the least remarkable incident connected with this arrangement [two boats on the ferry] is the retirement of Captain Hunter from the command of the ferry after a hard service of 18 years and four months. Were Captain Hunter's situation the most agreeable in the world, instead of being a singularly monotonous vexatious and harassing one, he could not have discharged his duty with more diligence, attention, and punctuality, than he has done by day and night, in all seasons and all sorts of weather, during the long period of his employment in crossing the harbour. Unless the harbour was frozen over now and then, which it has not been for 12 hours at a time within the last ten years, or that he was prevented by

64

temporary illness, Capt. Hunter has had but one day of relaxation from duty. Rumour says the SBC will allow him a liberal annuity in consideration of his long and faithful services on condition that he take charge occasionally of the boats employed on extra excursions.

Waggish readers of the late 20th Century may be inclined to wonder about the gold watch which seems not to have appeared on this occasion.

None of the fanfare explains why with three boats during a four-year period, only one was in regular passenger service. Excessive maintenance (boiler cleaning), towing charters and excursions might add up to one boat but surely not two.

In any event, the 1848 advent of two-boat service brought 20-minute service to the passengers. The company waited to see the outcome of this "experiment" before the next dividend was declared. It must have been considered a financial success, for at the annual meeting in 1849, a 3 pound per share dividend was disbursed, and the ferry schedule was extended from 9 to 10 p.m.

In 1850, the annual meeting of the Steam Boat Company was held in Dartmouth—another first. This may have been related to arguments between the company and the City of Halifax over taxes. In Dartmouth, where the company owned its terminal property, there were few such problems. On the Halifax side, however, through the entire history of the Halifax Steam Boat Company and succeeding ferry administrations, disagreement over taxation of terminal facilities continued, with arguments concerning the privately owned Steam Boat Company using the public landing and rents that should be charged. Property owners adjacent to the Halifax ferry terminal fought over damages they claimed to have incurred from passengers and vehicles passing through the narrow right-of-way to George Street. Disputes arose over titles of land the company wanted to purchase, and lawsuits dragged on for years. The most spectacular, was that with one C. Stayner.

In 1850, a newly elected Halifax City Council assessed the Halifax Steamboat Company on real and personal estate. The company denied ownership of personal property and refused to pay this portion of the tax bill. Thus one more scar appeared on the relationship between the company and the City of Halifax.

That summer, **Micmac** was kept busy on excursions. A newspaper advertisement stated, "The Dartmouth Steamer will go down the harbour on Friday of each week to East Passage, Ferguson's Cove etc. Trips to Sackville as usual on Monday and Thursday."

Strong drink was among the refreshments made available to passengers on these excursions. However the Temperance Society and the "Young Cold Water Army" gave the company a great deal of business and were able to persuade the company to apply the "temperance principle in the refreshment department."

The steamers were also still used as fire boats—not as fire boats today, with hoses, monitors and huge pumps—but as transporters of town firemen and their equipment to scenes of waterfront conflagrations. Mott's chocolate factory had a fire on May 18, 1850. The warehouse and steam mill were destroyed, in spite of the ferry's effort to bring Dartmouth firemen to the scene.

An interesting development began in 1850. Up to this time lighting on the ferryboats was by fish oil lamps. Halifax streets were lit by coal gas lamps, which were installed in 1849. However the Steam Boat Company was about to embark on an even newer system of lighting for their boats and terminals.

Halifax newspapers of the time had accounts of lectures given by scientists at the Mechanics Institutes of Halifax and Dartmouth. One of the more exciting lectures was given by Dr. Abraham Gesner, a medical doctor, who was also a knowledgeable geologist. He had been commissioned to do geological surveys of both Nova Scotia and New Brunswick in the late 1830s. Along the way he experimented with some of his mineral finds, and discovered a way to make gas from asphaltum, a thick pitch-like substance. In early production, the asphaltum used was imported from Trinidad. Pitch Lake on that island

31. *Mechanics' Institute, later Town Hall of Dartmouth, on Ochterloney Street. 1846-1948.*

consists of a "seepage of natural asphalt, viscous toward the centre but solidified around the edges."

October newspapers reported that "an Eastport vessel, the Brig **Zelica**, arrived at New York with 130 tons of asphaltum from Port of Spain, Trinidad, to A. Gesner. This alone is enough to show that the kerosene gas concern is going ahead in New York."

With this announcement, a fierce and wordy battle began in the newspapers on the merits of Gesner's gas versus that of the Halifax Coal Company. The latter was said to be "little better than the light of a dull, dim, penny dip or dingy old tin lamp half-fed with dog fish oil."

Directors of the Steam Boat Company favoured Dr. Gesner's gas. Lowe gave the following report at the annual meeting in February, 1851: "Accounts submitted show the earnings by each service including...The Gas Works entered upon at the close of last year (1850) and put in operation for lighting the Ferry Docks on January 14th.

Since that time arrangements have been into effect for lighting the Ferry Steamers and shops on the company's premises, which last have been supplied since 1st of July at quarterly rates amounting in the whole to 22 pounds ten shillings per annum. It has answered every expectation in the Steamers affording a cheap and clean light and giving general satisfaction. Five shops, two steamers, the office and dock and gate lights are all duly fitted and supplied and having two Gasometers the use of the Gas can be extended when necessary. I estimate the total cost at 150 pounds and that the revenue derived from the shops will support the whole giving the light used in the Boats free—I consider the whole a valuable addition to the company's property."

Technical details about how the gas was actually produced are absent or at least obscure.

The Gasometers were not for measuring gas flow, but were more likely small gas generating units that produced gas for immediate local use. This is deduced from the following account: "We were last evening favoured with a small quantity of kerosene gas sent to our office by Dr. Gesner. It was contained in a gutta percha bag, fitted up with a tube stopcock and burner. A book placed upon it furnished sufficient pressure, and a half cubic foot of gas gave a beautiful light for nearly an hour. The Doctor states that in such bags the kerosene may be hawked through the streets like bread or beer and delivered to consumers. We understand that the Halifax and Dartmouth Steamboats are to be lighted up by this novel method, for which the kerosene gas is admirably adapted, on account of its great density and superior illuminating power."

This was before Dr. Gesner had patented kerosene oil, but he took out patents for his kerosene gas discovery, and immediately encountered difficulties. His gas was made from "asphaltum" and therein lay a problem. Dr. Gesner classified asphaltum as vegetable matter. His opponents said it was mineral, and in New Brunswick entrepreneurs attempted to sell a supply of asphaltum to a gas company in New York under the name of coal, in order to evade Dr. Gesner's patent.

While this particular controversy raged on, the Steam Boat Company ran into difficulties with the lighting system with which Lowe had at first been so satisfied. Late in 1852 he reported that the "Gas Manufactory had to be discontinued a few months since for want of proper material, though sought for in Boston and New York. I have lately received information that a small quantity will be sent from New Brunswick which may serve for the Boats and Docks if not the Shops;—the return to oil and lamps has been found expensive and inconvenient."

That year, 1852, was the one in which Gesner resolved his nomenclature problems, and was granted another patent which won him world renown. This was for the discovery of kerosene oil, which became the forerunner of today's petrochemical industry.

Lowe reported at the annual meeting of 1854 that the gas manufactory had been resumed and that there was sufficient "asphalt coal" on hand for two years. When that time had elapsed, his 1856 report stated that "the Gas manufactory has been in operation throughout the year with safety and advantage—the high price oil has attained makes this a valuable addition to the company's property. I have no doubt there is a clear saving by it of all the light used in the steamers, besides the advantage of the cost, as compared with oil, of all other lights used on the premises."

Dr. Abraham Gesner, a foremost pioneer of the oil industry, thus played his part in the history of our ferries. Kerosene oil was introduced into the United States in 1853, after which Gesner did further research. This resulted in 1861 in his publication of "A Practical Treatise on Coal, Petroleum and Other Distilled Oils." Three years later, Abraham Gesner died, unaware of how his discoveries would revolutionize the world when the sequence of gasoline, diesel and jet engines followed through the succeeding hundred years.

Meanwhile, let us return to the mid-19th Century and examine the contribution made by another principal character in our story.

XIII.
Edward H. Lowe

While there were men of world renown like Samuel Cunard and Abraham Gesner connected with the Halifax Steam Boat Company, others not internationally famous deserve places of honour in its history. Such a man was Edward H. Lowe who served the company with much competence and integrity for 30 years.

"Rough and ready, chubby and chuffy, the Ferry Boat does its work well, without accident or delay . . . The bell rings at Halifax, you walk up and down a few turns, eight or ten minutes elapse, and again the ding-dong announces arrival at the opposite shore." So wrote an unknown commentator in 1850 in a Halifax newspaper.

Behind those words of praise lay the work of a quiet man, who had been appointed Agent or Superintendent for the Halifax Steam Boat Company, beginning work in 1832. Edward Lowe was the only one of four candidates who was willing to live in Dartmouth, rather than Halifax. His loyalty to the company and enthusiasm for his work very soon made him a most valuable employee.

In addition to being an efficient and devoted Agent for the company, Lowe was a diplomatic intermediary. On many occasions he improved relations between the company's directors (mainly Haligonians) and the travelling public (mainly Dartmouthians). His annual reports were factual and concise, and delicately included suggestions for improving the quality of the service. When his suggestions had been discussed and perhaps adopted, his next report never hinted that they were originally his ideas. One can imagine the directors patting their respective backs in self-congratulatory fashion for some innovative change in the system, when in reality it had been at Lowe's suggestion.

An important anniversary occurred during Lowe's tenure: 1852 marked the 100th year of operation of a

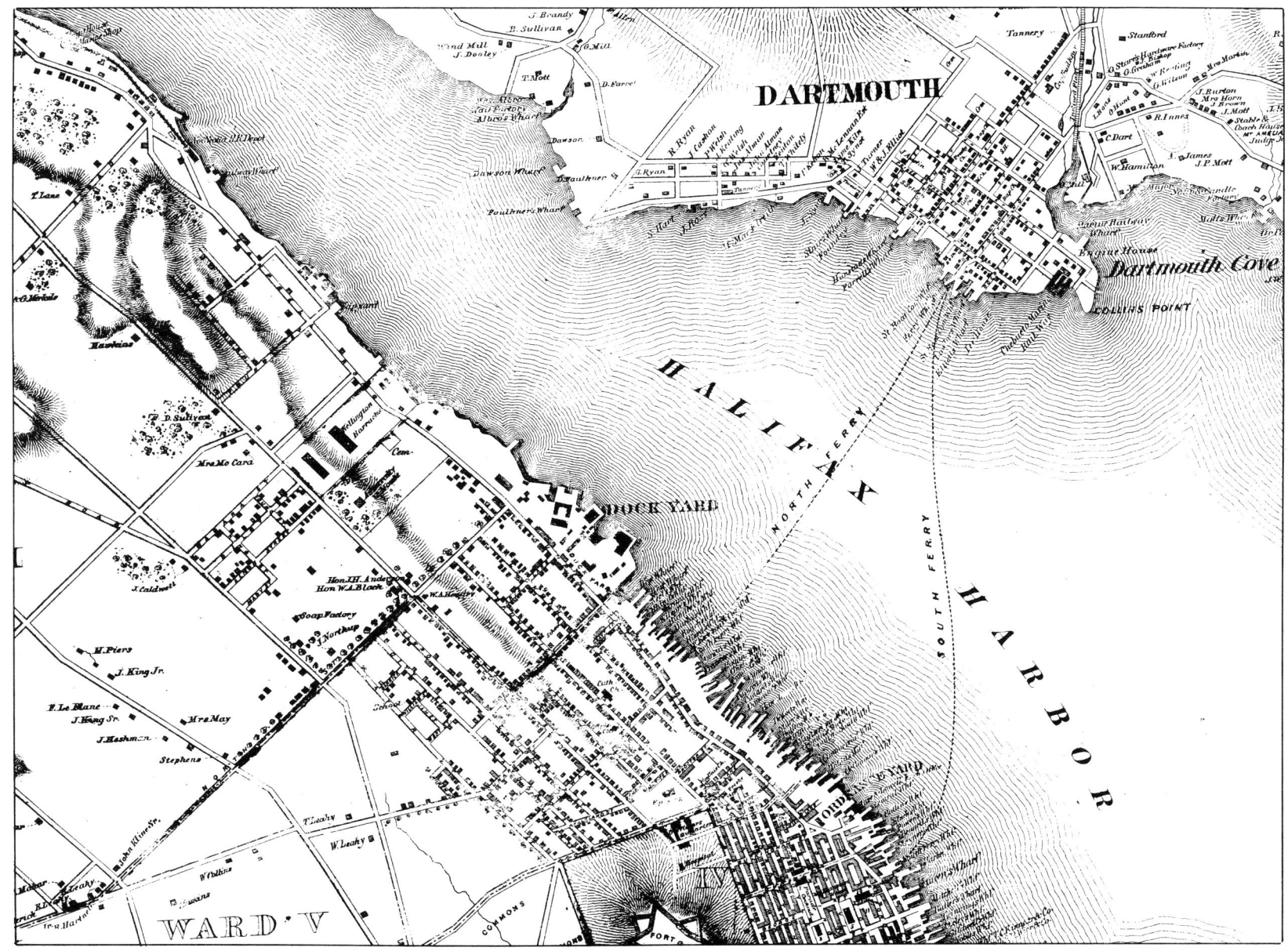

32. Portion of Township map of Halifax County showing North and South Ferry Routes, 1866.

regular ferry service, John Connors having been granted the original charter by the government of Governor Cornwallis a century before. The minutes of the Halifax Steam Boat Company did not specifically acknowledge this fact, but there was mention of a rather unusual award which may have been a subtle recognition of the anniversary. The directors voted to order from England a gold medal worth five pounds to be donated as a prize for the curling clubs of the area. There were no indoor curling clubs in 1852, so the game was played on various ponds and lakes—mostly by Scottish officers serving in the Army and Navy.

Like the original wooden model of the **Sir Charles Ogle** made in New York, this gold medal would be a priceless artifact should one turn up among the treasures of a descendant of one of those early Scottish curlers.

Along with the donation of the medal, another sign of the company's prosperity in this centennial year was the granting of semi-annual dividends of five pounds and three pounds per share.

In addition to the Gesner gas lighting of ferry property, other innovations appeared. The "inhabitants," according to Lowe, requested that the ferry cabins be heated. Coal stoves had been installed, but were quickly superceded by steam heating the following year. "The plan or method is by dome cylinders of galvanized iron," explained Lowe, "with copper tops and about ten inches diameter into which the waste steam is conveyed, assisted by a jet from the boiler. They appear to answer the purpose and will be much cheaper than pipes under the seats."

In addition to having the cabins heated, Lowe recommended that there "should be Station Rooms or Toll Houses. From October 1 to May 1 there is considerable time in the evening with but one Boat every 40 minutes and passengers must wait on the street. The consequences may be an order to run the second Boat an hour or two later which would be inconvenient and expensive." Whether Lowe was trying to save his company money, or whether he felt sorry for the waiting passengers is not clear. In any case, the following year, 1854, saw the construction of

station houses with "mutually beneficial results to publick and Company."

While the "publick" got their station houses, it was also the year of increased fares which the company blamed on the high price of coal. Instead of the friendly captains, men were hired to collect these higher fares at the gates. Their yearly salary was 75 pounds each. They immediately ran into opposition from the passengers. Lowe said that at the outset the fare collectors were too rigid in demanding payment for all freight, including even baskets. He maintained that previously the "publick had bullied the captains, in this respect."

A public meeting of the citizens of Dartmouth was held in the Mechanics Institute Hall. The following resolution was moved by Charles Robson, seconded by Jonathan Elliot and passed unanimously: "Resolved that a Petition as numerously signed as possible be presented to the Legislature earnestly requesting them to give the Sessions a more thorough control over the fares to be charged by the Steam Boat Company, with power to require from them an annual statement of their account."

The citizens' meeting took place on February 6, 1855. William Annand presented the petition to the House of Assembly three days later and then moved the appointment of a select committee, to consist of himself, Johnston, Wilkins, Howe and McQueen. The appeal failed. Lowe told his company that the magistrates when petitioned by the public had fully exonerated the company.

The Agent's comprehensive reports covered such matters as the real estate owned by the company, repairs to steamers and docks, freight rates, coal costs, accounts for excursion trips and towing jobs. The pleasure trips to Sackville were growing in popularity, but Lowe recommended that "a landing place in Sackville would save the trouble of throwing down the anchor." Captain Coleman was in charge of these trips and received praise for not having had "the slightest accident."

The company gave in to one request from Dartmouthians, and bought a dock in the north end of Halifax, at Richmond, near the foot of Cornwallis Street. The ferries

Ferry Between Dartmouth and Halifax.

No. *21*

SEASON TICKET, *terminating* *30th June* 1850.

AND SUBJECT TO THE GENERAL REGULATIONS.

THIS TICKET

Entitles to pass the Ferry as often as the Steamers may run :

Man and wife, unmarried children being minors, domestic Servants, and a One Horse Vehicle, owned by the proprietor of this Ticket. The privilege not covering the Lumber trade, or any business employing Teams constantly.

PROPRIETOR OF THIS TICKET. *J E Lawler*

Persons to Pass :

Edw H Lowe
Agent & Manager.

33. Season ticket, 1850, signed by E. H. Lowe.

then ran every 15 minutes. All boats left from the company's main dock in Dartmouth, but alternated between the old dock and the newer north end one on the Halifax side. A year after this new service started, Lowe's account was not enthusiastic. He said that the north ferry had "not increased receipts to any great extent. People go up to market on the north but return on the south." No doubt the people drifted down to the more bustling and commercial end of the city before their return to Dartmouth.

Apparently, local insurance companies' fear of boilers blowing up and other such disasters was diminishing, for in 1856 the company paid a premium of 360 pounds for coverage on the three ferries: 2000 pounds on the **Micmac**, the largest and newest ferry; 1500 pounds on the **Ogle**; and 1000 pounds on the **Boxer**.

Meanwhile **Ogle, Boxer, Micmac** and the docks were receiving careful attention. Lowe's constant vigilance must have added years of service from the boats. The following excerpts from his reports are evidence of extensive repairs and replacements. One wonders how much of the original boats was left in their final days:

1842:
Engine in **Boxer** "taken down."

1843:
Engine in **Ogle** requires new breast pipe, and Engineer thinks bottom of condenser is defective. Probably will require 10 weeks refit. Breast pipe pattern is partly made. Imported piston and boiler plate.

1844:
Repairs in **Ogle**.
Boxer now eight years old with original set of boilers,

1845:
Boxer now eight years old with original set of boilers, reported inefficient. The experience of the past year with the **Ogle** shows that repairs of steam engines and boilers occupy considerable time and therefore should be looked to early.

1851:
A new bridge float was built in the most careful manner with juniper timber and knees and sheathed with zinc. It was placed in the Halifax Dock. Its mate in Dartmouth has been thoroughly repaired and is good as new and ready for use.
Ordered a new smoke funnel or chimney for one of the steamers.

1853:
A substantial sea wall was built on the South Wharf. On account of the pressure of work in Scotland, the Boilers could not be obtained by the Spring ship as expected, and it was extremely fortunate that the old ones held out as they did. Their first cost amounting to 560 pounds currency is bearing interest of five per cent, and owing to **Mr. Stairs**, who assumed the debt. The two largest boats are in good order. The **Boxer's** engine requires repair.

1854:
Boxer's paddle wheel shaft broke. The wood sheathing on the sides of **Ogle** and **Micmac** was entirely worn through in winter storms, and was replaced by Yellow Metal. **Boxer** has a new rudder and her deck was renewed. She requires a new bed plate and other work

which will take eight to ten weeks.

1856:
Boxer's engine needs repairs again, but not the boilers. The build or model of the vessel is not equal to the engine which would drive one ten feet longer if better shaped. Our engineer has suggested she would be improved by adding some feet of length to each end. This may be true.

In 1856 the company indicated their appreciation of Lowe's services by raising his salary to 250 pounds a year. He must have received previous increases since his starting salary of 100 pounds in 1832. One of the directors, Mr. Falconer, moved a vote of thanks to Lowe for his valuable service to the company at the annual meeting three years later, in 1859. This was the year that the Agent had been sent to Pictou to look at a secondhand steamer, the **Lord Seaforth**. Although the price seemed right at $2,500, (the beginning of change from sterling to decimal currency), Lowe reported that the ship was not suitable for company purposes.

On December 4, 1861, a special meeting was called to notify the directors of the death of Edward H. Lowe, at the age of 63. The directors went on record in the minutes "to sincerely lament the loss they have suffered and desire to record the high sense they entertain of the valuable and zealous services of Mr. Lowe, during a period of nearly 30 years."

At that time pension schemes were non-existent. The directors voted to pay Lowe's salary to his widow for a further 12 months, a generous gesture for the times.

Edward H. Lowe was long remembered with respect by those who had known and worked with him, but no man is irreplaceable. Fortunately for the Steam Boat Company, he was succeeded by another dedicated and efficient Agent, Captain G. A. MacKenzie.

MacKenzie's tenure of office as Agent covered a period which included much of excitement and historical significance for both the harbour and its ferries.

XIV.
The 1860s and 1870s

34. Great Eastern.

The harbour was the stage for much of the great excitement of 1860 as famous ships and people visited the port.

Queen Victoria's 19-year-old son, who was to reign as Edward VII, was then Prince of Wales. Newspapers carried two-column notices devoted to the program arranged for his expected visit to Halifax late in July. The Steam Boat Company inserted an eye-catching display advertisement headed "Prince of Wales Visit." The **Micmac** and two other local steamers, the tug **Neptune** and the **Eastern State**, waited impatiently for a signal of three guns advising them to steam out the harbour to meet and greet the royal squadron. At the sound of the signal the three steamers departed for the harbour entrance, loaded with passengers, to meet Her Majesty's Ships **Hero, Ariadne** and **Flying Fish**. The **Micmac** carried the City Band as well. Passengers had paid five shillings for the privilege of being

on hand. A dozen Indian birch bark canoes, probably from Turtle Grove, near the present Narrows bridge, also escorted the visitors up the harbour. For the duration of the Prince's visit the regular excursion trips were suspended. Instead, the **Micmac** took a continuous stream of enthusiastic citizens on harbour tours around the visiting naval ships.

The excitement generated by this visit had barely subsided when a most famous ship arrived in the harbour. In August, **Micmac** and tug **Neptune** once more gathered passengers and went out to meet the **Great Eastern**. She was designed by Isambard Kingdom Brunel, who was known as "Little Giant," and who was perhaps the best known British civil engineer of his time. The **Great Eastern** was on her way home from New York. People came from miles around to get a look at the great ship and, if possible, to get on board for a closer inspection. Passengers on

Micmac and **Neptune** had a curious reception from the **Great Eastern's** crew. Some were curtly refused permission to come on board, while others were allowed. Still others made it on payment of a half crown. There seemed to be no rhyme nor reason regarding who might or might not visit on board, but as soon as it was learned that some visitors had been allowed on board, fresh crowds arrived.

A tragic incident occurred during the **Great Eastern's** visit. Thomas Graves, cooper, with his wife and two young sons, in their small sailboat, drew close to the great ship at her moorings near Cunard's wharf. Suddenly the wind died, leaving the sailboat unnavigable. The **Micmac** suddenly appeared and loaded with excursionists, she ran into the sailboat which overturned. The two little Graves boys were drowned. One of the directors of the Steam Boat Company happened to be on board **Micmac** at the time, and was much distressed. A newspaper editor chastised the Steam Boat Company, writing, "Dartmouth Ferry Steamers should keep on board boats and other means of rescuing people from drowning."

Today, more than a century later, visitors to London, taking the boat tour down the Thames to Greenwich, may be intrigued by the large orange words painted on a seawall at Millbank: "Site of the Building and Launching of the Great Eastern 1853-1856 length—892', 27,308 tons."

In 1864, at the time of the U.S. Civil War, an exciting naval event took place in Halifax Harbour. The Confederate gunboat **Tallahassee**, having been engaged in a blockade of Northern ports, came into the harbour to refuel and obtain stores. As it was a neutral port, she was allowed not more than 48 hours to accomplish this and depart. With the knowledge that eight or ten gunboats were waiting near the mouth of the outer harbour, the **Tallahassee's** captain, John Wood, attempted the only chance of escape available to him. A pilot with expert local knowledge, Jock Flemming, was engaged. Under cover of darkness, Flemming skillfully guided **Tallahassee** from her mooring at Woodside out through the narrow passage between McNab's and Lawlor's Islands and the little fishing village of Eastern Passage. **Tallahassee** slipped out through the shallow channel, normally used only by the small inshore fishing boats from the village, and passed well to the northeast of the waiting gunboats.

She had left her harbour mooring at 1:00 a.m., only a few hours after a moonlight excursion by the ferry **Micmac** "under the auspices of the Halifax Volunteer Band had passed close to the **Tallahassee**, which attracted much attention . . . The evening was beautiful and the steamer lighted up with variegated lamps." The much-told **Tallahassee** yarn is closed here by noting that at the end of the Civil War, Captain Wood of that ship retired to Halifax.

Not only were famous ships viewed by ferry patrons. In 1863, Joseph Howe bought "Fairfield," an estate in the north end of Dartmouth. During the years he commuted to Halifax, he made a strong impression one way or another on his fellow travellers. At the time of Confederation, Howe was anti-Confederate, and was elected member of Parliament for Hants County. There was a tremendous celebration, and throngs of people went to the railway station to meet the train bringing Howe of Hants, A. W. McLelan of Colchester and William Annand of Cumberland to Halifax. They were taken through the streets in "Casey's carriage" pulled by six greys, to the Grand Parade. When there was a lull in the cheering of the crowds, Howe spoke and received thunderous applause. From there he was taken to the ferry. On the Dartmouth side he was met by more crowds. A huge bonfire and an 18-gun salute made the occasion even more remarkable. A torchlight precession accompanied Howe to his home, "Fairfield," on Windmill Road.

Howe left Dartmouth for Ottawa in 1869, the same year that he became reconciled to Confederation and joined the government of Sir John A. Macdonald. As a tribute to the great Nova Scotian, the Dartmouth Heritage Museum has built a model of his study at "Fairfield," complete with a lifelike figure of Howe himself, seated at his desk.

35. Ogle *or* Boxer *approaching Halifax terminal (glass negative).*

In 1864, 97 "Canadian" politicians had come to Halifax for pre-Confederation and pre-Charlottetown talks. The Halifax Yacht Club sponsored an enormous hodgepodge and chowder party at Prince's Lodge where the visitors were entertained with "sports, feasting, song, eloquence and good fellowship." The visitors were transported by the **Micmac**, the revenue cutter and half a dozen yachts.

This was a time of intense gold exploration throughout Nova Scotia. Accounts of various gold mining companies and their directors appeared in the newspapers. Once again, directors of the Halifax Steam Boat Company were prominent. So the "Canadian" politicians were treated to a tour of the "Waverley Gold Diggins," on the day following the hodgepodge at Prince's Lodge.

The Halifax Steam Boat Company, in the years following the 1861 death of Edward Lowe, saw many changes. After a year as Agent, Captain George MacKenzie recommended that the old **Boxer** should not have too much money spent on her. Thus sounded the first knell of an old friend's impending departure from the ferry. Late in the spring of 1863, the directors called for tenders for a boat to replace **Boxer**. Her engine, built by Rigby of North Wales, was still in good working order, despite the use of salt water in her boiler. The engine was removed, and the hull (no longer **Boxer**) was sold to Lewis P. Fairbanks, who in turn sold it to Adam McKay, boilermaker. McKay had recently moved to Dartmouth from his previous location at Freshwater in the south end of Halifax.

McKay lengthened and repaired the hull, and presumably either he or Fairbanks installed new engines. The reconditiond ship was again "launched" in June 1865, with the name **Hope**.

It was reported in November 1872, that an arsonist attacked **Hope**, and that cabins, deck and paddle boxes were burned beyond repair. McKay had insurance in the "Royal" for $7000.

There are three versions to the end of the **Boxer** story and the reader is free to choose the one that has the most appeal:

A. "The **Boxer** was converted into a brigantine by Ebenezer Moseley and engaged in the West Indian trade," according to Captain James Graham in an interview on his 50th anniversary of ferry service.

B. "The old steamer **Boxer** was converted into a two-topmast schooner and was sold in South America. Until a few years ago she was employed on the Essequibo River, being of light draught, and suited to river work. The boat may still be doing duty."

C. "Some years after the **Boxer** was sold, she was changed into a lighter and employed in the West Indian trade."

In any event, the Steam Boat Company, acting on the new Agent's advice, voted in January 1863, to build a new boat. Alexander Lyle, who had built the earlier boats, had died in 1858. The new ferry was built in a yard near the Steam Boat Company's wharf by a Mr. Cameron of New Glasgow. The contract was for $3750 and the boat was to be finished by September 21, 1864.

The new boat was named **Chebucto**. Like her predecessors she had one lane which carried ten teams. Cameron did not finish her by September, as agreed, but there is no mention of the company retaining "liquidation damages" as a consequence. As if impatient at her builder's delays, in January 1865, the ferry was said to have "launched herself." Before the christening ceremony some of the shores were knocked loose. Without warning the boat slid down the ways and into the water "with a rapidity of movement which it is generally hoped may be characteristic of her future trips." Such hopes were apparently not realized. The same source reported on May 8, "Sorry to learn the new Dartmouth Steamer is decidedly slow, far behind the old boats. Yesterday two hours were occupied in making the passage across the harbour." Perhaps like the strawberry-picking-stop stories of our early trains, they stopped to take advantage of a mackerel run coming up the harbour.

Such difficulties were not mentioned again. **Chebucto** served the company and the travelling public for many years and was sold in 1893 for $395. A small attractive oil painting of her may be seen at the Dartmouth Heritage

Museum, painted by Dartmouth artist George Craig. It is the only record in colour of the early paddlewheelers.

In September of the year of **Chebucto's** self-launching, Lawrence Hartshorne died. Like Charles Fairbanks, the secretary who preceeded him, Hartshorne had served the company for more than 20 years. A. M. Uniacke was asked to prepare an expression of esteem to be sent to the Hartshorne family.

The company's 50-year Charter being due to expire in 1866, an application for renewal was submitted to the Legislature. The company was to be recapitalized to $8000—100 shares at $80. A new charter was granted in 1867 when, for the first time, dividends were paid in dollars. In 1866 the dividend had been ten pounds per share, while the following year it was $50. Seven years later, its capital structure was amended drastically—200 shares at $500—for reasons still unclear. There was, however, evidence of corporate shenanigans which will be reported later.

One of the effects of Confederation was felt in 1869. Tonnage duty was claimed by the Dominion Government— the first tax paid by the Steam Boat Company (except for property tax to the City of Halifax). Anti-Confederate feelings must have been dying, however, for the directors voted, in 1875, to invest $5000 in Dominion debentures toward the cost of a new ferry boat.

Since 1860, directors had received a stipend of 50 pounds a year. In 1869, this was changed to $200, with $20 going to the auditors, A. M. Uniacke and H. Y. Yeomans. In 1872 the president was voted $100 in addition to his director's fee.

While the shareholders' returns were increasing, the employees also were granted higher salaries. Captain MacKenzie's pay jumped from $1600 in 1870 to $2000 in 1875. Captain Coleman was granted a $6 a month raise in 1871, and the mates were given 50 cents a week more. In 1874, Captain Coleman, Captain Graham and Engineer Pearce received further raises of $5 a month.

A new ticket system was begun in 1874. When tickets are mentioned in the minutes, it is not clear whether quarterly commutation tickets are meant, or individual trip tickets. At any rate, female ticket sellers were hired and paid $3 a week. Two girls were for the Halifax office and one for Dartmouth. One of these was discharged in 1878, because she was $63.90 short in her accounts. Captain MacKenzie was directed to inspect the ticket rack not less than once a week from that time forth. As an added precaution, a small box for valuable papers was bought and kept in the company's bank. Ticket agent Corbett, a retired ferry captain, was given a raise in 1873 to $34 a month. In the 1877 minutes it was recorded that he had been pensioned off.

A new larger station house had been built on the Halifax side in 1870. This was located on the south side of the present main dock. The minutes of 1867 noted that a "water closet" was to be built at the end of this station house to connect with the ladies' cabin! Fire "exterminators" were ordered for the steamers, and the directors bought a "punching machine" for $400. This could have been for tokens, like the one in the Dartmouth Heritage Museum.

The Reverend Dr. Falconer, who lived on the upper end of Portland Street, and was minister of St. James' Presbyterian Church, applied for free passage on the ferry for the clergymen of the Presbyterian Synod, which was meeting in Dartmouth. This request was granted as was a request for a $20 donation to a bazaar at Bedford. The year 1876 was a time of improvements and generosity.

Services to the travelling public were increased from time to time, expecially if enough pressure was exerted by the commuters. Extra trips were run, according to the demand, starting in 1869. At the request of farmers travelling to the City Market, the boats began at 5:30 a.m. in the summer. Excursions continued to be lucrative. An advertisement of 1872 stated that excursion fares to Sackville on Monday, Tuesday and Thursday were 25 cents, with children travelling at half price. The excursion receipts for that year were $1146.

Cold weather still disrupted ferry schedules. In 1866 the tug **Neptune** cut a channel and took people across the harbour for three cents, when the regular ferries were

36. Chebucto *in 1870s. Oil painting by George Craig.*

frozen fast to their docks. By 1875 the price to cross by tug was considerably more. That year the harbour froze for 16 days, and the tug **A. C. Whitney** charged 50 cents per passenger. Tugs were used to tow a ferry off the shore at the Narrows where it had been driven during a severe snowstorm.

The same ice which caused the ferries so much trouble and loss of revenue provided pleasure to hundreds of skaters. Many present-day residents of Halifax and Dartmouth recall hearing stories of their immediate forebears either skating or walking to work across the harbour. When the harbour itself was not ice covered (the normal state), the ferry company contributed to the whims of the skating enthusiasts. Haligonians as well as Dartmouthians enjoyed skating on the many lakes of Dartmouth. The minutes of the Steam Boat Company record that a flag was to be hoisted at the Halifax Station when there was good skating in Dartmouth. This was in 1874, shortly after John Forbes' invention of "Acme Spring Skates." They were manufactured in Dartmouth at the

Starr Skate Factory, and were known the world over. In the U.S. Centennial Year, 1876, Starr Manufacturing Company sent a custom-built display case to Washington. The case contained samples of all Starr products, but the Acme skates were highlighted at the industrial exhibition.

From time to time accidents occurred, both on board the ferry boats, and between the ferries and other ships. One of the early onboard accidents was recorded in 1848. During a raw March day an unidentified man, who had travelled in on the long rough road from Preston, probably on his ox team, went to the engine room to warm himself. He fell into the main engine and was instantly killed.

In 1864, a fireman was severely injured while he was cleaning part of the machinery and the engines were started up. Like the Prestonian, he was not identified by name.

Newspapers of February 1871, carried the obituary of George Webber, 36, who was killed in a paddle box, where he was clearing ice off the paddles. The captain ordered the engine started, unaware of Webber's whereabouts, the paddlewheel turned and Webber suffered a fractured skull. At the inquest a verdict of accidental death was brought in. The Steam Boat Company donated $400 to the Webber family, and at the same time asked Agent MacKenzie to draw up a code of regulations for the guidance of the captains and the engineers.

In spite of this, a similar tragedy occurred in 1876. Eli Vienot, a carpenter told to wait until the boat was fully stopped, ignored this and entered a paddle box only to have both legs crushed. He died at midnight. The company voted to pay his widow $4 a week, and to urge employees to take out accident policies. A further resolution was passed to the effect that no man should enter the paddle boxes without orders from the captain or the engineer.

Accidents to the boats themselves were frequent. Minutes of the August 1870 meeting refer briefly to the "late accident to the Chebucto." Strangely, no mention of this appeared in the newspapers of the day.

During our research we thought for a moment that the Ogle had touched a ship which has since become a legend in Nova Scotia. However, the date of the accident made this impossible. The ship was the brigantine Teazer, a namesake perhaps of the ghost ship of Mahone Bay. A special meeting of the Steam Boat Company was called in October 1870, to interview Captain Graham of the Ogle with regard to a collision between the ferry boat and the Teazer. Captain Graham explained that as the Teazer was headed up the harbour in the same direction as those at anchor, and since she displayed no running lights, he assumed that she was at anchor also. Then he was alerted by the whistle of the tug Henry Hoover, which was alongside the Teazer, but hidden by the larger brigantine. The tug would have just missed the Ogle if the tug's captain had not altered course in a panic. She smashed into the Ogle's paddle box. The evidence submitted to the directors by Captain Graham, and corroborated by that of Mate Alex Marks and Engineer Mott, apparently convinced the directors to exonerate their captain and crew. The directors resolved to seek damages from the owners of the tug.

Two years later, in dense fog, the Ogle was again in a collision, this time with her sister ship Micmac. As Captain Graham was at breakfast, Alex Marks was in command. The damage was more serious on this occasion—a paddle box, the ladies cabin and the gentlemen's cabin all suffered. One young lady fainted from fright and was slightly scratched. After losing each other in the fog, the Micmac searched for and found the Ogle and towed her to a dock. The Chebucto immediately replaced her.

A near disaster occurred in the summer of 1873. It happened on the evening excursion trip of the Micmac. She was returning from McNab's Island with a reported but hardly believable 400 on board, and was turning into the north dock at the foot of Cornwallis Street to disembark her passengers. A very large plank, used as a fender to prevent damage to McKay's wharf, which was just to the north of the ferry dock, had sprung loose at one end. This projecting end struck and severed one of the wire guys staying the Micmac's tall black smoke stack. It toppled carrying a steam pipe with it and crashed into a life boat on the deck. The smoke and roar of escaping steam did not entirely obscure the fuss that the passengers were making. People scrambled up the sides of the ferry and jumped onto the pilings of the dock. They pulled and pushed their friends and family to "safety" as well. It is amazing that no one was seriously injured or drowned. Accounts stated that the passengers were shaken by the incident, but probably no one was as greatly disturbed as the unfortunate captain.

The accidents continued.

The boats were again involved when in December 1875, the **Micmac** and **A. C. Whitney** collided. Then, just a week later, the **Ogle's** machinery was disabled just after leaving the Halifax dock. She drifted with tide and wind, blowing her whistle continuously. The **A. C. Whitney** started to her asistance but **Whitney's** boilers developed trouble. Meanwhile, a line was thrown from the **Ogle** to the brigantine **Westwood**, lying in the stream. A boat was lowered from the **Ogle** and help brought from the **Micmac** which towed her sister ship to the dock. Another week passed when a similar problem occurred, and once more **Micmac** was the heroine.

It is not surprising that tugs and ferries collided when one considers the character of harbour traffic of that time. While the steam age was well advanced, the days of sail were still far from over. Thus at this time in the harbours and estuaries of the western world, the sight of large sailing vessels (without auxiliary power) under tow by small steam tugs was common, a most ungainly unit of traffic in relatively confined waters. These tugs were used mainly for towing sailing ships to and from their berths or anchorages. In July 1881, the tug **Henry Hoover** rushed off to recover a schooner stolen from her berth just shortly before. In the excitement of the occasion, the **Hoover's** captain claimed he simply did not see the **Ogle**. The resulting damage was reported as "slight."

In these pre-automobile days, one of the universal ways in which the Halifax Steam Boat Company contributed to the local economy was its purchase of brooms. Deck hands standing by with birch brooms, waited until the last vehicle had disembarked, and then swept the manure down the lanes and into the harbour. The brooms were made by residents of Preston and neighbouring suburbia, and sold in the city market, from door-to-door, or on order. They were skillfully made of many birch twigs bound around a debarked sapling, and were very useful for rough cleanups. Every household had at least one for sweeping the barn, garage, stable, basement or sidewalk. They were cheap, although considerable labour went into their manufacture.

As early as 1831, if not before, birch brooms were in demand in Halifax. Hence the following advertisement in a newspaper of the day:

BIRCH BROOMS
Office of Ordnance
Halifax, Nov. 28, 1831

Persons willing to furnish the Ordnance Department with One Thousand Five Hundred Birch Twig Brooms; One Hundred and Fifty to be delivered on the 14th December next, Six Hundred on the 1st February, 1832, and the remainder on the 1st April following; will send sealed tenders to this office, on or before the 8th December next, at 12 o'clock. The Brooms to be pegged in the handle, agreeably to a pattern which may be seen at the Ordnance Yard.

Until World War II, there were still many horse-drawn delivery vans—ice carts, coal carts, milk and bread wagons. On the traditional market days, Friday and Saturday, farmers brought their produce in from surrounding areas. Most travelled by teams pulled by horses or oxen. There was, as a result, plenty of work for the deck hands with their birch brooms.

Before 1865 it was possible to carry loads of manure on the ferry boats, as long as the trip was undertaken before 9:00 a.m. At a meeting of the directors in June 1865, it was decreed that this practice would have to stop. A lengthy newspaper editorial fairly presented the two sides of the ensuing controversy. While "very few like to be cooped up with all manner of filth in a small steamer on a warm summer day," in spite of this, wrote the editor, "that is no reason why the judicious regulation hitherto in vogue shall be revoked . . . We sincerely hope that the company will see the importance of withdrawing the 'offensive order,' and allow the old rule to prevail."

The directors must have felt more pressure from editorial and agricultural interests than from fastidious citizens, since in the minutes of the October 1874 meeting, it was announced that loads of manure would be charged "five cents instead of seven cents as heretofore." The following month this was amended—teams owned by non-ticket (season) holders and carrying manure were to be charged the regular fare. Then, in the following February, it was once more stated that manure carts would be allowed on the ferry until 9:00 a.m. except on Saturdays.

About this time, Dominick Farrell, a prominent Dartmouth businessman, was a director of the Steam Boat Company. He was a grocery, liquor and lumber merchant, and owned considerable property in the town. One of his establishments was located where the bus terminal is today, adjacent to the Steam Boat Company's property. Running towards the harbour, beside his property was a lane, apparently used by the company, and as well by a man who drove the first cab in Dartmouth, John Leadley. A dispute arose between Farrell and the company in regard to the ownership of the lane. Farrell took the offensive, and had several loads of manure dumped across the lane. An emergency meeting of the Steam Boat Company was called. Farrell, like John Skerry before him, won this

round. The Steam Boat Company gave in, and ordered Leadley to move his cab to the other side of the road leading to the steam boats.

So in several ways, manure, a scarce commodity today, created headaches for the directors.

Although the Steam Boat Company's Charter had been renewed in 1867, three years later the Legislature granted one George Washington Corbett the right to run a competitive ferry. The terms were set out in great detail and published in the press. The fact that nothing came of this particular rival ferry was substantiated by the following account: "It is understood that the projected opposition Ferry Boats have fallen through and the original projector George Washington Corbett is at present in Oldham, vaccinating possible smallpox patients."

In 1881 another north end ferry service was actually begun. The "steamer **Siena** ran between Smith's wharf at the foot of Round Church Hill (St. George's Church on Cornwallis Street) and Dartmouth, calling at Young Street." Young Street went right to the harbour, immediately south of Fort Needham. Evidently the experiment tried by the Steam Boat Company back in the '50s of running alternate boats to a north end dock was discontinued.

The fact that rival ferry services were able to establish suggests that the old Steam Boat Company was not providing adequate ferriage to the growing population. At one meeting of the Dartmouth Town Council it was stated that the ferries were unsafe. The directors tossed this criticism aside, while they continued to prosper, and the ferries bustled back and forth carrying ever increasing numbers of passengers and vehicles.

XV.

The Company, Its People and Some Events

The days of the Halifax Steam Boat Company were numbered. None of its charter members were still around by 1875. The most active shareholders of the company in the late 1870s and the 1880s were its president, Dr. D. McN. Parker, Dominick Farrell, J. F. Stairs, J. P. Mott, W. H. Greene, M. G. Black, Robie Uniacke, Judge J. W. Johnston and Captain G. A. MacKenzie, the Agent.

A greater proportion of these men were Dartmouth residents than in earlier days. Dominick Farrell, mentioned in connection with the manure incident, was a Dartmouthian as was W. H. Greene, a coal merchant and owner of a livery stable. He lived in the house which had once been John Skerry's Inn. J. F. Stairs was the manager of the ropeworks, and lived in "Northbrook," an estate near the ropework factory.

Neighbourly connections existed between Dr. Parker, Judge Johnston and J. P. Mott. An 1878 plan of Dartmouth shows that these three men lived on large estates adjacent

to what is now Pleasant Street. Only one of their houses remains today, "Sunnyside," the home of Judge Johnston. Dr. Parker's house was "Beechwood" to the immediate north of Johnston's. Next north, on the other side of the Old Ferry Road, was J. P. Mott's "Hazelhurst." All three estates swept down a gradual slope to the harbour amid large shade trees, and for size and location these properties could not have been more beautifully situated. All three had originally been part of the James Creighton land grant—and site of the Lower Ferry.

Shortly before the second James Creighton died, he had advertised for sale his "Land, Wharf and Water Lot which comprize the Ferry House and Wharf and premises long known by the name of the Lower or Creighton Ferry." The notice was put in the paper by Creighton's solicitor, J. W. Johnston. Soon after this the property was bought by Johnston himself.

Johnston, later a judge, and then Premier of Nova

37. Dr. Daniel McNeill Parker, 1822-1907.

history, when, in 1848, he pioneered the use of chloroform as an anaesthetic. A young colleague who witnessed the operation was Dr. Daniel McNeill Parker—the same Dr. Parker who now, years later, was playing a prominent role in the Steam Boat Company.

Dr. Almon's son, Mather Byles Almon, had also played his part in the history of the company, acting as treasurer from 1836-1857, and as president from 1860 to 1867.

In any small community nepotism is a fact of life. So it was with the prosperous shareholders of the Steam Boat Company throughout its history. We have seen that Dr. Almon's daughter Amelia, was married to "old" Judge Johnston. Their daughter Eliza married Dr. Almon's assistant at the chloroform operation, Dr. Parker. Eliza did not live long, dying soon after their first child, a son, was born.

Judge Johnston had a son, also James William, who became known as "young" Judge Johnston. The latter and Dr. Parker, both Steam Boat Company directors, and son and son-in-law of "old" Judge Johnston, either bought or were given their large adjacent properties by the elder Johnston. The old Judge may have persuaded his son-in-law, Dr. Parker, that land was a good investment, since an 1878 plan shows that the latter was the holder of many large tracts of land, mainly in the south end of Dartmouth.

When a schoolboy, Daniel Parker, later a long-time president of the Steam Boat Company, made a lifelong friend in the person of Charles Tupper. They met first at Horton Academy, and again at Edinburgh University. Dr. Parker was appointed to the Legislative Council in 1867. Tupper was Premier at the time, and he too bought land in Dartmouth. Two parcels of land were owned jointly by them. While on a visit to Winnipeg in September 1881, Parker wrote to his wife, "Every visitor goes in for land, but as I have had enough of such speculations in Dartmouth I am not likely to embark my capital in any such wild undertakings."

During sittings of the Legislature, Tupper stayed at "Beechwood" with his friend. This is somewhat confirmed

Scotia, married Amelia Almon, daughter of Dr. Almon, one of the most active of the early Steam Boat Company shareholders. Johnston built his house well back from the harbour, on the Cole Harbour Road part of his newly acquired property, and named it "Mount Amelia" in honour of his bride. His father-in-law, Dr. Almon, made medical

by the ferry records which show he had been issued commutation passes.

The year 1878 saw a great Conservative sweep to power in the federal government. Tupper was elected member for Cumberland. After the election he boarded the train for Halifax, and on arrival at the station there was the "greatest political demonstration ever witnessed," even more impressive than the one for Joseph Howe 11 years earlier. After a lengthy parade and speeches in Halifax, the procession, preceded by the band of the 63rd Regiment, rode down to the Steam Boat Wharf. They crossed on the ferry, from which there was a spectacular view of Dartmouth. The people of Dartmouth had placed lamps in as many windows as possible, and a great bonfire "crowned the hill." At the Dartmouth ferry terminal, 150 young men on horseback were lined up, each with a blazing torch. The Town Warden read a speech and Tupper replied. The band then led the whole procession on a long circuitous route—it went as far north as Lyle Street, and then wove back through the downtown area and then out on Portland Street, down the Eastern Passage Road to Dr. Parker's home, "Beechwood." A newspaper reporter congratulated Dartmouth for the display as being even superior to the one in Halifax because of the men on horseback.

A wealthy chocolate and soap manufacturer, John P. Mott, another Steam Boat Company director, was owner of "Hazelhurst" which occupied most of the land between the present "Old Ferry Lane" and Albert Street, and from Pleasant Street to the harbour shore. The old French prison mentioned earlier housed the soap factory, while new brick buildings were built for the chocolate and broma manufactory. This whole property was taken over as an Army training camp in World War II, and subsequently levelled and turned into a housing development. The name of Hazelhurst Street is the only reminder of the once park-like estate.

Dramas of crime, courtship, collision and rescue have occurred throughout the two-century span of our ferries. An example of the first of these involving J. P. Mott, is of interest.

One evening at his home, Mott received a letter addressed to him in pencil. The handwriting was large and childish, unfamiliar to him. He read as follows:

Mr. John Mott:
  I am in urgent need of six hundred dollars, which I must have before Tuesday, or I will be ruined, and as I have an old grudge against you and know you to have plenty, I am forced to demand it from you, and if you ignore the proposition that I am about to make or place it in the hands of detectives, I will shoot you dead before the expiration of a month. Just as sure as you are born, I will do it. Get six (600) dollars in gold 5 $ pieces and bring it over in the 8 o'clock boat on Monday night next, and take it in the smoking room,—and put it behind the door on the floor, and then your mission is ended. Mind you do not tell anyone about it or have anyone watching, or by the earth that is under me, I swear you will repent it. Roll it up well in some old rags, and shove it well in the corner, and mind that no one sees you put it there.

                                    remember
                                    sure death if
                                    you fail to
                                    do so.

The letter was unsigned of course. Mott knew of no one who would so threaten him. After initial shock and disbelief had worn somewhat, he took the letter to the City Marshall (the police chief) who advised him to follow the directions in the letter, but substituting pennies for gold pieces. Detective Nicholas Power was assigned to the case, and was to catch the extortionist when he picked up the bundle.

Mott followed all instructions. Detective Power, disguised as a drunken old tramp and appearing to be sound asleep, sat where he could see the bundle of pennies in their rags. Several people went in the smoking end of the cabin but no one appeared to look for anything until the ferry neared the dock. Then a young man with a cigar went in, stooped down and picked up the bundle. He came out

38.   Captain William Coleman, 1813-1886.

and went to the bow of the ferry, with the detective following closely behind. Suddenly aware of his "shadow," the young man dropped the bundle. Detective Power gathered it up with one hand, and seized his prey by the collar with the other. He marched him straight to the police station.

Warren P. Herman, age 20, at first denied all knowledge of the extortion attempt. He was well dressed and intelligent. When the case was tried in Stipendiary Magistrate's Court a few days later, on January 27, 1881, Herman confessed. His lawyer, however, raised an objection and the case was adjourned. When the adjournment was heard, Herman was committed for trial in the Supreme Court.

At the spring session, the trial was short, and the conclusion, surprising. The jury found the defendant not guilty, because there was no proof that he had written the letter. Was it a stupid jury or was it misdirected by the bench?

Interesting little items in the minutes illustrate the working relationship between the directors and employees of the Halifax Steam Boat Company. Since crew members and commuters were well known to each other, frequently captains or mates would not bother to inspect commutation passes when they were shown at the gates. They knew from long experience who could be trusted to have a paid up pass. From time to time instructions were issued from the directors, such as "Commutation tickets must be shown to the Mate or Captain. There must be a tightening up of rules and a check made of tickets sold." And "Captains must not detain the last boat [11:05] for any person."

One of the best-known captains of this period was William Coleman, who served on the ferry for almost 50 years. Like his grandfather, Seth Coleman, the leader of the Nantucket Whalers who settled in Dartmouth in 1785, Captain Coleman began his working life in the whaling business. He later joined the Steam Boat Company, hired by Edward Lowe. In his report of 1854, Lowe gave Coleman a rare (for Lowe) compliment, writing, "He has had charge of the Sackville trips for several years without the slightest accident."

In later years Coleman incurred the displeasure of the directors on two occasions. Once, in 1881, he was reprimanded for not appearing on stormy or foggy mornings. This may have been a protest of some kind on Coleman's part. After the reprimand he was told that he could have a man from the machine shop to assist him on mornings when the weather was bad.

On the second occasion, in 1884, Captain Coleman and the winchman, Adam Green, were interviewed at a special meeting about an accident incurred by the horse of one Mr. Beck. The horse had to be destroyed because it broke its leg while boarding. The two employees were held responsible. Green was fired, but given $30 gratuity because of long service with the company. Coleman got away with another reprimand.

Probably worse than the reprimand was a fall from a tree

39.   Micmac *on excursion.*

in his yard which caused him to be laid up for a time. Absence from duty through sickness was rare with Coleman. When the Halifax Steam Boat Company finally wound up its affairs, Coleman decided to retire. This was in August of 1886. The company paid him $100 as a tribute to his long service. The following December, at the age of 73, he suffered a stroke and died. A fine tribute to him appeared on the editorial page of a newspaper of the time.

A mate who served under Captain Coleman was James Graham. He also had been hired by Agent Lowe, in 1857, and when Captain Corbett retired in 1859, Graham took his place. Captain Graham was a rather brusque man, large in

build, and with a full sandy-coloured beard. He was well respected by the travelling public, and took no nonsense from anyone. A lady whose husband was a colonel of the militia once asked him to carry a parcel of fish on board the ferry for her. He refused, pointing out that it was not one of his duties. The lady was incensed and wrote a letter to a local paper, airing her grievance. Captain Graham wrote an equally indignant letter in reply, defending his position.

He served for over 50 years on the ferries. It is not surprising that during that period he had at least one serious encounter with the directors. This came about as a result of an accident on the evening of January 7, 1885.

Graham, in the **Micmac**, waited in the Halifax dock knowing that Coleman in the **Chebucto** was running about ten minutes behind and would not yet have left Dartmouth. Being winter time it became dark early. When Captain Graham and **Micmac** had almost completed their return journey to Dartmouth, Graham realized that he had not passed **Chebucto** in the harbour. Neither did he see her in the Dartmouth dock, so he assumed that she was in the lay-up dock. His acting mate, William Martin, later gave evidence that when passing a barque anchored in the harbour about two-thirds of the distance across, he saw the **Chebucto's** lights in the dock. He called out to warn Captain Graham, but did not receive any acknowledgement. As the **Micmac** was "making for the dock" Captain Graham suddenly "saw the **Chebucto's** lights coming out, commanded reverse, and blew the whistle, but the boats were so near each other that they came into collision. Although both were reversing [the collision] carried away the bow stanchion and some of the bulwarks in the **Chebucto** and damaged rudder on board **Micmac**. Damage not sufficient to prevent either of them running on the ferry."

At the conclusion of the hearing, Captain Graham was judged responsible for the accident and he later received the following communication:

Steamboat Office
Dartmouth 14th Jany 1885

Capt James W. Graham
Dear Sir:
    The Directors of the Halifax Steamboat Company having heard the Evidence in the Matter of the Collision between the "Micmac," under your command and the "Chebucto," on the Evening of Wednesday last 7th Inst. have come to the unanimous conclusion that you were entirely to blame in the matter, and should not have run so near the dock, without ascertaining that the "Chebucto" had left the dock knowing that she was behind time—
    I am directed to inform you that you are expected to make [good] the damage done, and the Directors having in mind their responsibilities to the Public and the Shareholders of the Company, feel that in case of Accidents occuring from Carelessness or the want of proper supervision or forethought on the part of any of their Officers, in the future, such officers must not expect to be continued in their service—
    In the case in question had lives been sacrificed, the decision of a Court of Justice would with moral certainty have been Manslaughter against you as the Officer in charge, While the Company would have been legally liable for damages, and a jury would without doubt have awarded a large sum of money to the families or heirs of those killed— Or had any passenger or passengers been injured, an Action at law would have resulted adversely to the interests of the Company— Had one or both of the Boats at the time of the Collision had but a little more headway, both might have been seriously disabled & the ferry left without any means of carrying on the large traffic between Halifax & Dartmouth, as the "Sir C. Ogle" was then as you are aware laid up & undergoing repairs—
    It is essential that the handling and general management of the boats when on the harbour or in the docks should be such as to retain public confidence and with this object in view, the Directors have requested me to thus seriously address you on a matter which they consider to be of the greatest moment—
    The Directors regret the necessity that has arisen for such a communication as this, and trust that at no future time will they be called on to request me to perform a similar duty—

I am
Yours & etc
G. A. Mackenzie

No mere slap on the wrist was this. In those days it would constitute a major reprimand only slightly short of summary dismissal. It might have crushed a less hardy soul, considering the financial implications as well, but

Graham remained on the job for 24 more years. In 1907 he was honoured on the occasion of his 50th anniversary, and presented with $50. Two years later, a special meeting was held to make plans for his retirement. He was also interviewed for a report of his experiences which was published in the local press.

During Captain Graham's time there were two mates who demonstrated widely contrasting attitudes in respect to their employment. One was Alex Marks, later Captain, who early in his career with the ferry was given a $10 reward for "exemplary conduct in saving Mrs. Brown on a Sunday evening." In 1882 he was given a $1 a week raise, bringing his salary to $9 weekly. He had to wait three years for his next raise—also $1. At this time Captains Coleman and Graham were on a monthly paid salary of $60.

The other mate was in perpetual trouble, in one way or another. In 1879 he was chastised for "being negligent in securing the boat to the bridge, refusing to assist the Captain admit passengers, using insulting language, and for making nets while crossing the harbour!" Even horses disliked him as he was bitten by one the following year. After another year passed this mate was dismissed for hitting the government wharf at McNab's Island, doing $60 worth of damage. He asked to be reinstated shortly after but the request was turned down. However, 18 months later there was evidence that the directors relented and rehired him, as he was in command of the **Ogle** which hit Stayner's wharf in October 1883. The company must have been hard pressed for captains, because on this occasion he was merely threatened with dismissal.

In comparison with today's hours and wages, employees then worked long hard hours for what seems to be very small wages. Holidays were almost nonexistent. The Chief Engineer, William Pearce, being a religious man, asked for some relief from his Sunday duties, because he wanted to attend church. After a lengthy discussion, reported in the minutes, it was decided that Mr. Siteman, who worked in the machine shop, could take over as engineer on alternate Sundays. Captain G. A. MacKenzie, the Agent, thought Siteman should be paid 50 cents extra on these occasions, but the directors said that 37½ cents would be sufficient. Generally, engineers' wages were on a par with those of the captains. In 1885, Pearce's salary was $65 monthly.

Small gestures towards the comfort of employees appear in the minutes. A little stove was purchased for the girls in the Halifax ticket office so they could heat their food. In 1880, a further $20 was voted for Captain Hunter's widow, to be paid in five monthly installments of $4. Two years before she had been given a lump sum of $50. In view of the latter installment payments, one wonders if the directors thought that she could not manage properly such a large gratuity if paid all at once.

When Captain Corbett retired from his wheelhouse duties in 1859, he was made a ticket agent. Almost 20 years later he retired on pension.

John Graham, carpenter, who rented a small house on ferry premises, was discharged because of age, and given a gratuity of $120 in 1885.

Both Chief Engineer William Pearce and Engineer William Morton were absent due to illness at the same time in 1883. Morton's death occurred in December of that year, the same month in which watchman William Ring was drowned. The company paid the funeral expenses for both men. The following month, a Miss Morton was hired in the Halifax ticket office, one of the Misses Gates having been transferred to the Dartmouth office to make a place for her. William Ring's widow was given $50.

Generally, the Steam Boat Company showed concern for its employees. Support and interest seems to have been based on a merit system. Financial benefits appear small when related to today's "cradle-to-grave" type of social security and its huge cost. However, in the late 1800s, when widows and pensioners lived with relatives, the Halifax Steam Boat Company was regarded as a good and fair employer.

XVI.
The Final Days

Since the Halifax Steamboat Company's charter was renewed in 1867, the business was going very well indeed. Directors and shareholders were pleased with profits, and with the "perks" as well. The four directors, elected annually, still received $100 a year as an honorarium. A system of free ferriage was derived on the following basis: the owner of one share got free passage for himself; two shares covered shareholder and wife; three—wife and family (regardless of size); and four shares or more entitled the shareholder, his wife, family, servants and his pleasure carriage to free ferriage. For commuters of that day, mostly businessmen and students, this meant a considerable saving in the course of a year. In addition, the semi-annual dividends of from three per cent to six per cent on the $500 shares would be considered a most satisfactory return in the late 1800s.

No wonder a smug complacency emerged in the company's attitudes towards other businessmen and governments of Halifax and Dartmouth. As an example, for many years a contentious correspondence was kept up by John Stayner (of Stayner's wharf, immediately to the north of the Halifax dock) and the Steam Boat Company. In later years this escalated to a long drawn out legal battle. When in 1876 Stayner asked the Agent to move a part of the dock fence, a resolution was passed at a meeting of the directors "to make no reply." There was more discussion in regard to this boundary in 1880. In 1883, when Stayner's wharf was hit by the **Ogle** in the fog, Stayner claimed $120. The directors ordered the Agent to offer him $80.

A new business tax was imposed by the City of Halifax in 1884. The company was charged $100 but the directors refused to pay it on the incredible grounds that they did not do business in Halifax.

The directors at this time were Dr. Parker, president,

Dominick Farrell, Judge J. W. Johnston, J. W. Stairs and Robie Uniacke, who was also president of the Halifax Banking Company.

The company was under another pressure from the Dominion government which it could not ignore. By 1878, the steam boats and their crews were showing the strain of long years of service. The **Sir Charles Ogle** was nearing 50 years of age (the present boats have a design life of 25 years), the **Micmac** 34 and the **Chebucto** 13. This was the year when steamship inspection became mandatory. Accordingly the **Ogle**, **Micmac** and **Chebucto** were hauled

out, in turn, on the Chebucto Marine Railway, and were gone over by an inspector of hulls, an inspector of machinery, and later by a Lloyd's surveyor.

These inspections resulted in a frenzy of activity as major repairs, neglected for years, were carried out. Boilers, engine parts, smoke stacks and deck planks were renewed. The boats were painted inside and out. In an attempt to make the interior decoration last longer the "cabins were varnished instead of being painted, grained in oak, because it is easier to keep clean." On the marine railway, the old copper sheathing was stripped off, planks

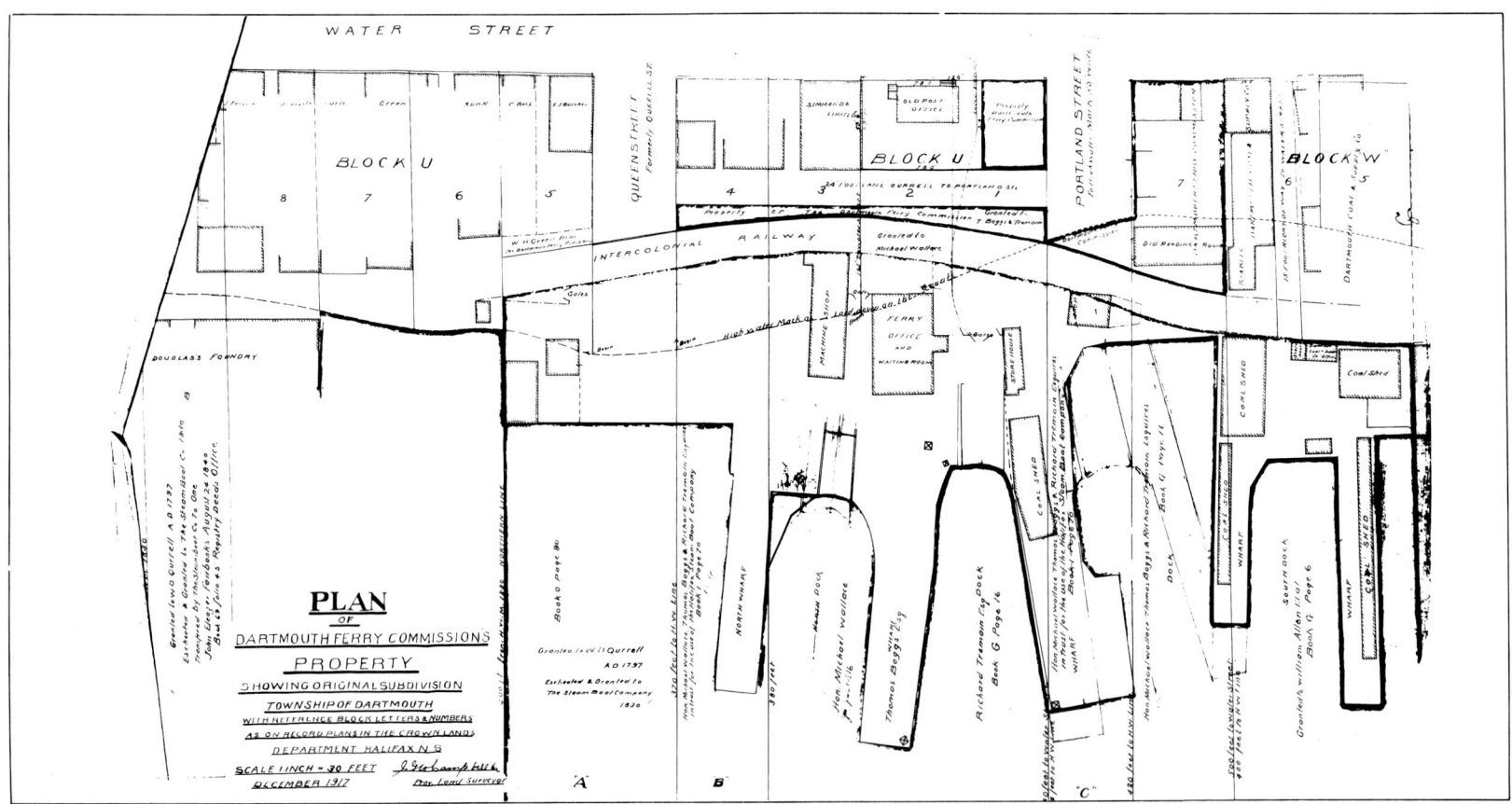

40. *Plan of proposed Intercolonial Railway Right-of-Way through ferry property.*

90

and keelsons repaired or renewed and the bottoms were caulked and recoppered.

In addition to the work on the boats, the docks and other real estate had a great deal of money spent on them. A breakwater was built at the south wharf with 800 tons of stone, at 20 cents a ton. A new coal shed was built on the Dartmouth side for $1,150, and a Mr. Blagden was almost continually at work on the wharves and floats.

The Intercolonial Railway came to Dartmouth in 1884. Company directors held a special meeting to examine a plan of the right-of-way through its Dartmouth property.

They passed the following resolution: "It is expedient that a Right of Way over the property of the Company of 25 feet by 500 feet as laid out in the plan herewith submitted be granted by the Company to the Government, they putting in a coal siding and trestle work as suggested by them and marked on said plan, and also removing and putting in good order at their own expense all buildings necessary to be removed or cut away and that the Directors of the Company be authorized and empowered to carry out the objects of this Resolution."

This railway represented a potential threat to the Company's revenues. At that time the rail terminus in Halifax was the North Street Station (later levelled in the 1917 Halifax Explosion). This proposed new branch line to Dartmouth was to cross a planned bridge at the Narrows, and then southerly along the shoreline to the new Woodside Sugar Refinery. Halifax and Dartmouth commuters, who were located along this route, would almost certainly use the railway rather than the ferry.

The Steam Boat Company also had a freight business, carrying heavy loads between the two communities. The railway successfully competed for some of this business, and the company's fears about diminished revenues were substantiated in later financial reports.

Another change in real estate came about when Peter Douglass of Atlantic Foundry, leased the North (Skerry) Ferry property in 1881 for 20 years. Five years later, in August of 1886, it was purchased outright by the same company for $5,000.

At various meetings, preliminary plans for a new boat were discussed, but never seemed to get beyond this stage. Funds set aside in a reserve toward the purchase of a new boat grew each year, but were never used for the intended purpose. By 1885 they had reached $36,720 in various debentures, building societies and banks.

In 1875, Captain MacKenzie was instructed to write to Lindsay and Co. in Glasgow in regard to engines for a new boat. He said, "We have heretofore used side lever engines in our boats, but are of the opinion that the inclined cylinder will answer better." The new boat was to be another side wheeler, 140 feet long, 320 tons.

Much time went by. At the February 1884 meeting, "a long discussion ensued with reference to the necessity of building a new boat, but it was decided to postpone it for the present." It came a little closer the next year. This was to be the year to buy timber and materials for the new boat, the model, specifications and working plans of which were to be furnished by Ebenezer Moseley. There the matter rested.

There were signs that others were anxious to start an opposition ferry service. The motives were varied: the public was dissatisfied with the service being provided; businessmen were jealously aware of the profits the Steam Boat Company was making; and conscientious citizens thought the harbour crossing should be a public rather than a private operation, and wanted one or both of the connected communities to assume responsibility.

As far back as December 1874, there was a proposal from a Mr. Troop and associates, of Dartmouth. In March 1875, the directors were informed that the citizens of Dartmouth wanted to purchase the ferry boats and property. The company set the purchase price at $120,000. Nothing more transpired until 1879, when it was alleged at a Dartmouth Town Council meeting that the boats were unsafe. A joint committee from Halifax and Dartmouth came to a special meeting to discuss purchase of the ferry boats, but the Steam Boat Company directors refused to negotiate on the grounds that this committee had no legal status.

From time to time the company was asked to allow free

41. *Halifax—1890, panorama.* Sir C. Ogle *in foreground,* Chebucto *leaving Halifax dock.*

carried free," but the factory was later built in Halifax in the Kempt Road vicinity. Undoubtedly Dartmouthians felt that the Halifax Steam Boat Company had not offered enough incentive.

A year later in August, the **Micmac** (which hired out at $40 per day) was let to a Sunday School convention free of charge. This privilege was granted rather than the reduced fares asked for as that "would interfere with the ticket system at present in operation on the ferry."

An excellent skating rink was in operation in Dartmouth by 1885. The band of the 66th Princess Louise Fusiliers travelled from Halifax to provide music for the skaters, and the bandsmen were granted a rare privilege: they were allowed a return trip on the boats for the price of a single fare. On band days admission to the rink was 15 cents, on ordinary days ten cents. Tickets were on sale in Halifax at the Steam Boat Company's office only, and these tickets included ferriage. The secretary of the rink was A. C. Johnston, son of director J. W. Johnston of the Steam Boat Company.

passage to groups or individuals. Each request was decided on its own merits, and no doubt friends, relations and politics were among these merits.

An unscheduled meeting was held in June 1881, when a letter was read from A. C. Cogswell of the Dartmouth Town Council. The directors were asked what privileges they would be willing to grant a proposed cotton factory if a Dartmouth site were selected. (Comparative shopping for industrial incentives is no new thing.) The reply was that "material used in the original construction of such a factory and all workmen engaged in its construction would be

In spite of these gestures to improve its image, the company's days were numbered. The Legislature passed on April 24, 1885, an Act granting "The Halifax and Dartmouth Steam Ferry Company" the right to incorporate.

Business appeared to be as usual for another year, at least until the 1886 annual meeting in February. This meeting was unusually well attended, with 15 shareholders present. The president, Dr. Parker, read an "exhaustive" report on the history of the company. The report was a curious one. On the one hand, it congratulated

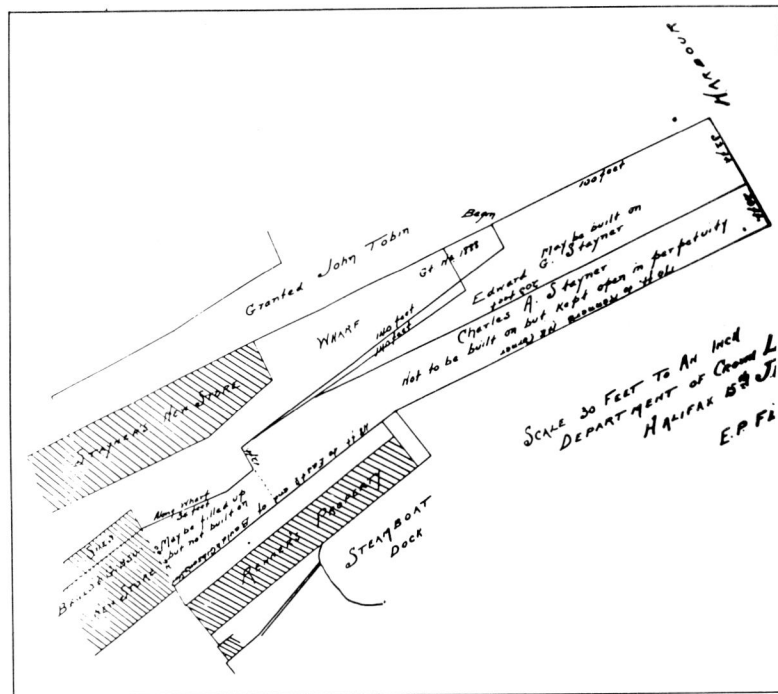

43. Plan of Halifax wharves made about the time of contemplated purchase.

management for having raised the share values from their five shillings in 1836 to their present price (which was not mentioned). On the other hand, the report stated that "dividends have never been as large as has been supposed by the public," and went on to mention all the difficulties of running such a business: want of population, expensive repairs to the boats and wharves, the "powers of the worms that infest the waters" of the harbour, the constant cry for new ferries, competition from the new railway, shortness of the excursion season, number of privately owned steam launches now on the harbour, fuel consumption costs and wages of crew members.

Less than a week had passed before the newly incorporated Halifax and Dartmouth Steam Ferry Company inserted an extraordinarily sarcastic reply in a competing newspaper. "The promoters of the Halifax and Dartmouth Steam Ferry Company (Ltd.) congratulate the directors of the Halifax Steam Boat Company, that after so many years of profound reticence, they have at last been so gracious, even at this (to them) critical period as to apparently show the public how money has not been made by their long existing monopoly."

The new company might be excused for its sarcasm in the light of the following sample figures for the years 1882 to 1885 found in the minute book of the Steam Boat Company. They are shown together with the corresponding figures published in the newspaper report:

1882	Minutes	Published
Receipts	$35,057.79	$32,171.27
Expenses	24,430.20	27,529.65
Net Earnings	10,627.59	4,641.62
Reserve	25,425.35	
1883	Minutes	Published
Receipts	$36,786.66	$34,190.52
Expenses	33,404.42	26,431.02
Net Earnings	3,382.24	7,759.50
Reserve	28,500.00	
1884	Minutes	Published
Receipts	$37,210.01	$34,401.53
Expenses	25,806.20	26,728.50
Net Earnings	11,403.81	7,673.03
Reserve	33,000.00	
1885	Minutes	Published
Receipts	$37,304.38	$34,113.20
Expenses	29,601.68	32,090.49
Net Earnings	7,702.70	2,022.71
Reserve	33,000.00	

Readers may well wonder just what was going on. Towards the end of February 1886, two unscheduled meetings were called. The first of these was for the purpose of discussing whether to renew the lease of the city dock. The directors decided to attempt to buy it instead.

The second of these special meetings heard an inquiry from the new ferry company requesting the asking price for the boats and real estate. The directors declined to name a figure, but asked the new company to make an offer, which would then be considered. At this same meeting it was resolved to run the ferries until midnight—a concession to public demand. Previously the company had maintained that the crews could not be asked to stay on duty so late, out of consideration for their health, a factor now ignored in the face of imminent competition.

The old company was refused any opportunity to purchase the city dock. Other docking facilities were investigated, and Tobin's and Connor's wharves were on the point of being purchased for $26,000 ($16,000 for Tobin's and $10,000 for Connor's). Suddenly in a surprise move at the March 19 meeting, the Agent, Captain McKenzie was directed to write to the Halifax and Dartmouth Steam Ferry Company offering it the entire property, including boats and the new wharves for $110,000.

A search into the titles of the wharf properties revealed that there was a flaw in one of them. The new company was therefore dissuaded from accepting the offer. In a further move, on April 10, 1886, a resolution was passed that an offer be made for the sale of "boats, real estate in Dartmouth and plant of the Halifax Steam Boat Company to the Halifax and Dartmouth Steam Ferry Company Ltd. . . . for the sum of Eighty-Four Thousand dollars . . . and that the Directors be empowered to convey the property as above as soon as the money is paid therefore."

The new price was less because the Tobin and Connor wharves were not included. The deal was consummated and when the papers had been duly signed, Dr. Parker resigned his presidency and left for England.

The following was written about Dr. Parker and the occasion, "The Halifax and Dartmouth Steam Boat Company [a minor error] of which he was President, sold out its entire undertaking, and this proved to him a salutary relief. To fiduciary offices of a charitable or philanthropic character he adhered longer, giving to them the preferential claim upon his services." Dr. Parker's biographer (his son), either ignored, or was unaware of his total association with the company which spanned at least 16 years. Captain MacKenzie, a 24-year veteran, was persuaded to stay on until the first of June when E. P. Story took over as secretary and cashier for $40 a month. Captain Stanley Swain was made responsible for the crews and physical plant—real estate and boats. A set of rules was drawn up to guide him, and these were recorded in the minutes of the old company.

The directors of the new company requested an extension of time to take over the operation. Their administration began on August 1, 1886.

In a final gesture of generosity, the old Steam Boat Company gave the crew of the excursion boat extra wages. In addition it allowed all employees, their wives and minor children free passage. The Fund for Relief of the Sick, instituted at a time when the company had felt pressured from too many sick and infirm employees, was "presented" to them. Since the employees wages had been docked 50 cents a week to build up this fund, the presentation was hardly a magnanimous gesture.

Story wrote the last minutes of the Halifax Steam Boat Company on September 20, 1886. There was mention of one more meeting to be held, but documentation of this meeting has not been found. This was the general meeting of all shareholders, held on Thursday, September 23, 1886. Presumably this was the occasion at which the proceeds of the sale were distributed, and perhaps the last financial statement was distributed to the shareholders as well.

In written reminiscences of the old ferries, an elderly Dartmouth resident remembered the details of his mother's shares. She owned three $500 shares, inherited from her father. When the old company sold out she received $2,200. Even if the recollection was conservative, it suggests that the shareholders of the Halifax Steam Boat Company had not invested unwisely.

So ended a major era in the corporate history of the Halifax Harbour ferries.

XVII.

The Halifax and Dartmouth Steam Ferry Company Ltd.

The Act to incorporate the new ferry company was passed by the Legislature in April 1885. S. E. Woods, James R. McLean and Henry G. Woods were named as original members of the company. These men who applied for the incorporation do not appear again in surviving ferry records. Entries in the Halifax City Directory of the time show that S. E. Woods managed the Seven Cent Store at 131 Granville Street, while McLean was listed as James R. McLean, M.D., Oculist, 91 Hollis Street. The only link betwen the three was that they all boarded at the International Hotel.

"The public will be pleased to learn that the new ferry company between the City and Dartmouth have arrived at practical results, having already secured over 300 shareholders, principally from among the residents of Dartmouth and surrounding country. In a few days they will publish their prospectus and Directory at the same time offering the balance of the stock. Besides supplying a first class ferry service, it is proposed to provide excursion facilities of the most approved kind during the summer, so that one great drawback to the appreciation of our beautiful harbour, basin, arm, etc., by strangers as well as our own people, may be removed. The desire is to interest the people at large in this enterprise, and the shares have therefore been placed at $10 each."

A prospectus was printed by the Halifax and Dartmouth Steam Ferry Company Ltd., dated February 1, 1886, and another on May 1.

(From here on, the new company will be referred to as the Steam **Ferry** Company, or the **Ferry** Company, as opposed to the old or Steam **Boat** Company.)

The inclusion of "Dartmouth" in the corporate title was probably a political move. Citizens of Dartmouth were by

95

44. *Burrell-Johnson Iron Company, Yarmouth. Ferry* Dartmouth *on the stocks, 1888.*

far the greater users of the ferries, and therefore potential purchasers of the new shares.

The provisional directors named on the prospectus were: J. C. Mackintosh, Mayor of Halifax, Banker; Alderman H. F. Worrall, Merchant; B. W. Chipman, Warden, County of Halifax, Merchant; Robie Uniacke, Esq., President, Halifax Banking Company; Charles Annand, Esq., Publisher; C. F. Fraser, Esq., Journalist; F. C. Elliot Esq., Merchant; George A. Pyke, Esq.; Dr. A. C. Cogswell.

Of these, only the last three lived in Dartmouth, and they worked in Halifax, commuting each day. Dr. Cogswell, a dentist, built the beautiful house "Locust Knoll" across Pleasant Street from the homes of Dr. Parker and Judge Johnston.

Capital stock in the Ferry Company was $100,000, as in the former company. The new shares however were $10 instead of the former $500. Consequently they were more available to the average citizen. By the time the May prospectus was issued, however, two-thirds of the shares had already been subscribed.

The new company promised to improve the service as soon as it took over, including "the purchase or building of two first class modern ferry steamers, with covered lanes, plus comfortable waiting rooms."

Forgetting the pessimistic report published by the Steam Boat Company as to why its business was not really as profitable as might be thought, glowing accounts were given in the prospectus of growth possibilities of ferry boat stock. These included the fact that ferries were necessary for people to cross the harbour; the City Green Market was supplied by people from the eastern side of the harbour; increasing population; and, supposedly the most convincing argument of all, shareholders in the old Steam Boat Company had realized a large return, and were now buying shares in the new company, the implication being that they knew a good thing.

One newspaper expressed the hope of many when it reported that a new company was to take over the "antiquated steam tugs" and "it is believed ere another year rolls around, some of the ear tickling promises made by the new ferry company will have been redeemed."

Like the proverbial new broom, the Steam Ferry Company swept some old complaints away, by immediately placing an order for a new ferry boat with a Nova Scotia company, the Burrell-Johnson Iron Company Ltd. of Yarmouth, a thriving and progressive industry, which had already produced 25 steamers. The ships were designed and built at the Burrell-Johnson plant, and even more amazing was the fact that the complex engines for the ships were also designed and manufactured there. "With the exception of two that are lost, we believe all are in service today and giving satisfaction" wrote the editor of the Yarmouth Herald.

The vessel being built for the Steam Ferry Company was another double-ended, side wheel ferry steamer. "Her dimensions are as follows: Length overall, 140'; breadth of beam, hull, 28'-8"; over guards, 46'; depth of hold, 11 feet. The hull is constructed of first class materials, the frames

45.   Dartmouth *at opening of Halifax Shipyard's Graving Dock, 1889.*

being of hacmatac; the deck, deck beams, topsides and ceiling of pitch-pine, and the bottom planks of hardwood. The fastenings are locust treenails, with copper bolts up to the water-line; bolts above water-line galvanized iron. She is thoroughly strengthened with iron and hacmatac knees.

"The steamer has two saloons for passengers, one on each side—94 feet long and 11 feet wide, fitted with comfortable seats along the sides. Leading from each

saloon are toilet rooms, well ventilated and fitted with every convenience. The saloons are commodious, airy and convenient, and fitted with steam heating apparatus. The floors of the saloons are of pitch pine, finished in oil.

"A central house extends 65 feet along the deck, on each side of which is a passageway, 8½ feet wide for teams. In the centre part of this house is the engine room. A stairway leads from one end of this room to the upper or promenade deck, and another to a saloon below. The promenade deck, 68 feet long and 22 feet wide, has a rail and rope netting running completely around it, with seats extending the whole length on each side. The pilot houses are situated on this deck near each end. As the steamer is to be run as a pleasure and excursion steamer during the summer months, this deck forms a very pleasant feature and one that cannot fail to be appreciated by all who patronize her.

"The **Dartmouth** is fitted with compound surface-condensing direct inclined engines of 76 nominal horsepower. The boilers, two in number, are of steel, are very heavily built and stayed to carry 90 pounds of steam, 60 pounds being the ordinary working pressure.

"The Halifax and Dartmouth Steam Ferry Company are to be congratulated on the successful completion of this beautiful ferry boat which is said by experts to be one of the finest steamers of the kind ever to be built in the Dominion."

In a published letter to the Halifax Board of Works, the Steam Ferry Company wrote (mainly regarding its lease with the City) that the cost of the **Dartmouth** was $36,000.

Among the guests at the launching of the **Dartmouth** were Chief Engineer William Pearce and Captain Swain. The latter had been appointed by the old Steam Boat Company directors at the time of Captain MacKenzie's resignation.

"The steamer **Dartmouth** was launched from the yard of the Burrell-Johnson Iron Company on the Queen's Birthday. There was a large concourse of spectators. The steamer slid down the ways without the least noise or difficulty and as she struck the water the paddlewheels began to revolve from the pressure against them, adding an unusual interest to the scene. It was one of the finest launches ever witnessed in this county."

Contemporary accounts said the "trials" took place on June 13, when 100 people were taken for a cruise in the Yarmouth area, loose terminology since guests would never be taken on The Trials. The managing director of the Steam Ferry Company, Engineer William Pearce and several ladies were on board. Electric lighting was an

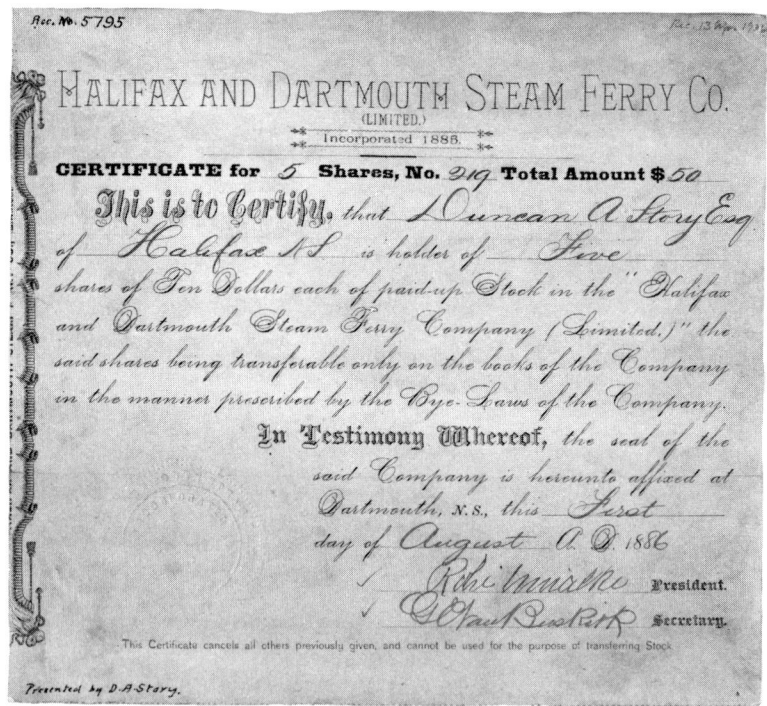

46. *(top) Briggs' model of* Dartmouth's *inclined compound engine.*
47. *(bottom) Share certificate.*

exciting feature of the new boat. In an early recollection of the older boats, a Dartmouth citizen observed, "What little cabin they had was lit with kerosene lamps. People crowded around with their newspapers trying to see." Evidently Abraham Gesner's kerosene gas had been replaced by his later discovery of kerosene oil, but apparently it was no better a source of illumination.

"The boat illuminated by the incandescent lights made a magnificent appearance . . . The electricity is supplied by a 50 light dynamo driven by an independent 6 H.P. engine."

The **Dartmouth** left Yarmouth on June 14, and docked at the Halifax Ferry Slip early the next morning. Captain Parker of Yarmouth was in charge of her, and Mr. Johnson of Burrell-Johnson was also on board.

On June 16, seven or eight hundred delegates—a scarcely believable number—to the Presbyterian General Assembly eagerly crowded on board for a sightseeing trip from York Redoubt to Bedford Basin. The water was rough, since in the open waters the **Dartmouth** "shipped a sea that slushed the main deck." The reporter who went along for the cruise grumbled that he was unable to get a good look at the new ferry because of the crowd.

The first excursion for the general public took place on June 21. Mr. Belcher of the Argyle Fruit Store supplied Jersey Ice Cream, New York Cider and other refreshments.

Subsequent excursions were advertised for various clubs and lodges. In 1889 a "Carnival Week" centered about activities on the harbour was held. The **Dartmouth** took excursionists each day, and made one very special trip. "The dry dock last Friday afternoon was visited by a large crowd, most of them proceeding thither by land. Steamer **Dartmouth** with 100 passengers left Central Wharf at 5:15 and at 5:30 steamed into our great dry dock—the first vessel to enter its portals. She proceeded up to its extreme end and then returned back into the open harbour, and turning, landed her passengers at the wharf above the dock."

These excursions were pleasant for those who had time and money to take advantage of them. The citizens were

48. Dartmouth, *cabin interior (glass negative).*

hardly getting the service promised them by the new company, and there was no sign of the second new boat, mentioned in the prospectus of 1886. Public resentment against the Steam Ferry Company grew, as its policies grew increasingly similar to those of the old Steam Boat Company.

Judge Benjamin Russell, at this time Magistrate for Dartmouth, later wrote in his autobiography a colourful impression of the trials of commuters, including his own. He had a court appearance scheduled before a judge known to be inflexible on time of appointments. Fearful of being late, Judge Russell, who lived in Dartmouth's Johnston Avenue area, went to catch an earlier ferry than he needed to. When he arrived at the terminal, he found that there was no ferry; it was being used as a tug. This was 1890 but it could have been 50 years earlier. Judge Russell tried to explain to the Exchequer judge why he was delayed, but

49. Dartmouth *as later altered.*

although he was only ten minutes late, the case was not heard. The senior judge, with severe tones, told him, "Mr. Russell, this Court does not wait for its officers."

The situation between the Ferry Company and the public became more strained with the lack of any improvement in the service. Cries of outrage issued when quarterly commutation tickets were abolished in January 1890. The company directors felt that they were losing money on the quarterly family tickets in particular, and wanted to sell single fare tickets for five cents each. To the travelling public, this was just one more evidence of the greediness of the shareholders, whom they already suspected of being in the business more to line their pockets than to give an efficient ferry service.

Rates for the old Halifax Steam Boat Company at February 1, 1867, the last recorded in the minute books

had been: Foot passenger, $4.50 per quarter; man and wife, $5.50 per quarter; and man, wife and unmarried children, $9.00 per quarter.

If there was a considerable number of unmarried children, it is easy to see how abolishing the quarterly ticket would cause a hardship in some families. It is equally obvious how the hardheaded businessmen of the company would have regarded it as too great a bargain.

So, because of its unfulfilled promises, poor service and withdrawal of quarterly tickets, the Halifax and Dartmouth Steam Ferry Company Ltd. had raised the ire of Dartmouth citizens to the point where they were in a near state of rebellion, and on the point of taking matters into their own hands. A public meeting was called to be held at the Town Hall on January 21. This was to be the beginning of a whole new chapter of the ferry story.

XVIII.
Dartmouthians Revolt

The January 21, 1890 meeting to protest the change in fares proposed by the Halifax and Dartmouth Steam Ferry Company was larger and more enthusiastically attended than the organizers had anticipated. Benjamin Russell suspected that some of the protesters attended in the hope of starting another profitable company, rather than being motivated by public spirit. The idea of a new company was quickly squelched by the majority desire for a "people's ferry", controlled by Dartmouthians as the users of the service, rather than by businessmen whose only motive was profit.

At the Halifax City Council meeting a week or so later, a letter was read from George Van Buskirk, secretary of the Steam Ferry Company, asking that the company's lease of the city dock be extended a further five years. A heated discussion followed. One alderman said he thought it would be unwise because of rumours that Dartmouth was going to run a free ferry. When Alderman Mackintosh supported the company's request, he was accused of having a personal interest since his brother was a director. In fact, the brother was the original president of the company. As if the waves of unrest and desire for reform from the Dartmouth side of the harbour had been contagious, the Halifax Council meeting was rancourous.

A committee had been appointed at the Dartmouth ratepayers' meeting to look into the costs of establishing a public ferry. It was ready with the facts in early March, so the ratepayers gathered once again. The chairman, B. A. Weston, presented figures:

"Gross earnings of the Halifax and Dartmouth Steam Ferry Company Ltd.:

General ferriage	$29,894
Commutation	9,472

Excursions	2,203
Rents	11,662
Wharfage	180
	$53,411

Based on estimated annual receipts of $39,000, and annual expenditures of $32,000, the committee felt that $110,000 would be needed to establish a ferry service. J. Howe Austen made a resolution that the Town Council be asked to petition the Legislature for the power to borrow $110,000 for the purpose of establishing a public ferry. George Shiels, J.P., seconded the motion. The resolution was passed without a dissenting vote. Presented to the Town Council, the resolution again received unanimous approval. approval.

On March 27, the committee on private and local bills of the Legislature heard the citizens of Halifax and Dartmouth who supported the bill that would enable the Town to borrow $110,000 to run its own ferry. Judge J.W. Johnston, W.C. Bishop, Benjamin Russell, Lewis P. Fairbanks, J.W. Allison and Robert Worrell spoke for the bill, mentioning the hardship that would be felt by shopgirls and Academy students if it did not go through, and if the Steam Ferry Company were allowed to abolish the commutation rates.

J.C. Mackintosh and Robie Uniacke, original president and director of the Steam Ferry Company spoke against the bill.

Arguments continued the following day. J.C. Mackintosh argued for a whole hour. However, he had a powerful opponent in Benjamin Russell who spoke "Brilliantly for fifty minutes" on behalf of the Dartmouth people.

Judge Russell later wrote, "there was loud laughter when the title was read which proposed the establishment of a ferry 'between Dartmouth and Halifax.' The House was amused by the order in which the termini were named."

That very evening a "red hot meeting" with "ladies present" was held. C.E. Creighton moved and W.C. Bishop seconded that "since the Halifax and Dartmouth Steam Ferry Company will not sell commutation tickets, and since

50. *Benjamin Russell, 1849-1935.*

51. Acadia, *left to right, C. E. Creighton, Dr. Cunningham, Mjr. Humphreys, (or Col. Weston), Dr. M. A. B. Smith, Walter Creighton, unidentified.*

NOTICE.

A PUBLIC MEETING

Of the RATE-PAYERS of the TOWN of DARTMOUTH

WILL BE HELD AT THE

REFORM CLUB HALL, DARTMOUTH

On TUESDAY,

The 18th DAY of MARCH, 1890, at 8 P. M.

For the purpose of voting upon a proposal to borrow the sum of $110,000 to establish a PUBLIC FERRY between the Town of Dartmouth and the City of Halifax, and to apply to the Legislature for the requisite authority to carry on the said project.

FRED. SCARFE,
MAYOR.

ALFRED ELLIOT, Town Clerk.

52. *Handbill by Russell for "The People's Ferry," 1890.*

the meeting thinks the new rates are too high, and since some other means of crossing should begin at once, a committee of five ratepayers be appointed to inquire into other transportation and report.'' The motion was passed unanimously.

John White, Benjamin Russell, B.A. Weston, W.C. Bishop and C. E. Creighton were appointed as the committee. The sum of $1500 was subscribed on the spot. The five, wasting no time and determined to outwit the Steam Ferry Company before the April deadline for the withdrawal of the commutation passes, went promptly to work. They bought the steam tug **Arcadia** which had been used for carrying

freight and passengers between Lunenburg and Halifax, making two trips a week.

The committee was extremely quick and efficient in this transaction, but unfortunately the **Arcadia** had to have some repairs and alterations before she could be put on the ferry service.

It was an interesting coincidence that the **Arcadia** was built at the Burrell-Johnson Iron Company in Yarmouth, and had been launched in 1888, only a week before the Steam Ferry Company's **Dartmouth**. The **Arcadia's** engine was also a compound surface condensing engine, which gave her a speed of 10 m.p.h. She was built for Captain Kinley of

Lunenburg, and had room for 250 barrels under decks. As well she was certified to carry 20 passengers in her two steam heated cabins.

The delay occasioned by the need for repairs and alterations caused the committee some embarrassment. No competing ferry by April 1? Unthinkable! Thus without official sanction, C.E. Creighton made arrangements to hire another steamer for the day. He was able to obtain the **Bridgewater**, which like the **Arcadia**, also ran on the south shore route. He paid the $85 rental fee from his own pocket. That night there was a meeting of ratepayers in the Reform Club Hall, where quarterly commutation tickets were being sold at the usual rate, for travel on the new People's Ferry. Such was the demand that Creighton easily recovered his $85.

Meanwhile, the Halifax and Dartmouth Steam Ferry Company had held a panic-stricken meeting on March 29, and set ticket prices a little lower than previous schedules had shown.

The following was published in the morning papers of April 1, 1890:

Halifax and Dartmouth Steam Ferry Company Ltd.

Commutations
To Come Into Force 1st April

100   3 cent tickets for $2.50
500   3 cent tickets for $10.00
1000 3 cent tickets for $17.50
100 12 cent tickets for $10.00
100 15 cent tickets for $13.00

To Shop and Working Girls, School Children,
Apprentices and Shop Boys
$100 tickets for $1.00
Other rates as before published
G. E. VanBuskirk, Manager

Presumably the "other rates" were for single teams, double teams, carriages, hand barrows and the like.

These were attractive prices, except for the absence of the quarterly commutation ticket, the cause of the final disillusionment. On the same page as this announcement was the far more exciting one inserted by "The People's Ferry Boat" interests.

PUBLIC NOTICE! The People's Ferry Boat **Bridgewater** will leave Campbell's Wharf Dartmouth at 6:15 a.m. making half hourly trips until 8 p.m. load passengers at Central Wharf for today only. The **Electra** will run on Wednesday from Campbell's Wharf to City Wharf. Commutation tickets can be purchased at the Town Hall at the old rate. The Town Clerk's Office will be open to receive payments and to issue tickets during regular office hours and on this Tuesday Evening from 7:30 to 9:30. Single Fares **Two Cents.** Further Information at the boat.
W. C. Bishop, Secretary.

Campbell's Wharf was located just south of the present Dartmouth City Hall.

As mentioned in the advertisement, the steamer **Electra** took over for a few days, and **Bridgewater** returned to her previous service. Next, the **City of Monticello**, a New Brunswick steamer which ran from Saint John To Annapolis, and finally the **Arcadia** were ready for service. Undercutting the Steam Ferry Company even further, it was announced that quarterly commutation tickets for schoolchildren would be $1 on the **Arcadia.**

In the House of Assembly the bill concerning the Town's borrowing for ferry purposes, was ready for third reading. Premier W.S. Fielding said a mistake had been made in the past in granting charters without some regulation in the ferriage rates, and he proposed a clause requiring that fare increases be approved by the Governor-in-Council. Apparently with this amendment the bill passed into law. The people of Dartmouth now had the means and the right to establish a public ferry, but with public control over rates. Before the dust had completely settled, and the final votes counted, another meeting of the committee on private and local bills heard further argument between the opposing

SHOULDER TO SHOULDER.

THE BILL TO ESTABLISH THE CORPORATION FERRY has passed the Legislature in spite of the threats of Directors and of all the influences that they could bring to bear. It has passed in a better shape than its most sanguine advocate dared to hope for. It now rests with the people themselves to say whether they will carry on the work so nobly begun, or whether by division in their counsels, or lukewarmness in their support they will throw away the successes that have already been achieved, and give the victory to their foes. The little boat put on the route at the beginning of the month has thus far fulfilled and more than fulfilled the predictions made in our last issue. The daily receipts have more than paid the expenses, and the Commutation fund is still to the good, to be handed over to the public, in whose interest the boat is run. If the patronage thus far extended is continued for the next few weeks, the Peoples' Ferry is an assured success. In the meantime the commission which will be organized at once will no doubt take immediate steps to put another boat on the route to accommodate both teams and passengers. The Ferry will then be entirely in the hands of the people themselves, and the monopoly that has heretofore been the curse of the Town will be broken up forever. Nothing is impossible if the people of Dartmouth will continue to maintain the same unbroken ranks with which they have up to this point fought their battle. The company's reduction of fares announced this morning is due entirely to the pressure of the peoples' agitation. Remove that pressure to-morrow and the rates will immediately spring back to the old figure and the company sit firmer in the saddle than ever before. The magnificent steamer "Dartmouth" which was promised on the route on Wednesday (wind and weather permitting) will go back to her dock and wait for the excursion harvest while the people of Dartmouth will be left in a worse condition than they were before the fight began. It behoves us then to close up the ranks and not give way a single inch until the victory is complete. Let the aged and the infirm travel on the company's boats if they must, but let not those of us who can possibly avoid it be tempted on any consideration to furnish the company with patronage and funds to fight their way back to their old monopoly.

Dartmouth, April 16th, 1890.

53. *Notice of meeting, 1890.*

factions. The Steam Ferry Company presented five reasons why the bill should not be passed, but Mayor Scarfe of Dartmouth defended the bill.

The City Council of Halifax gave the People's Ferry Committee permission to erect a temporary ferry house, charging $2 rent.

Finally, on April 15, 1890, the Act was passed. Essentially it gave the Town the right to borrow $110,000 "for the establishment and operation of a public ferry between Dartmouth and Halifax."

This marked yet another turning point in the corporate history of the Dartmouth-Halifax ferries. In spite of this, the battle was not considered as won. The People's Ferry Committee had, all month, been waging a campaign to get Dartmouth citizens to use the **Arcadia**, in order to drive the Steam Ferry Company out of business. Benjamin Russell wrote and had printed and posted handbills exhorting the commuting public to support the People's Ferry.

In his autobiography Russell noted that "only two men could be seen marching backward and forward on the deck of the ferry steamer. They deserve to be remembered—Ted Elliot, the architect, and Lewis Parker, a clerk in the savings bank." Apparently the controversy split families. Benjamin Russell's father Nathaniel, and Edward Elliot's father, Jonathan were stepbrothers. The Elliot family was further split because Frank Elliot was a director of the Steam Ferry Company, while Alfred Elliot, the Town Clerk, was busy selling tickets for the People's Ferry at the Town Hall.

All signs pointed to the struggle being won by the People's Ferry. The Steam Ferry Company was disheartened. A meeting of the shareholders was held in the YMCA on April 22 at which W.H. Newman, C.H. Harvey, W.C. Silver, Mr. Bissett, Alderman Mosher and Harry Romans were appointed to effect a settlement. As Benjamin Russell wrote, "The day came when the company was glad to be quit of the struggle against the townsmen."

The organization meeting of the Dartmouth Ferry Commission was held the next day. The commission was composed of Mayor Scarfe, Councillors Maclean and W.H.

Stevens, an appointee of the Governor-in-Council, John Donald, the Chief Justice's appointee, John White, and Byron A. Weston appointed by the Town Council to represent the citizens at large. For the first few meetings, Town Clerk Alfred Elliot acted as secretary for the commission.

At the first meeting, the most urgent business was the acquisition of a new boat, one which could carry teams as well as passengers. Commissioners Weston and White were appointed to travel to New York to look for a suitable vessel.

The next few meetings were taken up by negotiations with the Steam Ferry Company and its committee "to effect a settlement." Chairman Silver offered to sell all the Steam Ferry Company's property for $121,700. When the commission's counter offer of $75,000 was rejected by the Steam Ferry Company, the commission raised its offer to $105,000, on a "take it or leave it" basis. The old company came back with $118,193, not much of a reduction from the original $121,700. Finally, J.C. Mackintosh wrote a letter mentioning a figure that the commission felt could be accepted. Mackintosh's letter was signed by shareholders Robie Uniacke, Samuel Brookfield, Henry Romans, W.H. Newman, A.C. Cogswell, Saul Mosher, H.W. Brown, D.C. James, J.H. Renner, F. Elliot, James Starr, T.G. Stevens, D. Waddell, J.W. Turner, G.A. MacKenzie (the Steam Boat Company's erstwhile Agent), J. Ritchie & Co., and W.H. Brookfield. The asking price had been driven down to $110,000—"a figure so moderate that it occasioned serious loss to a recent purchaser of company stock," wrote Russell.

It was the same figure arrived at in the estimate of the committee appointed at the ratepayers' meeting of the previous January, and also the amount that recent legislation empowered the Town to borrow for such purposes.

The letter from the Steam Ferry Company also contained the stipulation that its employees be kept on by the Dartmouth Ferry Commission.

Finally, on July 16, 1890, six months after the campaign to organize the People's Ferry had begun, the Dartmouth Ferry Commission formally took possession of the property of the Halifax and Dartmouth Steam Ferry Company Ltd.

Another era in ferry administration had begun.

XIX.
ANNEX 2 and Tragedy

While the battle between the two opposing factions raged on at home, the delegation sent to New York to buy a new ferry boat was busy with the search. It did not take long to find what was believed to be a suitable ferry, and the newly organized Dartmouth Ferry Commission arranged to borrow $35,000 from the Union Bank in order to be in a position to negotiate the purchase of a "new" boat. This was prior to its takeover of the Halifax and Dartmouth Steam Ferry Company.

Annex 2 was purchased for $25,000. She was built at New Baltimore, N.Y., for the Brooklyn Annex Company, and ran between Brooklyn and Jersey City. Like the new **Dartmouth, Annex 2** was a double-ended, side paddlewheeler, with two lanes for teams. She was unique in that she was the only ferry on the Halifax Harbour service with a beam engine.

Marine application of the beam engine was largely an American development, presumably because of the extensive inland and relatively sheltered waterways in the United States, where stability would not have the same importance as it would on the open ocean. Thus the British concentrated on the development of the side-lever engine in which the main mass of machinery was installed low down in the hull.

Illustrations of the **Annex 2**, when she first arrived in Halifax Harbour, depict the large diamond shaped beam protruding through the canopy over the upper deck. Later, a house was built to enclose the beam, presumably to protect its working parts from our severe winters. The massive vertical connecting rods at each end of the beam must have been sources of wonder and delight to mechanically minded passengers, but perhaps strange and rather frightening to the timid, who would have been used to the engine being hidden under the main deck.

It seems unusual that the bill of sale for the **Annex 2** was

54. Annex 2 *with exposed beam, 1890.*

made out to James F. Kinley, and not to the Dartmouth Ferry Commission or even to one of the commissioners. This was the same Captain Kinley of Lunenburg who had been the original owner of the **Arcadia**. Now that the **Arcadia** was on the Halifax-Dartmouth ferry, instead of her previous Halifax to Lunenburg run, Captain Kinley had been asked by the commission to pilot the **Annex 2** from New York to Dartmouth. The bill of sale was signed June 26, 1890, in New York.

Feelings were still running high in Dartmouth at the time. The **Arcadia** was crowded with enthusiastic and patriotic Dartmouthians, as she continued her opposition to the boats

of the Steam Ferry Company. When word spread that a new, large ferry would arrive shortly from New York, the excitement became intense. The prospect of two large ferries running in opposition was intriguing. Who would win the battle for supremacy in the ferry war?

A news item aroused more interest in the expected arrival—a report from Yarmouth, where the **Annex 2** had arrived earlier in the week. "The new-old ferry boat was brought into Baker's Wharf yesterday. She is a large and handsomely built boat, with electric light and all modern improvements, decidedly showy in appearance and will be a welcome addition to the boats on the line. She has been

55. *Model of beam engine by William Pearce.*

coming along the coast in 'easy stages' and was delayed by fog three days at one port in Maine. She came to Yarmouth direct from Bar Harbour. The captains in charge are delighted with the boat, and they have reason to be. Though Yarmouth could have built them another fine boat, there was not time to wait, and we congratulate the people of Dartmouth on their palatial purchase. She will be a delightful excursion boat.''

When this account was followed by the news that the new ferry was expected to dock that evening, excitement became even greater. She was seen coming up the harbour in the early evening, and the word spread like wildfire. Families of the crew of the **Annex 2** were especially eager to be reunited, perhaps even to be treated to an unofficial tour of the boat.

She was due to dock at the new lay-up wharf, Warner's, one south of the Steam Ferry Company's dock. A light platform, held up by half-inch galvanized chain had been lowered from the head of the wharf so that the new ferry boat could draw up to it as a gangway. A welcoming committee of ferry officials was on hand—Byron A. Weston,

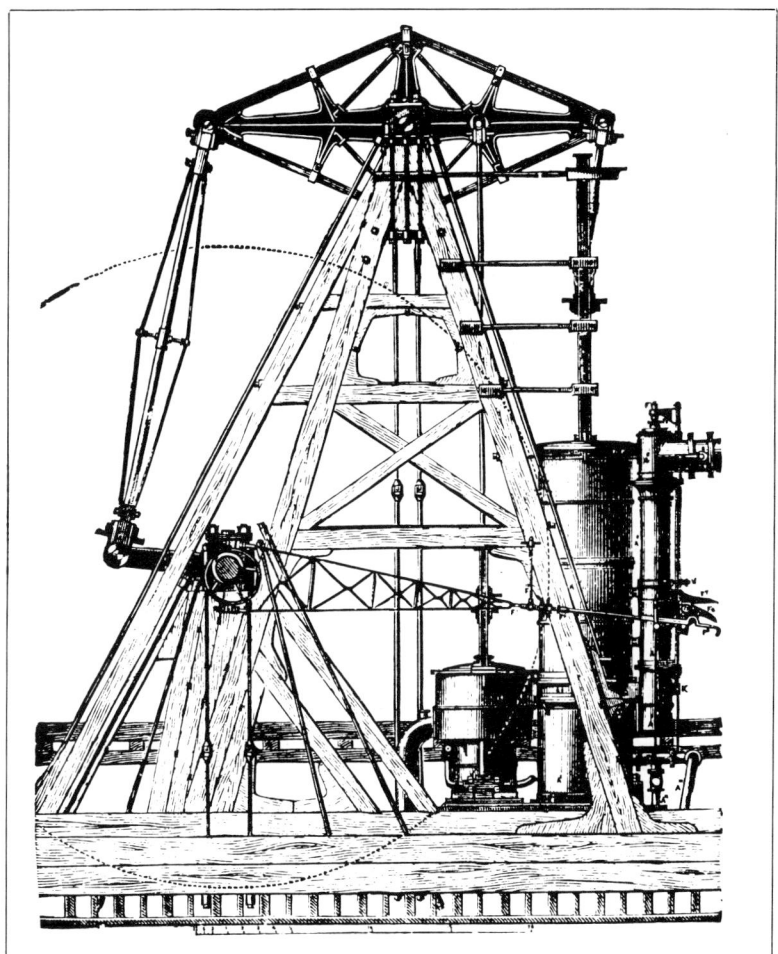

56. *Drawing of marine beam engine.*

W.H. Stevens and Henry Watt, the newly appointed Superintendent of the ferry commission. The gate at the entrance to the wharf was locked, but in their wild exuberance, the crowd forced it open and surged onto the wharf. Police Chief MacKenzie and Constable McLennan, as well as the ferry commissioners shouted to the people to stay back, but as Henry Watt said, ''The people seemed to be perfectly crazy. There was no keeping them back.''

As the **Annex** approached, she did not come up to the head of the wharf as the crowd expected. Captain Kinley had seen the size of the waiting throng, and knew it would be difficult to get his lines ashore through that mass of humanity, so he gave orders to go astern, and to tie up nearer the outer end of the wharf. At this, the crowd pushed out on the flimsy gangway which was about 18 feet long and 10 feet wide. Those who were pushed to the outside edge had no protection and some were tempted to jump to the deck of the **Annex**. Only one person made the leap successfully, the high-spirited wife of a clergyman. Her split-second timing may have been heaven guided, for at that precise moment the chains holding up the gangway snapped. All the other unfortunate souls were immediately plunged into the cold waters of the harbour, in a very small space, and where the depth of water was 20 feet.

It was dusk when the joyous and quite unscheduled celebration was transformed into pandemonium. On the wharf "women shrieked and fainted, strong men turned pale with fear; others shouted orders and advice of various kinds. There were but few cool heads in that terrible moment."

Fortunately there were some who did keep cool. Life preservers were thrown from the ferry by Mate Frank Rudolph and a young man named Wilson. This idea spread and the people began tossing heavy pieces of cordwood into the confined area of thrashing humanity. The wood hit some of the victims, knocking them unconscious. In the growing darkness and wild confusion no one was aware of their plight. Several young men either jumped in, or climbed down the side of the wharf to rescue those in the water. Names of some were given in newspaper accounts, including Alex Lloy, James Collins, County Constable James Burbridge, David Tait, Bill Fawson, George May and William Broadhurst. A raft and two or three small boats were quickly at the scene as well. Torches were called for, an men went to prepare them

Among those reported rescued were:

"-Elliot, Alfred, Town Clerk, and his two children.
-Broadhurst, Mrs. William, rescued by her husband, who was one of the first to jump into the water.
-Isenor, Mrs.
-Warner, Mrs. James.
-Logan, infant of Mrs. Logan, wife of the engineer of the boat who was anxious to be one of the first to get aboard.
-Lawlor, Michael.
-Foster, Edward, secretary of the East Halifax Agricultural Society.
-Waddell, Mrs. Alexander.
-Silver, Mrs. Henry. Mrs. Silver is a very heavy woman. While in the water Mrs. Waddell and Mrs. Silver grasped hold of each other, had a very narrow escape from drowning, and it was with the greatest difficulty that they were hauled out. Mrs. Waddell is reported to have had a child in her arms. (Probably Mrs. Logan's)
-Settle, James.
-Leadley, Grace.
-Leadley, Hattie.
-Wilson, Annie.
-Murray, Francis.
-Garrison, Annie. Daughter of W. A. Garrison, surveyor of customs, now absent in England on the Wimbledon team
-Bayers, a young boy.
-Falconer, Miss.
-MacKenzie, Lizzie.
-Mumford, Miss. Daughter of Francis Mumford.
-Carroll, Ellie. This young lady was thought to be dead when she was taken out of the water, but was resuscitated after half an hour's hard work."

Newspaper reporters of the time were given to expressing personal opinions and to writing intimate and often irrelevant details, but the writers of the foregoing account and that which follows might be excused on account of the unusual circumstances. Accidents of this nature and magnitude were rare, so that matters of ethics, sensitivity and public taste, had perhaps not yet arisen.

The following account gives a vivid picture of the event.

THE DEAD
No one could tell the number of the dead last night.

110

Four bodies were recovered, but a strong current was running, and there might be a dozen or score carried in among the piles of the wharf, under the boat or out into the harbour. Various opinions were expressed as to the number that must have perished; but one opinion that the number would not exceed half a dozen was based upon exactly the same evidence as another opinion that the number would reach a dozen or another that it must be a score. The bodies recovered up to 11 o'clock were as follows:

—Boyle, Peter, aged about 60 years, an old pensioner, engaged in the Ropeworks. He leaves a large family. This body was taken on board the Annex, placed in one of the cabins and covered with a blanket. His countenance presented a ghastly appearance.

—Sinnott, Ella, aged 17, a bright young girl, daughter of Michael Sinnott. Her body was removed to her parents' residence almost immediately after being recovered.

—Bundy, John, aged 11, colored; father dead; lived with his mother. Every one appeared to know little "Johnnie Bundy," and to be sorry that the little fellow was among the victims.

—Foster, Bessie, aged about 27 years. The body of this girl lay in the cabin of the Annex for an hour before being recognized. At half past 10 the body was moved into the waiting room of the ticket office, where it was viewed by several hundred persons. One declared it to be the body of Miss . . . , school teacher; another Ellie . . . , yet another said it was Bessie . . . .

The chief of police, Captain Graham, Henry Watt and others said the face was familiar to them, but they could not think of the name. When the boat arrived from Halifax at 10:30, one of the passengers recognized the body as that of Bessie Foster. Her features were very much swollen. She was said to be the daughter of Edward Foster (mentioned above as among the rescued) and was standing close to her father at the time of the catastrophe. Both went down into the water together; but the daughter drowned while the father was saved. At least, this was the current report when the boat left, and the story is published as received, without an opportunity of being verified by the writer.

The news of the catastrophe spread like wildfire on both sides of the harbour and the greatest excitement prevailed. The scene in Dartmouth was one not soon to be forgotten. Little groups of people stood on the sidewalks, in the streets, on the wharves recounting the story of the horror. Women and children cried and moaned. Big burly men with stout hearts rushed about to look for their missing ones, or ran home with blanched faces to tell the story of the horror and see that their families were safe. On the Halifax side, the approach to the ferry dock was crowded with anxious ones, eager to get the latest news, and every arrival from Dartmouth was compelled to tell the story anew.

——————— Searching For the Bodies ———————

Willing hands with grappling hooks, torches, etc., were working until midnight searching for more bodies. Someone telephoned to Diver Stone to engage in the work. He got over on the 11 o'clock boat, but when he arrived none of the ferry commissioners were on hand to give him instructions or to assume any responsibility in regard to his work, and the diver declined to do anything; and was indignant at the way he was treated.

——————— Men's and Women's Hats ———————

The great majority of those on the gangway were women. This was evidenced by the headgear which floated in the water and was picked up and ranged in the cabin of the Annex. There were 13 women's hats, of various shapes, mostly straw, and 7 men's hats. These were ranged along the seats of the cabin, and served rather as an evidence of the number precipitated into the water than a means of identifying the victims. Most of those rescued left their hats in the water. But scores and hundreds of people who feared that some member of their families or some friend had gone down, critically examined these pieces of clothing with a view to identification.

——————— Responsibility for the Calamity ———————

The responsibility for this terrible calamity will be

57. Halifax (Annex 2) *with enclosed beam, ca. 1895.*

enquired into by a coroner's jury; and 'tis hoped the enquiry will be a searching one by a coroner in whom the public have confidence. But it may be added here that the chain that held the gangway is supposed to have been capable of little more than operating the bridge itself; not to speak of also supporting the weight of half a hundred human beings."

Some sought to take advantage of the tragedy. A florist with a recently acquired telephone arranged to have the following notice inserted at the bottom of one of the press accounts: "Telephone 252, for Roses, Bouquets, etc."

Then as now rivalry between the ports of Halifax and Saint John was keen. One Saint John newspaper had the scathing comment:

The dreadful accident which caused the deaths of so many persons in Halifax last evening seems to have been one that might have been prevented by proper precautions. The people of Halifax must be little accustomed to novelties when they rush in such crowds to see an old New York ferry boat. The Town of Dartmouth might have built its own ferry steamers, as Saint John has always done, and if this had been the

case the accident would not have occurred. We regret that so many valuable lives should have been lost without any apparent necessity.

Another Saint John paper was kinder:

Last night's tragic occurrence at Halifax is one which everybody will say might have been prevented, but which after all belongs to a class of events that are not prevented because they are not foreseen. The people might easily have been kept off the floats if precautions had been taken in time, the structure might have been made strong enough to withstand the pressure, or the people might have heeded the warning of the officers. It is easy to see now how the loss of life might have been prevented. But there are very few accidents that could not be prevented if responsibile persons could always say beforehand how the victims, or those who cause the accident would act in all possible circumstances. The action of purely mechanical forces can be estimated with something like accuracy by skilled men, but the behaviour of the human element can never be exactly foreseen. Perhaps in this case there was undue negligence. If so it will be determined later. What is known is that a calamity has fallen on the Town of Dartmouth and the City of Halifax, and that sorrow has come down suddenly on several homes.

There were grossly exaggerated reports from Quebec and Boston papers: ". . . precipitating a crowd of six or seven hundred men, women and children into the water." "About 700 men, women and children were precipitated into the water. Many of those rescued were severely injured, and some will doubtless die from the effects of their wounds."

It was an unfortunate beginning for **Annex 2** on the Halifax-Dartmouth ferry, but better times followed. When inspected locally the following spring, Mr. Coker would not pass her hull until it was strengthened. Probably this was due to ice in the harbour. The hull work was done at G. and J. Young's Shipyard, and finally, with her name officially changed to **Halifax**, the "old-new" ferry boat was ready for service.

XX.
Vignettes of the Nineties

After the shock waves of the **Annex** disaster had rippled away, the new ferry commission got down to regular business. Town Clerk Alfred Elliot, part-time secretary of the hastily organized new administration, was soon succeeded by a permanent secretary, G.E. VanBuskirk. The starting salary for VanBuskirk was $800 a year, for which he worked long, hard hours. The first ten days of each quarter of the year was the time set aside for the sale of commutation tickets. On those days the secretary's hours were from 7 to 1, 2 to 6, and 7 to 8. The remainder of the quarter was less strenuous—from 9 to 1, and 2 to 5. His salary was raised to $1000 in 1892, which action caused the following to be written: "one extravagance our ferry commission is guilty of is in having a secretary at a salary of $1000 per annum... I do think a young lady could do all the work necessary... at a salary of less than one half that paid to the present secretary." The letter went on in a manner that was oddly prophetic: "My idea has been that the Town Hall should be nearer the ferry and all the clerical work of the town (ferry and water works included) be done from there."

VanBuskirk resigned in 1895 to operate a fuel business, and was replaced by John W. Jago, whose salary began at the former figure of $800 until he had proved his worth.

Solicitor for the commission was Benjamin Russell, who had spoken so brilliantly in the cause of the "People's Ferry." His salary was $150 a year. This was a part-time position since Russell was still one of the original professors of the Dalhousie Law School. He was later appointed as a Judge of the Supreme Court.

With two excellent large boats (**Dartmouth** and **Annex 2**) in service, and the **Micmac** in use for excursions and emergencies, tenders were called for the sale of **Ogle, Chebucto** and **Arcadia.** Negotiations were carried on with prospective buyers for several months. The **Arcadia** was sold in February 1891 for $3,500, the **Chebucto** in May of 1892 for $300. The **Chebucto** was later registered in the name of Wm. E. Sproull, Pictou Landing, and the **Arcadia** to Mrs. Elizabeth Beatty, Pictou. The Government of Canada expressed interest in the **Ogle** and the commissioners thought they would ask $2,500 for her. In view of the fact that she was 62 years old, this seemed optimistic indeed. No sale was made at this ridiculous price: instead, the **Ogle** was leased to the government for a period of six months. She was taken to the deep water terminus and prepared to do fumigating and disinfecting work, if necessary, on vessels coming to Halifax from infected ports. Meanwhile, a hospital and wharf were under construction at Lawlor's Island, as a permanent quarantine station. A Dr. Wickwire was the government's representative who negotiated this transaction with the **Ogle**. The last days of the **Ogle** came in December of 1894 when she was purchased by Nathaniel Evans, boilermaker, for $200. It was mentioned previously that her old hull became part of the crib work at Evan's wharf.

The commission's commutation rates were published in the summer of 1890.

Single teams—loaded	25
unloaded	20
Double teams—loaded	35
unloaded	25
Double teams exceeding 2 tons—loaded	45
unloaded	25
Double teams exceeding 3 tons—loaded	50
unloaded	25
Vehicles only	15
Horse and rider	12
Cattle and horses	10
Sheep and hogs	3
Wheelbarrows and handcarts	5
Barrels and packages of merchandise	5
Bicycle (May, 1891)	3

Unlike the old Steam Boat Company, the Dartmouth Ferry Commission decided to allow the carrying of manure on the ferry at any time as long as the carrying vehicles were properly covered. One writer of letters to newspapers objected strenuously, saying that on one trip on the **Micmac** there were four loads of manure, and it was impossible to escape the odour anywhere on the boat.

The monthly meetings of the commission must have been fairly lengthy until commutation rates, single fares and excursion rates were set. In the spring of 1891 rates were set for the hire of boats for excursions:

		(Raised in July to)
Halifax and **Dartmouth**	$75 per day	$100
Ogle	$40 per day	$ 50
Micmac	$60 per day	

If the boats were kept out after 8 p.m. the rate would go up by $10 for each hour.

The following year, a new mayor and councillors voted to have no excursions. Excursion policy seemed to vary with successive councils.

Henry Watt had been appointed Superintendent at a salary of $800. A sign of the times was that a telephone was installed in his house for emergencies.

Adult foot passenger (per quarter)	$4.50
Man and wife	5.50
Man and wife and 5 minor children	9.00
Each additional child	.50
Adult males of the same family	4.00
Single females	2.00
Apprentices and clerks (minors)	2.50
Pupils attending the Academy	FREE
Domestic servants on employer's business	1.00
Commercial travellers (at Dec. 1, 1891)	3.00
Bicycle (at May, 1891)	2.50

SINGLE FARES	Cents
Adults	3
(But raised to 4 cents, or 3½ cents for 20 or more tickets in November 1891)	
Children under 15	2
Coloured people and Indians	2

58. Halifax (Annex 2), *ca. 1900.*

The masters, mates and deckhands were to wear uniforms "whilst on duty." They were each to have two uniforms, one being paid for by the commission. Pictures of captains in the Steam Boat Company era show the crews in everyday clothes so these uniforms must be considered a new departure.

There were stirrings of labour unrest, since the minutes of the 1890s recorded a number of firings, and continual requests for raises in salaries. In 1890, captains were paid $50 a month, mates and fireman $35. The Chief Engineer received $80 and two other engineers $60. Some of these salaries were increased in 1892—$55 for captains, $40 for mates, and $8 a week for deckhands. Engineers' salaries, however, were not mentioned. Two engineers had recently been dismissed, and a third censured for refusing to do required repairs on Sunday.

In June of 1893 when the commissioners decided to run a 4 a.m. boat on Saturdays to accommodate farmers going to the market, the engineers were upset. They had not been consulted, and objected strenuously to the length of their day. They usually worked over 11 hours. The shortest possible engineer's day was ten hours, and the longest, 12¼ hours. With the new Saturday arrangement, this day was drawn out to 14½ hours. This was particularly trying, they claimed, on the **Dartmouth** since the engine room was poorly ventilated, and had only four oil lamps for lighting. (Whatever happened to the magnificent new electric lighting system?) Further, the engineers said that if they were on a sea-going ship, they would be working only eight hours a day.

Things came to a head in February 1894. Engineer Short was dismissed for disobeying rules, and for the first time, a labour union entered the picture. The commissioners were called to a special meeting to hear a powerful letter from the Canadian Marine Engineers Association. The commission was persuaded to reconsider its position, and as a result rehired Engineer Short, but saved a small bit of face by demanding and obtaining a promise from him that he would, in future, obey the rules.

The personnel had undergone many changes since Steam Boat Company days. Captain Alex Marks, aged 53, died of consumption in February 1892. He had been a popular captain, and had saved more than 20 people from drowning. His obituary rather plaintively mentioned that he was entitled to the Royal Humane Society's medal, but had never received it.

A year later another captain left the service. On a foggy morning, Captain Hamm in command of the **Micmac**, left Dartmouth at 6.45 a.m. but did not reach Halifax until 10:00 a.m. The **Micmac** struck the recently arrived steamer **Camellia** which was at anchor in the harbour. This blow heaped insult upon injury to the **Camellia**, which had just had a difficult crossing from Antwerp, taking 24¼ days. **Micmac** sustained damage to her rails and gates. **Camellia's** damage amounted to $45. As a result of the inquiry following the accident, Captain Hamm was dismissed.

The reporter who wrote this story must have still been smarting at the story in the "Saint John Gazette" at the time of the **Annex** disaster, since he added the following paragraph: "(It is understood that based on the above, something like the following has been dispatched to Saint John): 'You will be glad to hear that our harbour is frozen over; that the Dartmouth ferry was delayed two hours crossing this morning. Please notify morning and evening papers and Board of Trade. If the harbour remains in present condition the next mail from England will probably have to be landed at Saint John.' "

Two weeks later the same Captain Hamm was a passenger on the **Dartmouth**, on his way to his new position as second officer of the S.S. **Barcelona.** His former mate was now the captain of the **Dartmouth** and according to newspaper accounts "there was so much 'barber' (foam? lather?) in the harbour that the **Dartmouth** ran into the head of Musgrave's (Power's) wharf at the foot of Duke Street and carried away several piles. The ferry was damaged and the commission became liable for $120 damages to the wharf."

This accident occurred even though "a large bell had been purchased by the Ferry Commission and placed at the head of the wharf as a fog guide."

Crews of the boats, and shore employees had no holidays until 1894, when they were granted a munificent three days a year. When one of the captains pointed out that it took one day to go even a short distance, and one day to return, and that the third day was really not much of a rest, the commissioners decided that a full week was justified. All employees were given this privilege in 1896.

It did not take long for some Dartmouth citizens to feel that the ferry service should be entirely under the control of the Town, with no appointees of the Governor-in-Council. A bill was introduced in the Legislature to this effect, but was defeated.

Newspaper reporting was rapidly becoming more sophisticated, with telegraph and telephone service adding an element of timeliness to the printed word. Older and more conservative town councillors objected to reporters invading the council meetings because they felt that inaccurate reports had been published at various times. Since some of these councillors were also on the ferry commission, reporters received an extremely cool reception when they tried to attend commission meetings. Of these reporters, two were J.W. Regan of the "Evening Mail" and H.S. Congdon, editor and reporter of the "Atlantic Weekly," a Dartmouth newspaper.

There was a particularly contentious issue in 1893, when once again Inspector Coker refused to pass the **Halifax** (**Annex 2**). She had to have all her machinery taken out for close inspection, while the hull and superstructure were thoroughly examined. Coker's suspicions had been correct, and the commission heard the sad fact that she "presented a decayed condition." People were shocked that their "new-old" ferry, only three years on the local route, was in such a sorry state, and there was discussion on the street corners about the poor deal made in New York. For this reason, the two rival local reporters wanted the "inside" story, straight from the commission meetings. This was not to be. VanBuskirk was advised to write them a formal letter stating that it was "not convenient" for them to attend the meetings. This prompted a strongly worded editorial from Congdon, but it was not until some months later that the commission gave in, and then went so far as to furnish two small tables "for the use of the Press."

59. *(top)* Halifax (Annex 2), *at Dartmouth dock, 1890s.*

60. *(right)* Dartmouth, *early 1900s.*

The pendulum swung further as the commission allowed reporters to publish in detail accounts of its meetings. In addition reports were sent in itemizing the total costs of the **Halifax** to date, and a pay sheet covering all employees. In March 1894 it read:

	Per Annum
G. E. VanBuskirk	$1000
Dennis Murray, Chief Engineer	960
Superintendent Watt	800
	Per Month
3 Engineers	67
3 Captains	55
	Per Week
3 Mates	9.25
3 Firemen	9.00
3 Deckhands	8.00

4 Ticket Girls	4.25
John Keefe	12.50
M. Storey	12.00
M. McCabe	9.60
H. Siteman	9.00
Watchman	8.00
John Webber	7.50
E. Wentzell	7.00
T. Bowser	7.00

In the meantime experts were consulted in regard to the **Halifax**. Should she be repaired or replaced? J. B. North of Hantsport said she could be repaired, and John Zwicker of Mahone Bay thought it would be possible to repair her, but that the specifications were too vague (a complaint one occasionally hears today). Ebenezer Moseley of Dartmouth thought it would be better to build a new boat. As the vote stood at two to one, she was repaired with the work all being done in Dartmouth. Young's Shipyard repaired the hull for $6,500. W. & A. Moir supplied the parts to put the engine in working order for $2,600.

The Ferry Commission called for tenders for the construction of a new station house in Halifax in September 1890. A contract was awarded to Messrs. Brown and Horton, for the sum of $1,255. The station house was a single-story flat roofed structure located on the south side of where the main dock is today. There seemed to be a problem at the Halifax terminal on Saturday afternoons, since a letter was written to the City of Halifax requesting a policeman to be on duty there. Later, an electric alarm bell was installed to connect the Halifax ferry station directly with the police station.

On the Dartmouth side there had been many changes in the vicinity of the ferry terminal since the advent of the railway in 1886. Several buildings were moved or torn down to make way for the tracks, and a rail siding was added to facilitate the delivery of coal. Immediately to the south of the main Dartmouth dock was the small, flat roofed waiting room and ticket seller's wicket. This was on the side opposite to the present-day terminal. Just a little to the southeast of the waiting room was a fairly large wooden building which had been the site of George Wright's bar. While liquor licenses were abolished in 1886, coincidental with the arrival of the railway, the building did not remain idle for long.

A group of progressive Dartmouth citizens held a public meeting in the Town Hall in January of 1886 for the purpose of establishing a public library. Those involved were Mr. Frazee, John Y. Payzant, J. Walter Allison, Alex McKay, Benjamin Russell, Harris J. Congdon and Alfred Elliot. They were not successful in organizing a true library, but they did achieve a Public Reading Room, which opened in George Wright's erstwhile bar on New Year's Day, 1889. "This is a great boon to the town," wrote the editor of the "Acadian Recorder". "It is used as a waiting-room by ladies and gentlemen who find that they are just in time to be late for the boat, and who can very profitably occupy these moments towards self advancement, (and) it is used by a large number of citizens, old and young who go there for the sake of getting information from magazines and periodicals, in addition to merely gazing at a few pictures or peering into the dailies. One is very much struck with the frightful picture (that is if those in the "Graphic" are a criterion) of the celebrated but fickle-minded nobleman Lord Randolph Churchill which adorns the walls of this useful room."

When it was time for the passengers to embark for Halifax, tickets were shown to the captain or mate just outside the little waiting room. In the case of single fares, they were simply stuffed into the employee's pocket, and then a bell was rung as a signal that the ferry was departing. "This clanging brought a rush of commuters out of the Reading Room where most of them lingered until the last." It is not to be wondered that they lingered in the Reading Room, because the list of magazines and periodicals was most impressive: Popular Science Monthly, Forum, North American Review, Fortnightly Review, Contemporary Review, Nineteenth Century, Review of Reviews, Atlantic Monthly, Century, Harper's, Scribner's, Cosmopolitan, St. Nicholas, Frank Leslie Popular Monthly, Outing, Harper's Bazaar, Frank Leslie's Illustrated Weekly, Illustrated

London News, Graphic, Sketch, Grip, Punch, American Machinist, Carpentry and Building, Scientific American, The Metal Worker, Youth's Companion, Canadian Manu-facturer, Moniteur du Commerce, London Times, and all Canadian newspapers.'' All these were available and after they were a month old, went into circulation for a fee of 3 cents a week. Apparently the men who had first met to discuss a library decided that they would make this modest beginning and hope to add books later on. "Twelve persons pay the whole shot," said the editor of the "Atlantic Weekly."

Water pipes were installed in Dartmouth in 1892. The Young Cold Water Army members who formerly hired the ferries for excursions had grown up, and the ladies' branch, which became named the Women's Christian Temperance Union donated a novel three-way drinking fountain which was installed near the bottom of Steamboat Hill. It was provided for the convenience of "humans, horses and dogs". The top was adorned with a lamp, and the whole was imported from New York.

Another difficulty at the foot of Steamboat Hill was the railway track. "The boat is in the dock, a long string of teams is coming off and crossing the track, while men, women, children, dogs, cats and cattle are mixed up with the teams of the hackmen on and about the crossing. Suddenly the end of a box car (the engine always comes last) appears from around the curve and thus all is in confusion, horses bolt, drivers swear, cattle stumble, women scream, dogs bark and cats howl. In the midst of the scrimmage the train goes by and the spectator heaves a sigh of relief when he sees, to his amazement, that no mangled corpses cumber the track. Luck must be with the people of Dartmouth for as yet no lives have been lost on this spot but it strikes me that we are trusting too much to luck if we let this thing continue much longer." Thus wrote a reader to the editor of the "Atlantic Weekly".

The branch line of the Intercolonial Railway ran from Richmond in the north end of Halifax, across a bridge at the Narrows, and south along the shore of Dartmouth to the Sugar Refinery, then to Woodside. "The bridge measures six hundred and fifty feet in length, and is built in water from sixty to seventy-five feet in depth. Mr. M.J. Hogan, of Quebec, was the contractor and builder of the wood-work; the Starr Manufacturing Company, of the iron super-structure of the draw-bridge; and Mr. Duncan Waddell of Dartmouth, of the stone pier on which the iron draw swings." During a September gale in 1891 (probably a hurricane) the bridge was swept away. A second bridge was immediately begun, and completed a mere four months later. However it only lasted a year and a half, when it simply drifted away, six hours after a train had crossed it. Some time later the Dartmouth branch line was extended to Windsor Junction, avoiding the harbour altogether. These catastrophes did not assist the railway's competitive position with respect to the ferry.

Having put the **Halifax** back in order, and returned to service, the **Micmac** was the next to fail inspection. The commissioners were told at the 1895 August meeting that she would not be allowed to operate after November 1, 1895, "certificate of **Micmac** which has been extended from time to time pending arrival of new boat having expired." This would leave only two ferries on the route—the **Dartmouth** and the **Halifax**. There was some discussion of the merits of buying another secondhand ferry from the United States, but instead, Lockwood Manufacturing Company of East Boston was asked to prepare a plan of a 140-foot long boat, wooden hull and propeller driven.

Six months later these plans were in the hands of the commissioners, and tender calls were placed in the following newspapers: Halifax Herald, Halifax Chronicle, Boston Advertiser, New York Herald, Toronto Mail and a Glasgow paper. It was decided that the hull could be of steel. Plans and specifications were to be sent to a responsible Glasgow firm which would act as agent for the commission, and tenders would be opened two months from the date of the first advertisement. Having made these arrangements, the ferry commissioners waited for the results of their inquiries. Another milestone in the history of the ferries was about to about to take place.

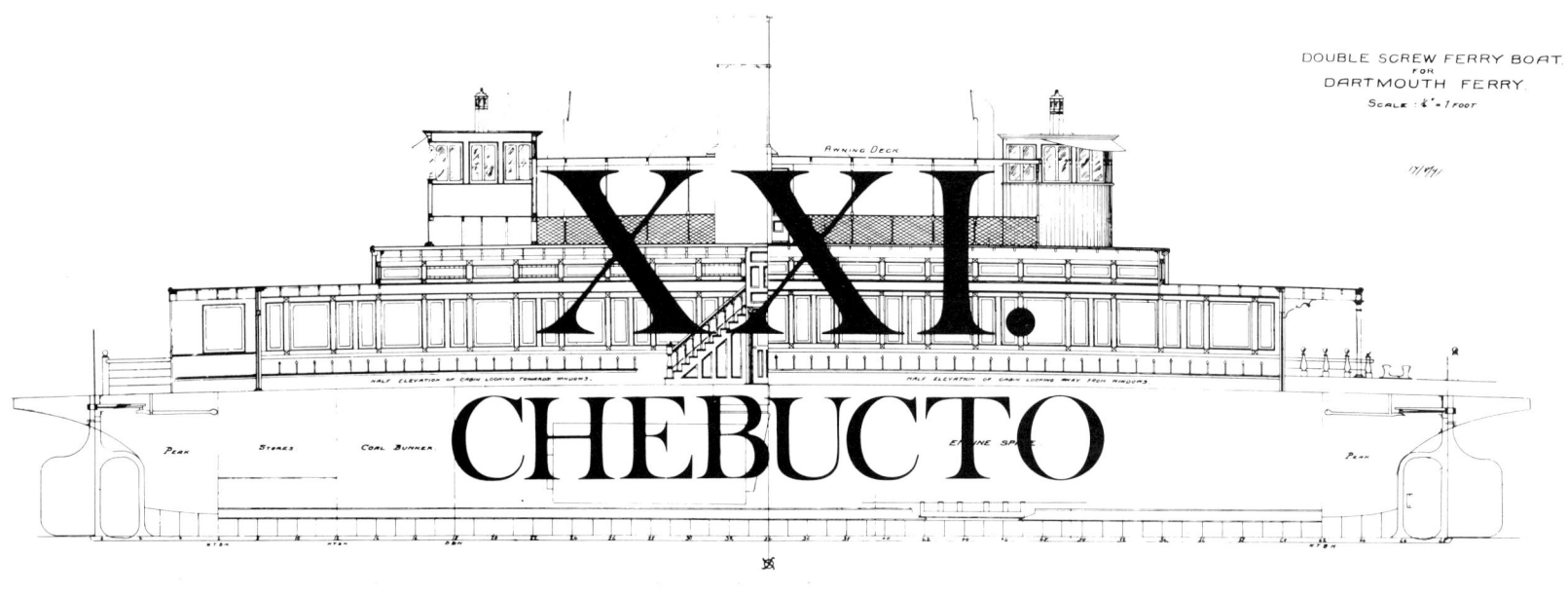

DOUBLE SCREW FERRY BOAT
FOR
DARTMOUTH FERRY.
SCALE : ¼" = 1 FOOT

XXI.
CHEBUCTO

TENDERS FOR A STEAM FERRY BOAT

Sealed tenders will be received at the office of the Secretary of the Dartmouth Ferry Commission at Dartmouth Nova Scotia until 4 o'clock P.M. on the 15th day of August A.D. 1896 for the construction and delivery at the dock of the said Dartmouth Ferry Commission at Dartmouth, duty paid if any, of a Ferry Steamer, to be built, completed and fitted in all respects in accordance with the conditions, plans and specifications now on file at the office of the said Dartmouth Ferry Commission and copies of which are also on file at the office of James Jacks of Glasgow G.B. and the Lockwood Manufacturing Company, East Boston U.S. a contract to be executed in accordance with the draft annexed to the said specifications.

Tenderers are to have the option of tendering for the construction of a steel ship in which case they will be required in the event of the tender being considered to furnish without charge the additional specification to the satisfaction of the Commission by the change from wood to steel.

The Commission do not bind themselves to accept the lowest or any tender.

In September 1896, the tender of John Shearer and Son, of Glasgow, was accepted. This firm offered to deliver a steel-hulled ferry to Dartmouth for 11,950 pounds.

A public meeting was called on October 15, at the Reform Club Hall "for the purpose of authorizing the Mayor to issue debentures for the sum of $30,000, the proceeds of which debentures to be used for the purchase of a new ferry boat." A hot and heavy meeting ensued. Two citizens, H. C. Walker and E. Williams, felt that the boat should be built in Dartmouth or at least in Nova Scotia, and of wood, not steel. J. Walter Allison and Benjamin Russell spoke of the

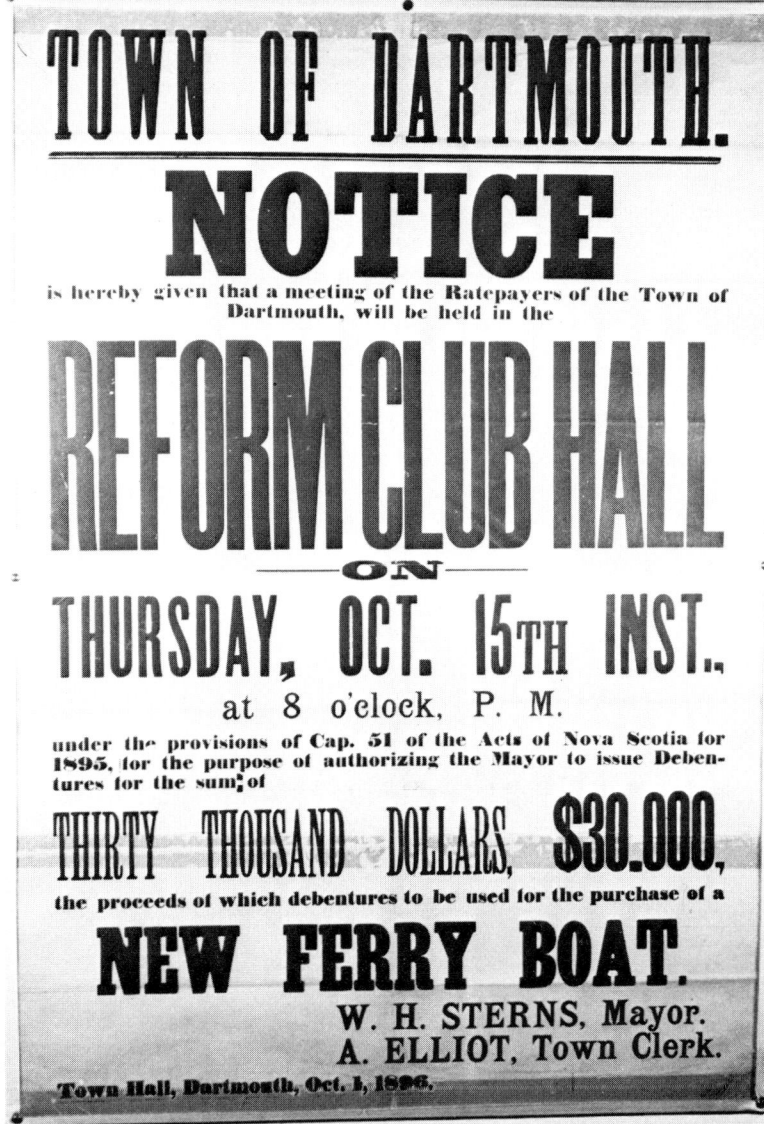

TOWN OF DARTMOUTH.

NOTICE

is hereby given that a meeting of the Ratepayers of the Town of Dartmouth, will be held in the

REFORM CLUB HALL

—ON—

THURSDAY, OCT. 15TH INST.,

at 8 o'clock, P. M.

under the provisions of Cap. 51 of the Acts of Nova Scotia for 1895, for the purpose of authorizing the Mayor to issue Debentures for the sum; of

THIRTY THOUSAND DOLLARS, $30,000,

the proceeds of which debentures to be used for the purchase of a

NEW FERRY BOAT.

W. H. STERNS, Mayor.
A. ELLIOT, Town Clerk.

Town Hall, Dartmouth, Oct. 1, 1896.

61. Notice of public meeting, 1896.

economy and durability of steel boats. By this time Russell was looked upon with great respect by the citizens, partly because of his leadership in the public takeover of the ferry system. The vote seemed to reflect their confidence in him, and as a result a special meeting of the ferry commission was called in November to complete the contract with John Shearer and Sons.

The plans prepared by Lockwood Manufacturing of East Boston were used by the Shearer firm. "The double-screw ferry steamer...both externally and internally has features of considerable novelty as far as shipbuilding practice on this side of the Atlantic is concerned, although in the main the vessel is representative of a type not uncommon on the American and Canadian seaboard." As work on the new ferry progressed, commissioners and commuters alike grew increasingly excited at the prospect of the arrival of the steel-hull, propeller driven boat, which they hoped would take place in the summer of 1897.

A good opportunity for a first hand report on the ferry's progress came in March of that year. The commission's Glasgow Agents, Messrs. Jacks and Company, were sent a letter written by secretary John W. Jago: "Mr. George Stairs is leaving today for England and will be at Glasgow at an early date, when he will be pleased to go over the plans and work with you and can explain fully any of the points which are not perfectly clear as he is quite conversant with the whole matter." By this time the keel had been laid and the frames were being constructed.

On this side of the Atlantic, small double-ended ferries had been a common sight for many years, on harbour and river crossings. But the little boat under construction at John Shearer and Son's yard was apparently quite a conversation piece, because she was unusual there. "She presents an exterior so striking and unusual that in passing down the Clyde she was the subject of curious comment on the part of shipyard and shipping workers who are certainly no strangers to maritime novelities," wrote a commentator in a maritime publication after her trials.

While the new ferry was nearing completion, there was another great occasion for excitement and public

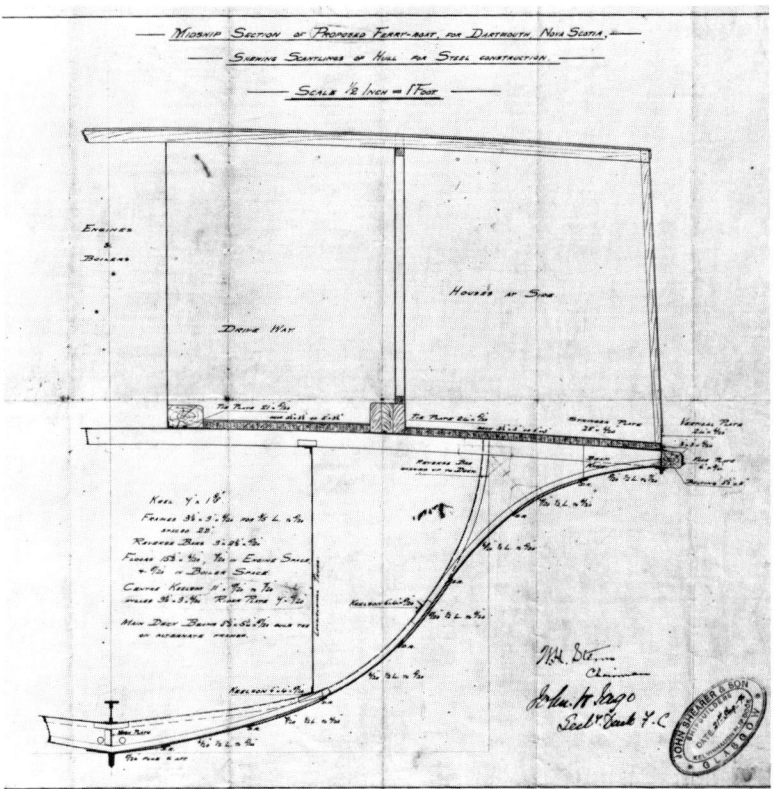

62. Chebucto, midships cross section, *1896.*

celebration, Queen Victoria's Diamond Jubilee. Not unnaturally, there were suggestions from many quarters that the little steamer under construction should be named **Victoria** to commemorate the event. By a narrow 3 - 2 margin the ferry commissioners felt that **Chebucto** would be a better name as there would be an abundance of **Victorias** throughout the Empire. So, **Chebucto** she became.

When the **Chebucto** was about ready for her trials, and excitement was beginning to mount on this side of the Atlantic, fate intervened in Scotland. A strike of engineers delayed her trials from July 15 until August 12. The two men who maintained that the boat should have been built in Dartmouth of wood, no doubt felt some measure of satis-

faction at this gloomy turn of events, for the hurricane season was approaching. The plans were to bring the little ship across the Atlantic under her own steam—no mean feat even with the most favourable of weather!

At last the strike ended, and on August 12, the trials took place

A fine descriptive account of the ship and related events was published in a Glasgow paper. When read in conjunction with certain of the illustrations of this chapter, a fairly complete picture of the **Chebucto** emerges.

The trial trip of the ferry steamer **Chebucto** took place yesterday, (August 12, 1897). The steamer has been built by Messrs. John Shearer & Son, Kelvinhaugh Slip Dock. The "Chebucto" is a vessel of 600 gross tonnage, and is of a novel type. Both ends are alike, and at each is a screw propeller and rudder. The underwater body and ends of the vessel are yacht-like in fineness. The vessel is built for special goods and passenger ferry traffic between Dartmouth and Halifax, Nova Scotia.

The main body is constructed of steel to Lloyd's highest class, with heavy deck beams, supported by longitudinal truss channel girders each side of the vessel, for cart and carriage traffic. These beams are carried out in one length to the extreme width of the vessel, forming a sponson deck. The wings are part of the integral structure, being supported by the outward sweep of the ship's frame and shell plating. On these wings are two spacious houses, each about one hundred feet long by ten feet six inches wide, by thirteen feet high, seated all round with handsome curve back settee chairs, divided by electro-plated elbows, affording seating accommodation for 222 passengers. The woodwork of the house is a combination of cherry-wood and yellow pine. There are two tiers of windows in the sides, the upper tier being filled in with cathedral glass. The ornament is very chaste, a fine effect being produced by the introduction of a light band of lincrusta of elegant floral festoon design. On the hurricane deck two pilot houses (one at each end) are placed, containing the steering gear for each end of the ship. Extending over the hurricane deck, and embracing the pilot-houses, a light awning dick is fitted, shading a very commodious arrangement of deck seats of elegant construction.

An installation of electric lighting has been fitted throughout. The cabins are heated by a thorough system of steam radiators. The engines, of which there are 13 [this must be a cylinder count] were constructed by Messrs. M'Kie & Baxter, Copeland Works, Govan. In this department the vessel is also novel. The fore and aft screws are driven by two pairs of compound engines, supplied by steam from two Admiralty type boilers with four Fox's furnaces. There is an installation, comprising five pumps, by the Blake & Knowles Steam Pump Works Company, including a duplex independent airpump, the first of its kind which has been fitted to a vessel in this country, a special form of feed pump, a donkey pump, a boiler circulating pump, and a sanitary pump. Hancock inspirators are fitted for feeding the boilers, and Hancock ejectors for clearing the bilges. The air pump discharges into a tank, from which the feed-pump draws through a filter, the speed of this pump being automatically controlled by a float. The exhaust steam for all the auxiliary engines is carried to the condenser, and the feed water passes through a heater on its way to the boilers. The centrifugal circulating pump was made by M'Kie & Baxter, is one of their "Challenge" patterns, and has a special balanced valve fitted, the invention of Mr. Baxter. The engines are reversed by direct-acting steam-gear upon an entirely new principle, the invention of Mr. Baxter and Mr. D. B. Donald, of Falmouth. The boilers supply steam to an electric light engine and to the heating appliances throughout the vessel.

The Company invited to the trip left the Central Station yesterday morning at ten o'clock, journeying to Gourock, where they joined the steamer. Among those present were Councillor Shearer, Captain D. Macpherson, and Messrs. M'Kie, Baxter, Wilson, Cochrane (Board of Trade), and Austin (of Lloyds). The trip was favoured with fine weather. The sun shone genially, and there was only the gentlest swell on the water. The steamer did the measured mile, and registered ten knots an hour—which for a vessel of her class is a thoroughly worthy performance. Afterwards a pleasant run was made up Loch Long. Luncheon was served on the homeward run, Councillor Shearer presiding. The health of the Queen was cordially pledged.

In proposing "success to the **Chebucto**," the chairman remarked on the novel character of the vessel, the contract for which was placed on this side of the Atlantic, after competition with the United States and Canada. (Applause) He recognized the assistance that Messrs. M'Kie & Baxter, the engineers, had rendered. The vessel was constructed for the purpose of carrying goods and passengers from Dartmouth to Halifax, in Nova Scotia. He felt sure that every item in their specification would be carried out to the letter. (Applause) The toast was enthusiastically pledged.

Mr. Wilson (representing Messrs. William Jacks & Co., the Glasgow agents for the Nova Scotia company), briefly responded, and remarked that there had not been the slightest hitch between the builders and the company. (Applause) He proposed the health of the builders, which was cordially drunk, and the chairman replied. The health of the engineers was also heartily pledged, Mr. Baxter replying for the firm. Other toasts followed. The company returned to Glasgow in the evening.

Two days after the conclusion of trials and festivities, Shearer sent a cable to ferry commission secretary Jago. "Expect boat to leave Saturday" (August 14, 1897). However, shortly after her departure, heavy seas damaged **Chebucto's** rudder, and she had to return to Glasgow for repairs. She departed again and after several days steaming was accosted by fierce gales, and with a strained and leaking hull, put into St. Michael's, Azores, in late September.

The ferry commission was much upset on receiving another cable, this one from their Glasgow Agent, Messrs. Jacks and Co., on October 29, 1897. "Fear delivery before next May impossible." Imagine the rage and feelings of frustration that must have been present at the meeting

63. Chebucto, *engine room telegraph.*   64. Chebucto, *builders' trials, River Clyde, Scotland, 1897.*

called to deal with this further disappointment. Jago was instructed to cable the Agent: "Give formal notice to hold them responsible for any delay or detention according to agreement. Boat must be towed. We are advised voyage via Florida is practicable."

Despite these instructions, it was not until the following spring that the **Chebucto** made her next departure, from the Azores to Nova Scotia.

Meanwhile the ferry commission was heavily criticized for the manner in which it dealt with the crowds of passengers wishing to cross to Dartmouth to celebrate the town's Natal Day. The Halifax waiting room was packed with people for a good part of the day, largely due it seems, to the fact that the commission had skimped on their purchases of life jackets. A consequence of this measure was that the boats were not permitted to carry as many passengers as could be physically accommodated. In spite of this, the commission's

receipts on that day came to $600. There had been a donation to the regatta committee of $100, but this did little to temper the criticism of what was seen to be poor service.

The following winter was unusually severe, and the harbour surface was heavily frozen over. The old paddlewheel boats made strenuous efforts to free themselves each morning, and to keep a path open across the harbour. Frequently, these efforts resulted in the breaking of their wooden paddles. The tug **Whitney** was again brought on the scene to assist, but eventually the ferries had to stop running for some days until tides, wind and milder weather combined to break up the ice.

Spring came late, and at the June 13 meeting the commissioners were made aware of the cable sent by Jacks & Co., advising that the **Chebucto** had left the Azores. Just 20 days later she arrived in Halifax Harbour, dirty with salt and coal dust, somewhat battered, but triumphant. Steam-

124

65.   Chebucto, *cabin interior, ca. 1900 (glass negative).*

ers which had passed the tiny **Chebucto** in mid Atlantic had shown great interest in her, and one steamer's crew had cheered her as they passed.

Shearer had come across ahead of the new ferry and assisted with her drydock survey on arrival. The commissioners appointed the following inspectors on their behalf: W. C. Moir, machinery; Superintendent Watt,

woodwork and fittings; and Chief Engineer Murray, electrical plant and boilers.

After some minor adjustments, she was officially taken over on July 21, 1898. The following day, members of council, former members of the ferry commission, representatives of the press, inspectors, ferry captains and engineers were on board for "trials," with Captain Williams

66. Chebucto, *entering Halifax dock, ca. 1930.*

in command. (Again, it is incomprehensible that passengers would be permitted on board for trials.)

She went south to George's Island and while returning "the fuel ran out and she put into the dock on this side (Dartmouth) to coal. In coming in to the dock it was found too narrow, not permitting the **Chebucto** to get within four feet of the bridge. After coaling she was further tested but the

reversing gear still acted badly. "The Mayor **refused to take** the boat until things were satisfactory."

Commissioner Dr. Cunningham must have become closely involved with these problems because he was congratulated by the editor of the "Atlantic Weekly" for hastening the needed adjustments so the **Chebucto** could be placed "on the ferry." He, in turn, congratulated the employees for their handling of the Natal Day crowds that year—18,000 people in one day. (Probably 9,000 round trips, still a substantial number.) Evidently the ferry commission had been anxious to avoid a repetition occurring of its bad image after the 1897 Natal Day. Not only were the crowds well accommodated, but $300 was donated to the Regatta Committee. A replica of the **Ogle** was entered in the parade—"the very spit of the old boat."

The **Chebucto**, now insured for $10,000, made her first excursion trip on August 16, hired by the Eastern Star Lodge. The rates for excursions that year had been set as follows:

All day - 9:00 a.m. - 10:00 p.m.	$100.
Afternoon and evening - 1:00 p.m. - 11:00 p.m.	75
Evenings - 7:00 p.m. - 12:00 midnight	50

The dock, which had been built to accommodate the **Chebucto**, had to be further altered. There was another problem involving engine room ventilation—an additional hatch was cut to provide "through" ventilation.

One day **Chebucto** was reported to have made the crossing in five minutes, assisted no doubt by quality coal, two firemen and a strong tail wind.

As with all technological advances, **Chebucto's** new equipment had initial bugs. The reversing engine, according to Chief Engineer Murray, did not always perform satisfactorily at the trials. He was contradicted by Engineer MacPherson who crossed the Atlantic in her.

A newspaper report in September confirmed Murray's comment. "The **Chebucto**... refused to reverse at the Halifax dock, the 'shock lifted gate posts and sent the old station house on a tramp up the street, and even the fish market started'."

Further trouble developed in September when the iron ring around the propeller was broken. The whole crew was charged with carelessness in docking, but the following month a diver was hired to clear the docks of obstructions.

When the first winter ice surrounded the **Chebucto** in her dock, one of her prime virtues became apparent. Instead of people having to chop the ice out from paddlewheels, her propellers not only ground it up, but when reversing on entering her dock, she thrust the broken ice out into the harbour, in a manner that the paddlewheelers could not achieve.

Chebucto and the crews who served on her soon adjusted to each other. The ship began service in 1899 with a clean slate. She was then destined to give solid service for more than half a century, a worthy example of Clyde shipbuilding in its golden age.

XXII.
The Turn of the Century

As the ferry service expanded, so did Dartmouth. Or was it the other way around? The population grew as more industries settled in the town. The ropeworks, Starr Manufacturing Company, a rolling mill, several foundries and the ferry commission itself employed many people. The growth of Dartmouth and of the ferry commission were closely linked.

Haligonians were acutely aware of Dartmouth and its ferries on at least one day of the year, Dartmouth Natal Day. Crowds jammed the boats to attend the annual races, parade, regatta and other festivities, and the revenue of the ferry commission was always unusually high (unless it rained). It became a routine gesture to donate $300 to the regatta committee. Throughout its history, the ferry commission made various attempts to attract the people of Halifax to the other side of the harbour, thus increasing its revenue.

Posters showing "points of interest" were painted and

67. Ferry passes, 1905-1906.

hung in the ferry cabins in the summer of 1899. As a further attraction for people to locate in Dartmouth, and to make tourists further aware of its charms, architect H. E. Gates suggested to the commission that a number of framed photographs be placed in the waiting rooms and on the boats themselves.

The waiting rooms were not particularly attractive, and it was in this connection that the same Gates along with Superintendent Watt travelled to New York in the fall of 1901 to observe station houses and ferry operations in that city (reminiscent of the Lyle and Leppert 1829 trip to New York in the earliest steam days). Gates and Watt reported on their observations the following February, but it was not until four years later that a plan of the Dartmouth station house, drawn up by Gates, with specifications written by Watt, was approved. Thomas Merson was awarded a contract to construct the new waiting room, (still in operation in 1979) in April of 1906. His tendered price was $4,066. The new building was opened that summer, and was complete with a newsstand, rented for a year by A. K. Herman for $75. The following year this concession was taken over by Marshall-Layton for only $25, theirs being the only tender.

When 1907 dawned it became evident that a new Halifax station house would be built as well. Once more, however, there was difficulty in obtaining a clear title to the Halifax property. While negotiations went on endlessly, the public complained loudly and frequently about the dirty, odoriferous and inadequate facilities on the Halifax side. The docks grew more and more dilapidated, and were subjected to further damages as the ferries continually crashed into them. Finally, in May of 1911, the city wharf collapsed completely. An emergency meeting was called. While the docks and landing were patched up there was still no progress in the negotiations between the Halifax Board of Works and the Dartmouth Ferry Commission. A newspaper report accused the Board of Works of "trifling" with the ferry commission, and stated that "the business interests of Halifax demand fair treatment for the Dartmouth ferry service."

In desperation, Commissioner A. C. Johnston met

68. *Dartmouth ferry terminal, ca. 1910.*

privately with the Board of Works and "arranged a contract to break the deadlock." This was approved by the real estate committee of the ferry commission in February 1912, but the arguments and hassling continued. In April 1913, Mayor E. F. Williams went directly to Ottawa to settle the issue once and for all.

C. R. Thorne, a Dartmouth architect, had drawn up plans and specifications for the new Halifax terminal. The contract for its building was awarded to C. E. Smith, who tendered a price of $6,900. The Starr Manufacturing Company made the iron gates for $525, the plans of which had also been drawn by Thorne. At the same time extensive work was done on the docks. It appeared that all the problems with the Halifax Board of Works and the Stayner family had been resolved. The "new station house (was) about finished," and was opened on December 9, 1913.

The commission was continually being requested to hire out the boats for excursions, or even to donate them free of

69. *Coaling schooners docked behind old Dartmouth terminal, ca. 1885 (Sinclair glass negative).*

charge. As an example, about one hundred newspapermen met in Halifax in 1899, representing leading American and Canadian newspapers. The Board of Trade and the ferry commission treated them to an excursion trip during their visit.

That was the year the Boer War started in South Africa. Many Nova Scotians enlisted, and were transported from Halifax in the troop ships **Laurentian, Koomeranian,** and **Milwaukee,** early in 1900. The **Chebucto** accompanied the troop ships out the harbour loaded with enthusiastic well-wishers, each of them paying 25 cents for the patriotic privilege. The proceeds from this venture went to the wives and children of the men from Halifax County who had enlisted. Nearly $70 was realized. The troops returned in October of the same year and the **Chebucto** took passengers out to greet the transports. Later in the month there was a parade in Halifax to honour the veterans. The entire Dartmouth Fire Department and its equipment, along with Colonel Vidito's 63rd Rifles were taken across to Halifax free of charge to march in the parade.

Another historic occasion took place the following year, 1901, when the Duke and Duchess of Cornwall and York (later King George V and Queen Mary) paid a visit to Halifax. Their itinerary did not include Dartmouth, but the ferry **Dartmouth** was used to take sightseers down the harbour accompanying the **Ophir** in which the royal couple had embarked. Tickets were 25 cents for adults and 15 cents for children. The proceeds were $400.

At the death of Queen Victoria there was a period of intense mourning throughout the British Empire since she had reigned for 64 years and was greatly revered. The Coronation planned for Edward VII was a cause for rejoicing in 1902. As part of the festivities, plans called for the ferry boats to be illuminated with coloured electric lights. However, on the very eve of the Coronation, the King was suddenly taken ill and hospitalized. The Coronation proceedings took place on August 9, instead of June 26, but were subdued due to the King's close brush with death and his slow convalescence.

Since the ferry takeover by the Town of Dartmouth, high-school students of the town travelled by free passes to attend Halifax County Academy for grades 10 and 11, there being no high school in Dartmouth at the time. This privilege was extended to students of St. Patrick's High School in 1899. At the request of Professor Sexton of Nova Scotia Technical College, students there were also issued with free passes in 1907. Students of Halifax Ladies College were included in 1914.

A retired citizen of Dartmouth recalls that when a pass was lost, students devised a way of carefully splitting apart their cardboard pass so that a friend could use the back part while the owner kept the front half to flash at the captain as they quickly passed through the gates during the morning rush hour. Eventually this scheme was discovered, but not before many students had taken advantage of it.

The discriminatory fare applying to coloured people and Indians remained in force until 1906 when it was repealed. Until then, they could travel at the reduced rate of 2 cents provided they did not use the ladies' cabin or the upper deck. It is difficult today to imagine how the ferry administration could so restrict the Prestonian ladies, having just made the long trip to market by ox cart on cold winter days, compelling them to the use of the men's cabin, and presumably its facilities.

In December 1898, ambulances travelling to the Victoria General Hospital in Halifax were given permission to cross without charge and to have priority over other vehicles. At that time, ambulances were horse drawn. It was not until May of 1909 that a commutation rate for automobiles was mentioned. The rates were set in November 1910 as 25 cents for a single fare, or $3.67 a month plus 5 cents per trip.

In the summer of 1904, for the first time, three boats were placed on the service on Saturdays to serve market gardeners and summer travellers. This was another indication of the growth of Dartmouth, and was presumably a response to a corresponding demand for improved ferry service.

A robbery attempt in the Halifax ticket office on October 10, 1898, was foiled by a Miss Huxtable, ticket seller. She was rewarded by the commission with a gift of $15. At the same time, Mr. Chaster wrote a letter to the commission stating that he had foiled the robber and felt that this should be acknowledged in some way. He was presented with $5. a month later, after an investigation.

There were many claims presented to the ferry commission. In November 1899, a ticket girl was reimbursed $2 for a counterfeit bill she had accepted. A $2 refund was given to a Robert Stanford whose horse had died after he had used his monthly horse and carriage pass only twice. A lady who lost her glasses overboard when the boat

70. *Ferry landing at Dartmouth, 1905.*

bumped into the dock was reimbursed, as were four passengers who were drenched when a hose ruptured. An elderly Dartmouth woman well remembers this occasion since it happened to her on a Sunday, when she was dressed in her best, and on her way to a Halifax church where she was a paid soloist. Her lavender muslin dress was suddenly soaked by the shower of icy water and the soft fabric clung to her like limp paper. She returned home, scrambled into her second best, and arrived at Fort Massey Church quite late, to the intense disapproval of the organist and the choir master.

Mate Ronald MacDonald suffered a more serious accident when his foot was crushed between ferry and bridge. He was off duty for a long period and eventually returned in the dual position of ticket collector and freight agent, and with a prosthetic foot.

Chief Engineer D. J. Murray kept an interesting log book, in which he noted ferry schedules, repairs, daily work and crews on the various boats. Noteworthy and irrelevant (to the ferry) events of the time also found their way into the log books—such as the arrival of a travelling circus, or a famous turbine-driven ship [**S. S. Victorian**] entering the port.

Occasionally, personal notes crept in—the Murray's rent had been raised, the insurance had been paid, they had moved to another house. A portion of his log book reads:

Feb. 2, 1904: Extremely low tide.
Feb. 16, 1904: Ice extends from Woodside Sugar Refinery in a South West direction almost to Western shore.
Feb. 19, 1904: Ice ½" thick all the way across the harbour.
Feb. 28, 1904: Harbour frozen entirely from shore to shore. People crossing from Dartmouth shore to Halifax dockyard.
Mar. 2, 1904: Diver Samuel Smith recovered three of the **Chebucto's** propeller blades and a length of winch chain from the Halifax dock.
Mar. 7, 1904: Storm signals were displayed from the Citadel indicating South East wind and rain.
Oct. 1, 1904: The Time Ball on the Citadel operated today for the first time at 1 p.m.
Feb. 19, 1905: Ferry steamer ordered to run all night (presumably to keep harbour open).
Mar. 10, 1905: An accident to the water wheel at Starr Works, Dartmouth, left the Town without electric lights.
Nov. 6, 1905: The first turnstile was put in operation at the Ferry Gates in Dartmouth.

Engineer Murray's log gives a clear picture of the coaling operations of the era. A continuous procession of schooners with romantic names, such as **Foaming Billows, Golden Dawn, Argosy** and **John Halifax** made their way to the Dartmouth ferry docks. Tied up, they unloaded their cargo of various Nova Scotia coals—Inverness Pea, Run of Mine Port Hood, Sydney Reserve Run of Mine, Gowrie Slack. The prices varied, usually from $3.10 to $4.10 a ton. Once, Murray refused to accept a load because it was "too slack" so the price was dropped to $1.75, and the schooner unloaded.

The usual loads carried were from 95 to 150 tons, in the schooners' holds, and it would take one to two days to unload. Then either one of Warner's teams, or a hand cart operated by ferry employees, would haul it on board and into the ferries' bunkers. Murray's entry for Jan. 31, 1905, notes: "Coal put aboard Ferry Steamers this night by Warner's Team - 19 loads at 2100 lbs. per load."

Once, after a more severe than usual February cycle of thawing and freezing, Murray made this entry: "February 14, 1905: Screened Port Hood coal put on board **Dartmouth** and **Chebucto** at Halifax ferry dock as they came across, by Halifax Coal Company. Inverness Pea coal at Dartmouth ferry wharves frozen so hard that men cannot break it out for putting aboard ferry steamers. Run of mine Port Hood coal supplied, 28,050 lb."

Logbook entries call to mind a great range of related activities of that era—bustling shipyards building schooners, diverse and active coal mines, loading and unloading operations at each end of the schooners' runs, Bluenose seamen working these little vessels through their scores of trips the year round, the work of coaling the ferry steamers and, lastly, the hauling of ashes and clinker from the stokeholds and the disposal of same. With respect to the last, these were always available for street repairs, landfill, icy streets and sidewalks, and even for muddy private driveways during the spring thaw.

The business of coaling and ash removal were normal operational activities. Occasionally the commission was faced with highly abnormal problems. In March 1904, the firemen went on strike. Murray wrote in his log on March 16 that the firemen had given notice to Superintendent Watt that they would not be reporting for work the next day, which happened to be St. Patrick's day. Murray's entry was hardly in keeping with certain of the traditions of the day, since it was written in brilliant red. To keep the service operating, one fireman was recruited from W. & A. Moir's for daytime duty, and one of the painters helped at night. However only one ferry, **Chebucto**, could be kept on the route on the 17th. The following day two boats ran in the morning, but the **Halifax** was laid off at 1:15 p.m. That afternoon the commission met, and shortly afterwards offered the firemen $9.50 per week. The offer was accepted and all was back to normal at 1:00 p.m. on March 19.

In April the following year, the commission was

71. *Ferry landing at Halifax, 1905.*

temporarily faced with the problem of having only one boat on the service, but this time for a different reason. At the time **Dartmouth** was undergoing her annual inspection, leaving **Halifax** and **Chebucto** on the ferry. Late one night Engineer Creighton reported a heavy knock in the **Chebucto's** engine, and in spite of Engineer Murray (with help) working through the night, the following day the knock increased to the point where she had to be taken off the service. The **Halifax** worked valiantly alone all the rest of that day, but she had help the next day. Murray's log notes: ''Tow boat **Togo** leaves Dartmouth as a ferry passenger

vessel 6:15 a.m., landing and rceiving passengers at bow of steamer **Chebucto**, lying in Middle Ferry Dock.'' The crank shaft of the **Chebucto** was taken to W. & A. Moir for repairs. It was a week before the **Chebucto** was running again, but meanwhile the **Dartmouth** had returned from her annual inspection.

A fourth crew was hired in 1906. At this time there were several changes in employees. Captain John Marks had died in 1901 after a long illness and the commission was involved in lengthy legal proceedings in regard to his sick pay. Captain Graham retired in 1909. New captains hired were

134

Bowser and Myrer. Superintendent Henry Watt retired in June of 1908 after 18 years service and was succeeded by Captain Charles A. Hunter. Henry Siteman, who had worked in the machine shop, retired at the end of 1910 after 38 years, and was given no superannuation pay.

A new and interesting experiment was tried in July 1899. Robert Moseley of the Dominion Paint Company, Dartmouth, had developed an anti-fouling, corrosion inhibiting paint for marine use. This was tried on the **Chebucto**, and when examined ten months later in drydock, she was found to be remarkably free of marine growth. As a result, two coats of Moseley's anti-fouling paint were applied. This was the beginning of a whole new concept in the war against marine growths on ships' hulls. Formerly, wooden hulled vessels were sheathed with copper to retard such growths, but painting was vastly cheaper, even in the early 1900s.

In the days of wooden ships, steam driven by coal-fired boilers, and some lit with kerosene lamps, fire hazards were very real. A letter written to the ferry commission by the Nova Scotia Fire Insurance Association and presented at the May 1896 meeting, claimed that two fires were started in Halifax waterfront buildings by sparks from ferry boats. The commissioners instructed the secretary to reply that the fires must have been caused by schooners with fires on the imaginative ground that the coal used by the commission's ferries did not produce sparks!

A new hazard became evident when it was discovered that the recently purchased life jackets were being set on fire by cigarette and cigar ends being carelessly disposed of between the seats of the **Chebucto**. Then a funnel fire occurred in the **Chebucto** in May 1904. Even more serious were three early morning fires on November 17, 1906. They took place within a few hours of each other—one on the **Chebucto** and two on the **Dartmouth**. An emergency meeting was called and as a result the Attorney General's Department was notified.

All was quiet on the fire front until December 9, 1909, when disaster struck the unlucky **Halifax** (ex **Annex 2**). She had just undergone major repairs, including having her bottom recoppered, and was due to have her boilers tested in the morning. They had been filled with water in preparation for the tests.

Early in the morning, at 4.45 a.m., Nixon, the commission's night watchman, looked out the window of the freight shed, saw a bright red reflection, and upon rushing out discovered that the **Halifax** was ablaze. He rang in an alarm, but the fire had made great headway, and it was too late to save the old lady. The fire lasted for several hours, and by the time it was out the engine room and stokehole held much water and there was a grave danger that she might sink at her berth. However, the Lady Dufferin fire engine set to work pumping out the water she had just pumped in, and this final indignity was averted.

Arson was suspected, since the boilers were cold and there was no fire in the below deck heating stove. There had been no workmen in the Halifax end of the men's cabin the previous day, where the fire had started. The last labourer had left the boat at 5.00 p.m., and the watchman, Nixon, had noticed nothing unusual when he made his rounds at 8.00 p.m. and 1.00 a.m.

After a thorough investigation and due consideration, the ferry commissioners decided that even if the old ferry were to be repaired and the machinery renewed, the resulting boat would still be an old ferry, not worth the cost of repairs. She was insured for $5,000, and her sale to Charles Brister for scrap brought $850. Altogether, the **Annex 2** had been an expensive investment, although her original purchase price of $25,000 had seemed a bargain in 1890.

The commissioners were facing a dilemma. Should the **Halifax** be replaced, or would the now aging paddlewheeler **Dartmouth**, and the 11-year old propeller driven **Chebucto** be able to carry the growing traffic? Should an additional boat be a secondhand one or a new vessel? If new, where should she be built? All these questions and the search for answers took up much of the commission's meetings following **Halifax's** unfortunate departure from the ferry fleet.

XXIII.

A Second HALIFAX

After the annual town election, the new ferry commissioners of February 1910 were still faced with the problems occasioned by the loss of the **Halifax** by fire. The new commissioners were Mayor Thomas Notting, chairman, E. M. Walker, John Ritchie, James Douglass, John Forsyth, James A. Calder and A. C. Johnston. There had been grumblings in the press with regard to the escalating costs of running the ferry service. However, one editor extolled the ferry operation because of the side benefits it brought to the town—employment, $2,000 in taxes and $600 for water. In 1909, another editor felt that a third ferry could be dispensed with.

About 60 years earlier, Lowe, the Agent for the Halifax Steam Boat Company, had been faced with this same problem and similar opposition. At that time, all was well when for short periods the **Ogle** and **Boxer** had been operating smoothly, but if one of them broke down for any

72. Halifax *engine builder's nameplate.*

reason, or was laid up for annual inspection, then there was a general outcry from the commuting public for better service. Lowe successfully persuaded the company of the need for a third boat to keep the service running continuously and to allow one boat to be used for excursions and emergencies.

Breakdowns, accidents and inspections occurred with equal regularity to the **Dartmouth** and **Chebucto**, thus it was decided in March that a third boat was mandatory. Chief Engineer D. J. Murray was sent to New York to search for another secondhand boat. Meanwhile the commission directed the Town Council to petition the Legislature for permission to issue bonds not exceeding $75,000 for the purpose of procuring another boat. Murray returned from New York to report that he had found only one boat that would be at all suitable, but her owners were unwilling to sell. This left just one option—to call for tenders for a new boat. Fortunately, the Lockwood Company's plans, drawn up for the **Chebucto**, could be used again with a few modifications. The **Chebucto** herself had proved to be a basically satisfactory design.

This decision seemed straight forward enough, but five months later there still had been no satisfactory bids, so a new tender call went out. In this way a whole year slipped by since the disastrous fire. Finally, early in December 1910, the tender of McKie and Baxter of Scotland (the firm which had built the **Chebucto's** engines) was accepted. Murray was delegated to travel to Glasgow to act in the dual role of the commission's Agent, and inspector of construction.

Troubles developed almost immediately on Murray's arrival. McKie and Baxter refused to sign the agreement even after the commission had made requested concessions. The best solution seemed to be for Notting, the chairman, to go to Scotland and negotiate directly with McKie and Baxter or other tenderers, such as the Ailsa Shipbuilding Company of Troon. Notting was given power of attorney, and in his absence James R. Douglass was appointed acting chairman.

Notting's personal approach proved much more effective than trans-Atlantic correspondence. He returned to Dartmouth in time for the April meeting two months later, with a signed contract between the commission and the firm of Napier and Miller of Old Kilpatrick, Scotland. The new ferry would cost about $67,000. Mayor Notting was given a hearty vote of thanks by the commission for his personal interest.

A notice was placed in the papers requesting suggestions for a name, and **Halifax** was chosen. The vessel was launched on June 29, 1911, and christened by Mrs. Murray, wife of the chief engineer of the ferry commission. A British maritime journal gave the following account:

On June 29th, there was launched from the yard of Messrs. Napier and Miller, Ltd., Old Kilpatrick, the double screw ferry steamer **Halifax**, built to the order of the Dartmouth Ferry Commissioners, Dartmouth, Nova Scotia. The dimensions of the vessel are: Length, 125 ft; breadth, 48 ft; depth, 13 ft. 1 in; with a gross tonnage of about 600 tons, built under the rules of Lloyd's Register for their highest class. The vessel has a complete main deck with promenade and awning decks above, three watertight bulkheads, and has been specially built for ferry service between Dartmouth and Halifax. Accommodation for passengers is arranged in large deck houses on each side of main deck, with a driveway in the center of ship for wagons and teams. The vessel has been fitted with electric light throughout. Machinery is being supplied by Messrs. Aitchison Blair Ltd., Clydebank, and consists of two sets of compound engines and two navy boilers."

In spite of labour troubles, the **Halifax** was finished in record time. She sailed for Nova Scotia with Captain Henry Wayman of Glasgow in command, leaving Clydebank on August 8, with a crew of 13 officers and men. Heavy seas did some damage to her shortly after she left the Clyde, and Captain Wayman decided to put into Loch Swilly in Northern Ireland for a check. The damage was minor, repairs were made, and on August 11 the little vessel set forth again. For ten days she made good progress, averaging 130 miles per

73. Halifax *about to leave Dartmouth dock, ca. 1911.*

day. There was a heavy swell and Captain Wayman had a nasty fall when the **Halifax**, bobbing like a cork, gave a sudden forward lurch. He was confined to his bed for several days and suffered a great deal of pain in his side for the remainder of the trip.

Then the weather deteriorated once more. The following account gives a vivid picture of the difficulties they encountered:

Strong gales were met on Saturday (August 19) accompanied by high irregular seas and thick fogs. The ship was plunging into a high head swell.

On Sunday, 20th, strong breezes caused the ship to roll. In order to ease the ship her speed had to be reduced. This was about 3:30 p.m. Eight feet of water was found in both compartments. The men kept working the pumps continuously. A heavy rain set in.

The speed of the ship had to be reduced on Monday because four feet of water was found in her forward hold. The ship's bow was sunk well down into the water. At 2:40 she was stopped to make repairs in the engine room.

Mountainous seas swept over her on Tuesday, August 22nd. The sea water poured into her compartments in tons. In order to trim the ship so she would ride the seas well the water tanks were filled. So heavy were the seas that swept over her that a portion of her wooden bow was smashed in. A large body of water was found in her hold. On Wednesday,

August 23rd, Captain Wayman was still suffering great pain from his fall. High seas still raged, and at times swept completely over the entire ship. The water poured into her different apartments in tons. The ship was hove to for a starboard tack. Towards the evening the seas became more moderate and the damage occasioned by the angry elements repaired.

Last Thursday, strong southwest gales prevailed, and high seas caused the ship to plunge heavily forward. The improvised wooden bow was considerably damaged.

On Friday, August 25th, the crew worked the pumps night and day. High seas prevailed. Even with the pumps kept going all the time it was impossible to keep the water in the holds lower than several feet. Similar weather prevailed on the following day.

Cape Race was passed on August 27th, at 10:50 p.m. The wire connecting the steering gear on the starboard side broke. The engines were stopped and repairs made.

On the 28th a dense bank of fog was passed through and very little headway was made. The Captain was still very ill.

Gales and thick fog were experienced on the 29th. Early in the afternoon the ship's head was swung in the direction of the southwest in order to ease the strain on her. Only 1½ knots an hour were made.

Heavy seas which swept over her on August 30th loosened the planks in her upper deck.

Cranberry Head was passed yesterday at 4:24 a.m. Light seas prevailed. The air pump engines broke down early in the evening and repairs had to be made. At 9:20 o'clock the engines were started and she proceeded.

The pilot from Halifax boarded her yesterday morning outside the harbour at half past twelve. At three a.m. she came to anchor, and at 8:50 she proceeded to her berth at the Dartmouth shore where she still lies.

In spite of the storms and her various problems, the vessel arrived a week earlier than expected. When she entered the harbour, Captain Hunter went out in his own launch to greet her.

Halifax had left Old Kilpatrick with 150 tons of coal in her bunkers and other unusual places for coal, and arrived with perhaps 40 or 50 tons remaining.

Captain Wayman, acting as Agent for the builders, remained in the port until **Halifax** was painted, cleaned up and made ready to be put on the ferry. He sailed for Glasgow, late in September on the **Pretoria**. Engineer Alex Donaldson stayed for six months as required by the contract, to instruct the commission's engineers. D. J. Murray, the chief engineer, had meanwhile returned from Scotland to take over his normal duties. He told reporters that the **Halifax** was much superior to the **Chebucto**, but had cost only $4,000 more. Asked in what respects she was superior, he said that the main shaft was 1½'' larger in diameter; the main engines had open columns rather than box columns; the cabins were constructed of pitch pine rather than spruce; and the wiring was steel clad, like that used in ocean liners.

The minutes recorded, on November 13, that the **Halifax** had been officially taken over. Like her stepsister ship the **Chebucto**, she was destined to give long and faithful service on her cross-harbour route, and did not retire until the first harbour suspension bridge rendered her obsolete, in 1955.

Shortly after the **Halifax** was put in service, Chief Engineer Murray suffered a period of ill health. After a leave of absence failed to restore his health, he resigned to accept a less arduous position as assistant inspector of boilers and engines for Nova Scotia. A Dartmouthian, Joshua Short, replaced him in September 1913. Short took on the responsibility for the operation of three reliable steam ferries, which during their lifetimes were to accumulate passenger/mile totals equalling that of many ocean liners. The steady rhythm of their engines was as much taken for granted by the hundreds of daily commuters as the beat of their own hearts. In a wider sphere, and across the Atlantic, the pulse of Europe was quickening with the threat of war. Halifax and Dartmouth would see great changes, and the ferries would soon have to contend with new and different problems, as traffic on and across the harbour increased.

XXIV.
Labour Problems and World War I

The acquisition of the second **Halifax** led to what ought to have been a golden period in the history of the ferries. The **Dartmouth, Chebucto** and **Halifax** were destined to carry all the traffic until 1935. For 24 years the fleet was stable—no additions or deletions. There were, however, disruptions through this period. Crew unrest on a scale not before seen and heightened harbour activities due to World War I were dealt with in their turn by the Dartmouth Ferry Commission.

In 1907, four aggrieved engineers requested that their $65 a month wage be raised to $70. Earlier that year, a fourth crew had been added, giving them better hours. Along with the improved hours went the suggestion that the pay scale would be raised shortly. Fourteen years previously, in that long-gone inflation-free era, engineers had been paid $67. Now the commissioners apparently reneged on the "suggestion." What was to be the last straw was the request that the engineers work overtime in the machine shop without extra pay.

On Wednesday, June 24, 1908, Engineers McLeod and Short refused to work in the machine shop. Superintendent Watt, whose resignation was to be effective at the end of that same month, when confronted with this insubordination, fired them on the spot, without consulting the commissioners. While Engineer Creighton kept one boat operating, the fourth engineer, James Ross addressed the commissioners at an emergency meeting held that evening. By word of mouth, many commuters learned that they might not be able to get to work next day.

Ross was a diplomatic intermediary, and the commissioners concluded that the engineers had a great deal of right on their side. The fact that Superintendent Watt was out of favour with several of the commissioners at the time also helped to sway opinion on the side of the engineers.

The Ferry Landing, Dartmouth, N.S.

74.   Dartmouth ferry terminal, late 1910s.

Not only were the dismissed engineers rehired, as a result of Ross' appeal, but their pay was raised from $65 to $67 a month, and they were to get 25 cents an hour overtime for work in the machine shop.

Minutes of all ferry administrations show lack of firm policies in many areas—arrangements with the City of Halifax in regard to rent of the docks, sick pay, ticket collection policy, excursions or the lack of them, pensions and gratuities. Commissioners of 1911 decided that as of October 1 there would be no further sick pay. The employees had been approached and asked to establish a benefit and pension fund but had refused to do so. Probably in an attempt to force the issue the commission now set this hard and fast rule. In fairness, it was made clear to the employees that the commission was willing to pay towards such a fund, but could not continue to pay the whole amount. This caused further discontent among the employees. A letter from the Ship Masters' Association complaining that the commission had broken its agreement in this regard was answered with a rather high-handed reply that the commission "was not disposed to enter a discussion" with them.

From time to time there were commuters' complaints about captains and mates not allowing them on the ferry when passes had been forgotten and left at home. It was an inflexible rule that no one was to be allowed to board a ferry if he did not have a pass or a transient ticket.

In May of 1912, one of the ferry captains was persuaded by a passenger to break this rule, and he was immediately suspended by Captain Hunter, the new Superintendent. In sympathy, the other captains, and the mates as well, indignantly walked off their jobs. This "strike" did not turn out as favourably for the sympathizers as had the engineers' trouble four years previously. Superintendent Hunter himself managed to keep the **Chebucto** going on half-hourly service until 11:15 p.m. Meanwhile, the commissioners, meeting in another emergency session, positively refused to take the captains and mates back, and dismissed them all. However, over a period of years many of the protesters were rehired as positions became vacant, but by this time the commissions' views on sympathy walkouts would have been quite clear.

Thirty-four years later, in 1946, part of this event became public knowledge for the first time. Miss Minnie Boutilier, cashier, was honoured on the occasion of her retirement after 40 years service with successive ferry commissions. She told a newspaper reporter of the most amusing incident in her career. Captain Hunter did not run the **Chebucto** alone on that day. Since it was illegal to run without a mate, Captain Hunter tried in vain to find one in a hurry. Commuters were pressing him to get the ferry running, so in desperation he persuaded Minnie Boutilier to dress in a mate's uniform and accompany him. For years this was a well-kept secret, but on her 40th anniversary, Miss Boutilier felt free to mention the part she played in the episode.

With the increase in automobile traffic at this time came the problem of transportation of gasoline. A rule was set down that it could be carried as freight on the ferry only in steel drums. The arrival on the transportation scene of the motorcycle, required another category in the rate schedule. It was set at five cents, plus the driver's ticket. In 1929, a commutation rate of $2 a month plus seven cents a trip for the driver was laid down.

For years, militia personnel, both permanent and volunteer, had been travelling on the ferry under an arrangement between their transport officer and ferry administration. A fee which varied from $100 to $150 per year was paid to the ferry, and members of the militia could cross when in uniform without further charge. It was found that this privilege was being abused, so in 1908 it was withdrawn.

With the outbreak of war in the summer of 1914, new arrangements were made with a Major Dean of the Transport Office. The secretary, Prescott Johnston, advised Major Dean by letter, November 19, 1914 that for the sum of "$250 per annum, men, gun carriages, horses, etc." could show their special passes to the captains at the ferry gates and travel "free" on the boats. Once more, however, this arrangement turned sour, since on August

15, 1916, Johnston wrote again, as directed by the commission: "This board does not intend to renew the agreement entered into with them [the military authorities] for the carrying of troops, and that on and after the 1st day of October next, all officers, soldiers and military vehicles will be required to pay the regular rates when using the ferry."

The war brought problems with navigation, as well as with transporting the military. On foggy days ferry captains had a difficult task weaving through vessels moored in the lanes used by the ferryboats. Even more dangerous was the likelihood of running into the many ships making their way up to the dockyard or Bedford Basin. That there were so few collisions as did occur was something of a miracle. However, after two such encounters, the **Chebucto** with the **S. S. Morwenna** on January 30, 1915, and the **Halifax** with the **J. S. Nelson** soon after, chairman E. F. Williams of the ferry commission went to Ottawa to "bring the matter of the ferries' rights in regard to vessels anchoring in tracks taken by the ferry boats" to the attention of federal authorities.

Late that summer came the very kind of accident that had been feared, but even it was not as disastrous as it might have been. The paddlewheeler **Dartmouth**, making a late supper hour crossing from Halifax, with about 60 passengers on board, was feeling her way cautiously through a thick fog. Captain Allan, Mate Bowes and the deckhand were keeping a sharp lookout for moving ships and listening for fog horns and bells. Suddenly they saw a warship headed directly for the ferry.

Captain Allan immediately ordered the engines reversed and put the helm to port. It was too late to avoid a collision, but because of the captain's quick action only the anchor and guns (trained outboard?) of **H.M.S. Sydney** struck the **Dartmouth**, raking along the side of the men's cabin. "The superstructure of the Dartmouth end of the men's cabin was smashed to kindling wood, and the Halifax end badly strained and twisted." The paddle wheel was injured, but all passengers were safe. They had taken out the lifebelts,

and amusing stories were told of an elderly Mr. Brown who draped himself with several, determined that he was not going to drown. The warship's crew swung out their lifeboats, but the little paddlewheeler managed to get to her Dartmouth dock safely and unaided.

When repairs costing $3,000 were made advantage was taken of the opportunity to improve the **Dartmouth.** Windows were enlarged on the men's side, and a stairway built to the upper deck from the inside of the cabin, rather than from the carriageway as it had originally been constructed. Almost three months later, November 15, 1915, the **Dartmouth** was back on the service.

At this time, Charles E. Pearce was acting chief engineer. Joshua Short wrote his last entry in the chief engineer's log book on July 12, 1915. Pearce, of the third generation of his family to be closely associated with the ferries, worked on his shift each day, but was relieved by another engineer at 2 o'clock to take over the administrative duties of the engineering department. It was his custom to make notations in his log of local events, and items regarding ferry personnel. On Tuesday, February 15, 1916 he wrote inside a ruled black border: "Chief Engineer and Brother Joshua Short Passed away to Rest after Intense Suffering at 12 noon today. The Lord Rest His Soul."

From that date until October of 1945, Pearce added these notes to his logs, which add interesting colour to the harbour's history. One of the next items dealt with the fire which destroyed old Pier 2 (from which World War I troops embarked). At this time Superintendent Hunter made the **Chebucto** ready to help out, at the fire scene, if needed.

Less than a week later, another note was made to the effect that the **Halifax** had run down a row boat with two men in it. One man, Chesley Hustins was drowned. His family asked for financial assistance from the commission, but the request was turned down.

Daylight Saving Time was introduced for the first time in May 1916. According to one elderly citizen it was regarded with disapproval by many, inspiring such remarks as, "There are only so many hours of daylight, and you can't make more by changing the clocks." "It's just for lazy people." "If you want more daylight, get up earlier, but don't put the clocks ahead."

Pearce's log records that the ferry clocks were advanced one hour on the evening of April 30, 1916, and put back to standard time at 12 p.m. Sunday September 3—Labour Day weekend.

On August 28 of that year the commission agreed to rent a ferry boat to military authorities to bring wounded soldiers from ship to shore. This only happened once, and seems a strange arrangement, when they could have been moved directly from the ship to an ambulance at a pier. Perhaps the fire at Pier 2 had some connection with this request.

The numbers of automobiles in Dartmouth mushroomed in spite of the war, and Pearce's 1916 log book noted that on September 11, all Dartmouth automobiles went to Halifax for the parade in connection with "Twilbee Fair." This seemed a strange little note, implying as it did frivolities at the height of the war. Further research brought it into perspective and its relevance to the times.

A group of Dartmouth men met and decided to hold a fair which they named "Twilbee" to aid the British Seamen's Relief Fund, thus it was related to the war effort. The planning, effort and publicity which went into the fair was intensive, and aimed at the population of greater Halifax. One of the committee members conceived the brilliant idea of having an automobile parade through the main streets of Halifax to promote the fair of the following day.

An extra ferry was laid on and a grand total of 50 cars plus motorcycles, decorated with flags, bunting, flowers and autumn leaves crossed to Halifax. Thousands of people lined the streets to watch the procession which took a lengthy route: up George Street to Barrington, south to Inglis, north along South Park to Spring Garden Road, west to Oxford, along Quinpool to Windsor, down North to Gottingen, down Cogswell, Brunswick, North, Lockman, Barrington, Pleasant, Morris, Hollis, and back to the ferry at the foot of George.

During the event, ferry officials had a moment of panic when one of the ferry dock floating bridges suddenly sank without warning. Fortunately there was nothing on the bridge at the time. The "Lady Dufferin" steam engine pumper of the Dartmouth Fire Department was brought into action to pump out a leaking pontoon, and the situation returned to normal.

The parade was not only successful in itself, but had the desired result of bringing hundreds of Haligonians over to "Twilbee Fair." An extra boat was run that day as well, and at 2:30 Mayor Williams officially opened the fair. There were huge dining tents erected in the Dartmouth Park, near the rink, and a "fakirs' row" with booths—wheels of fortune, grab bags, "Hit the Kaiser," Wild Man and various games of chance—did a rushing business. There were several civilian and military bands playing and several hundred sailors had helped in decorating and illuminating the park. The lights were turned on the night before the event to further promote it and to tempt the Haligonians to come across the harbour the next day.

The hopes of the committee were realized. The fair grossed more than $3,000, of which about $1,000 went for expenses. The men who worked on the committee were James Burchill, W. C. Bishop, A. A. MacDonald, H. R. Silver, C. W. Waterfield, Paul Creighton and John Misener.

Twice during the war, the commission invested in Victory Loan Bonds, $5,000 in November 1917, and the same amount again in October 1918.

The ferry boats were witness to the most dramatic and terrible occasion of the war on this side of the Atlantic in December 1917. On the clear sunny day of December 6, two ships, the **Imo**, a Belgian Relief ship, and the **Mont Blanc**, loaded with TNT, approached each other near the Narrows, the entrance to Bedford Basin from Halifax Harbour and about a mile north of the ferry lanes. For reasons never satisfactorily explained the two ships collided and the **Mont Blanc** burst into flames. The crew, knowing that she was literally a huge floating bomb, took to the lifeboats and rowed for shore. Unaware of the danger, people gathered along both shores to watch the

75. Dartmouth *after collision, 1915.*

burning ship. Passengers on the little ferries had an excellent view, and were totally unprepared for the force and roar of the explosion that ripped the air, surrounding the area for miles around with death and destruction.

Dorothy MacLennan of Dartmouth, later Mrs. W. H. Chisholm, on her way to work at the Royal Bank in Halifax, was on the deck of the ferry, where she and Henry Rosenberg, principal of the Nova Scotia College of Art, watched the fire on the ships at the Narrows. While they were remarking on what a very bad fire it seemed to be, and wondering what the cause had been, the ships blew up.

The canopy over the deck of the **Halifax** and the surrounding harbour water were peppered with debris, which splashed and hissed around the ferry. Utter bewilderment and confusion reigned among the passengers. Some thought the explosion was a result of German bombardment, while others, like Henny Penny, were sure it was the end of the world, and that the sky was falling.

A soldier took charge, ordering people to lie flat on the deck behind the shelter of the doors to the companionway. Miss MacLennan, found to her surprise that she was jointly in command with the soldier, as they herded people to this small area of slightly protected deck. As she lay on the top layer of passengers she found herself thinking that it would have been much safer to have been on the bottom of the heap.

She remembers nothing of the tidal wave, of which others spoke, but after a short while of waiting for further explosions, the pile of humanity was roused to a standing position once more when passengers from the cabin below rushed up the companionway to the "safety" of the open deck area. Many of the cabin passengers had been very badly cut when the windows blew in.

Meanwhile the ferry's engines throbbed on, and the passengers disembarked at Halifax. When Miss MacLennan reached the Royal Bank, the staff was instructed to return to their homes, so she once more boarded the ferry. The return trip was almost more frightening, because by this time the north ends of both Halifax and Dartmouth were ablaze with raging fires. A growing awareness of the immensity of the disaster dawned, as the certain knowledge that there were people trapped in the infernoes made the scene a nightmare.

In the afternoon everyone was ordered out of their houses, since there was a risk that the naval ammunition storage area might explode from fires near it. Miss MacLennan went to the north end of Dartmouth to see if her friends, the Stanfords, who lived in the vicinity of the present Angus L. Macdonald bridge, were safe. To her relief they were, although their house had suffered a great deal of damage. The Stanfords, in turn, were worried about their relatives, the Chisholms, who lived at the north end of Brunswick Street in Halifax. Young Miss MacLennan volunteered to find out. She ran all the way to the ferry, crossed to Halifax, and ran to the Chisholm's house. As far as the occupants themselves were concerned, all was well, but no house escaped unscathed on that day. She ran back to the ferry, caught a breath on the trip across, and made a final run, about a mile uphill, to the Stanford's.

The Stanfords, meanwhile, had moved indoors, and taken shelter in the safest part of the house—the coalbin in the basement. Mr. Stanford had built a fire down there and they were enjoying a cup of tea. Thankfully, Miss MacLennan accepted the one offered to her, and recounted her visit with the Chisholm family on Brunswick Street.

Many first-person accounts of the explosion as experienced by ferry passengers are still available. Another follows.

Among the passengers that morning were two young ladies who elected to remain in the cabin. One was Theresa O'Regan, on her way to her secretarial job in Halifax. The other was Agatha (Hattie) Gibson, now Mrs. W. A. Johns of Musquodoboit Harbour.

When Miss O'Regan entered the ladies cabin she saw the passengers kneeling on the seats to have a better view of the two ships on fire at the Narrows. Just as she approached a window the explosion occurred and the cabin window blew in over her face.

Hattie Gibson was with her sister, Marguerite. They were thrown back against the radiators by the force of the blast, and momentarily knocked insensible. When Hattie came to, she heard an elderly lady from Preston exclaiming that the end of the world had come. Then she turned and saw Theresa O'Regan, her face covered in blood, and she cried, "Oh Theresa, your good looks are gone forever!"

Miss O'Regan has the impression that the ferry stopped completely for a moment and then started up again. Mrs. Johns said that she felt it sink down as if the harbour's waters had parted in the tidal wave, and then bob up again.

As a postscript to the ferry/Halifax explosion story, it can be stated that Miss O'Regan did not lose her good

looks. Sixty years later she bears a most unobtrusive scar across the bridge of her nose—a proud souvenir on an almost patrician face.

Mrs. Johns was not cut, but was badly bruised, the effects lasting for several days. Her home was on the Old Ferry Road near the home of Dr. Parker, one-time Steam Boat Company president. In a turn of events of which Dr. Parker would probably have approved, "Beechwood" was put to use as an emergency hospital to accommodate the many injured.

Over 2,000 people died in the explosion, but once again the ferry boats seemed to have been given a special dispensation. No one was killed in them, although crew members and passengers were injured by flying glass.

Pearce's log book of that day reads:

> Thursday, December 6th, 1917. Weather Fine and Bright.
> **S.S. Halifax**   [This entry referred to the
> **S.S. Dartmouth**   on the service.]
> Mr. W. Pearce Machinist on **Chebucto** until the Great Explosion, then went home to fasten up windows and doors.
> Frank Green—Extra help on **Chebucto** until 9 a.m. went home badly hurt by the explosion.
> Ferry Steamers kept running all night.
> Ferry Boats and Property badly damaged.
> City and Dartmouth in ruins. Everybody boarding up windows and doors.
> Ferry hands doing all possible to relieve strain.

The **Chebucto** was not in service that day but was in the lay-up dock. William Pearce, Charles Pearce's father, and Frank Green were working on her at the time.

On the following day the log reads:

> Friday, Dec. 7, 1917. Weather—Gale blowing with driving snow.
> **S.S. Halifax**
> **S.S. Dartmouth**

76. *Arch of firemen's ladders for special occasion, 1920s.*

Wm. Pearce Machinist connecting up **Chebucto** main
engines.
Frank Green Machinist not working today. Do not
think he will lose sight of his eyes.
Ferry shop badly twisted—roof opened at top.

The minutes of the ferry commission show that
Dartmouth was anything but back to normal, even four
days after the explosion. "Dec. 10, 1917—The regular
monthly meeting which should have taken place this date at
4 p.m. did not materialize due to the confusion existing on
account of the great explosion of Dec. 6th."

The Superintendent and engineers were instructed by
the January meeting to have the glass replaced on the
steamers, but it was some time before there was enough
window glass to go around. Two years later the Dartmouth
Ferry Commission received a grant from the Halifax Relief
Commission for $3,000 against their explosion damages.

A resolution, passed at the March 1918 meeting, follows:
"Resolution: That this commission desires to place on
record its deep appreciation of the action of Superintendent
Hunter, and the crews under his charge, who during the
6th day of December stuck to their posts and kept up
communications between Halifax and Dartmouth the whole
of that day without interruption. This in face of the fact
that they were ignorant of the fate of their families was an
act for which courage and devotion to duty was
unsurpassed by any other body of men on that day."

Less than a year after the explosion, World War I ended.
The ferry boats and their crews had played their parts.

XXV.
Post War Years

By the time conditions in Dartmouth and Halifax had returned to relative normality after the explosion, the "war-to-end-all-wars" was over. Housing was in short supply, and so were men to keep the ferries running, especially firemen and oilers. To attract men to these jobs, a bonus of $3 a week was offered. A terrible influenza epidemic took its toll of crews, and substitute crews were sought. In an attempt to control the epidemic, no more than ten people were permitted to gather in public places such as the ferry waiting rooms.

While the commission had argued about raising engineers' salaries from $65 to $67 in 1908, in 1918 they were given a large increase—from $100 to $125. Other employees' salaries and wages in 1918 were:

	Per month
Captains	$105
Mates	90

	Per week
Deckhands	16
Ticket sellers	9

	Per year
Superintendent Hunter	$1,700
Chief Engineer Pearce	$1,650
Secretary Prescott Johnston	1,600

There were a few bright spots when the war ended as people everywhere looked forward to a future with peace.

The Governor-General, the Duke of Devonshire, visited Dartmouth on December 10, 1918. He was taken "across the harbour on the ferry steamer **Halifax** in charge of Captain Martin Murphy, and 1st Officer James Bowes, the steamer gaily decorated with flags and streamers. On his arrival the Band of the first CGR played the National Anthem. The 1st Dartmouth Troop, Boy Scouts, and the Church Lads' Brigade of Christ Church formed a guard of

148

honour. The school children lining both sides of the street, each with a flag added much to the welcome extended by the town." The Duke talked to the boys' groups and congratulated their leaders, Captain P. F. Ring of the Church Lads' Brigade and Scoutmaster A. B. Elliot. There was a civic arch of welcome at the ferry gates on the Dartmouth side, and also a fireman's arch of ladders. Firemen were mounted on the latter and gave three cheers as the Governor-General approached. He was taken to visit the Nova Scotia Hospital, the oil refinery and U.S. Naval Air Station (now CFB Shearwater).

From time to time, mechanical trivia surfaces in the records. Too many cars parked on both sides caused traffic congestion on Ferry Hill. An automatic cashier was given a month's trial but was soon removed because "it did not suit." Consideration was briefly given to running a ferry from Halifax to the new oil refinery at Woodside, but was decided against. Chief Engineer Pearce was interested in converting the ferries' boilers from coal to oil, but the manager reported at the March 1919 meeting that it "would not be in the interests of the ferry to convert to oil at this time."

To celebrate the 46th anniversary of its incorporation, and the return of its soldiers, sailors and airmen, the town fathers assigned to A. C. Pettipas the task of preparing a special Natal Day souvenir booklet. It included many illustrations of prominent citizens and businessmen, as well as historical sketches of schools, churches, the Shubenacadie Canal, the ferry and an honour roll of men killed in the war.

The popular fishing schooner races were begun in 1920, and in 1923 were off Halifax Harbour. Excitement in the area was high as the **Bluenose**, under Captain Angus Walters prepared to race against the Gloucester, Mass. schooner **Columbia**, Captain Ben Pine. An excursion ferry boat took enthusiasts to watch the race which was won by the **Bluenose.**

A highly detailed account may be found in newspapers of the time, October 29, 1923. The designer of the **Bluenose** was William Roue of Dartmouth, who later designed the ill-fated Dartmouth ferry, **Governor Cornwallis.**

In 1926 more excursion trips were provided when the **Bluenose** raced against another Roue-designed schooner, the **Haligonian.** "The Dartmouth ferry steamer **Halifax** will run on an excursion each day of the schooner races except Saturday, and will leave the Dartmouth ferry dock at 12:30 p.m. and the Halifax ferry dock at 1 p.m. This will give excursionists an opportunity to see the returning schooners and witness the finish of the race." F. W. "Casey" Baldwin, an associate of Alexander Graham Bell in the Aerial Experimentation Association, was on the race committee.

With each town election the members of the ferry commission changed, as required by its constitution. Ferry employees were hired, fired, replaced and retired. During the 1920s and early '30s, chairmen of the commission were Mayors Dr. H. O. Simpson, Colonel Vidito, Walter Mosher, and C. A. MacLean. A. C. Johnston, who had served as commissioner since 1892 (and had been chairman for five of those years) died in 1933, after a record 41 years of service. This was the longest period that any one commissioner had served the town continuously.

Commission solicitors, who were also usually magistrates for the Town of Dartmouth, did not remain for lengthy service with the commission, since they generally received promotions in their careers to other government departments. When Benjamin Russell resigned in 1904 to become a judge of the Supreme Court of Nova Scotia, he was succeeded by W. R. Foster. The latter was solicitor for the ferry commission until 1920, when he was appointed Registrar of Probate. His successor was R. H. Murray, a Halifax lawyer who had moved to Dartmouth in 1912. When he resigned in 1933 to become Judge of Halifax County Court, he was succeeded by W. E. Moseley.

Because of age and ill health, secretary Prescott Johnston resigned in April 1921. He had succeeded John W. Jago as secretary in 1901. Johnston was voted a pension of $400 a year, but this was raised only two months later to $800.

For some time the ferry operations had been running at a deficit. The newly appointed secretary, C. Hedley

Williston, C.E. swept into the commission's offices like the proverbial new broom, determined to improve both the financial picture, and the ferry service itself. Superintendent Hunter was reclassified "Marine Superintendent," and Williston given the title "Manager," and a salary of $3,000. Williston was undoubtedly relieved of a great deal of "administrivia" due to the presence of his assistant, Miss Clara Walker, who was a meticulous stenographer and bookkeeper.

Manager Williston made some innovative changes. Perhaps for the first time, coal tests were made, which showed that Acadia Run of Mine coal was more economical than Dominion Coal Company's Reserve Coal. Ticket clerks were bonded and a vault was built in the Dartmouth terminal—a large concrete room, at a cost of $500. Employees were paid by cheque. Crews were granted two weeks vacation with pay. The manager of the new Marks Cross Arena (the old rink had been destroyed in the explosion) arranged special transportation coupons on the ferry for Halifax patrons. These were to be redeemed at five cents each when presented at the rink. It was a further attempt to lure Haligonians to Dartmouth for the mutual benefit of the ferry commission and the Marks Cross Arena.

New broom Williston did not remain long with his employers. Three years later he resigned, leaving the financial picture somewhat improved. Captain Hunter took over again, this time as manager, but retaining the role of superintendent. Miss Walker, Williston's erstwhile assistant, was appointed secretary-treasurer, and she held this position for ten years until her resignation in 1934 due to ill health.

Real estate on ferry commission property in Dartmouth was also subject to changes. Although the Reading Room never lost its popularity, it was not a paying proposition, and its original founders gradually departed, leaving it a burden to the commission. In January 1916, $217.80 was owed for rent and water. Nothing was done about this situation until over a year later, when on May 1, 1917, the commissioners voted to take possession of the Reading Room. A delegation from the Reading Room Board pleaded with the commissioners to keep it open, but the pleas fell on deaf ears. It had been in operation since 1889, 28 years, and was sorely missed by the community. Just before the explosion, it had been rented to the "Unionists" for three weeks for $20. As part of the rental agreement, they were to provide heat and light. It seems likely that the explosion put an end to the problems associated with the renting of this building since there was no further mention of it.

For years the commission had carried on a freight business, mainly on small items. A little shed just to the west of the new Dartmouth terminal building was the "transhipment" point. Two of the freight handlers were James DeVan and John Hiltz. At the height of the war, the operation was closed down because they could not find any responsible boys to operate the service. The announcement in the press following this decision stated that the freight business would be discontinued, because it was operating at a loss—$9.05 for the previous month. Despite a citizens' protest meeting, the commissioners held firm and did not reverse this decision.

This action may have contributed to the beginnings of what became a thriving trucking and transport business across the harbour. One such enterprise was owned and operated by a Moir family of Dartmouth. It probably produced for the ferry commission far more revenue in commutation fares, than its own freight business had ever done. As for the freight shed, it became a telephone booth for cabmen in June 1918, when C. Naugle rented it for this purpose.

Newsstands in the ferry terminal buildings were remunerative businesses for the lessees, and for many years remained in the same hands. Mr. Langston ran the Halifax operation, and Mr. Horobin the Dartmouth one. Many were the snacks, newspapers and periodicals purchased by commuters who had rushed to the ferry without breakfast, or who were returning home after a long day of work, or shopping in the large department stores on Barrington Street in Halifax.

Perhaps due to the lessening of traffic in the harbour

after the war, and the building of the Deep Water Terminals at the southern end of the Halifax waterfront, the frequency of accidents between ferries and other shipping decreased. There were the usual number of mishaps to wharves and floats, particularly in stormy weather. The heavy two-lane car ferries now in service were capable of doing considerable damage to the wharves when they rammed into them, occasionally assisted by hurricane force southeasterlies in the autumn, or the northerly gales of winter.

The first car to go overboard from a ferry was driven by J. A. Fader, in 1918. He was saved from a possible drowning by William Morgan, a foreman for R. W. Mosher, wharf builder.

The **Dartmouth** collided with **S. S. Galtymore** of the Furness Withy Company in January 1926, because the latter was moored in the ferry lanes. The commission sent another protest to Ottawa, seeking further legislative safeguards against the causes of such accidents.

Throughout changes in management and shoreside properties, these three ferries steamed steadily back and forth with few interruptions to the reliable service they gave to the harbour commuters.

Even so, repairs, alterations and general maintenance often required the temporary absence of one of the three. For some reason, the propeller blades of the **Chebucto** gave considerable trouble. From time to time a blade would break off and a diver was hired to recover it. The ferry engineers, who were apparently machinists as well, were often called upon to turn out new blades. Then an agreement was reached with the Douglass, Fullerton Company, to make some blades of tougher material.

The **Chebucto's** single companionway was replaced in 1924 by two, one from each of the two cabins to the upper deck. This was the same arrangement as in the **Halifax**. The modification was done by A. M. Stuart for $695.

A major alteration was done to the **Dartmouth** in 1926 by the Halifax Shipyards. Her main deck was raised at a cost of $2,750. Not much later, her paddlewheels were altered and rebuilt for $790, and a year or so later her "roof" was recovered with canvas. These repairs represented modest efforts to prolong the life of the old steamer, but her time was coming to an end.

Until 1928, the **Halifax** had been used as the picnic and excursion boat. In an effort to cut expenses (coal cost $1,000 more in 1927 than in 1926) it was decided to discontinue picnics and excursions in 1928. Insurance for such trips would have cost $450, and that alone was deemed reason enough to cancel the former arrangement.

That same year a new method of collecting tickets went into effect. Every captain on each shift was to have a separate box to be turned in when he went off duty. According to the secretary, Clara Walker, this meant 32 boxes in all. The rule went into effect on May 1, 1928.

The fares went up twice during these post war years, once on April 1, 1921, and again in December 1924.

In 1930, several improvements were made to ferry property. The Halifax docks were repaired by W. R. Morgan—the North Wharf at a cost of $113,450 and the south one for $5,460. Ferry Hill (Dartmouth) was paved at a cost of approximately $1,000, in spite of the objections of the owners of two ice companies, Mr. Otto and Mr. Chittick. They wrote that paving would make the hill too dangerous in the winter months.

James F. Lahey was awarded a contract to paint the interiors of the cabins of all three ferries for $699. This was in February of 1931.

In 1928, the engineers began another campaign for higher salaries. They presented a very stiff letter at a commission meeting, pointing out the poor conditions they were working under for very low wages, which perhaps had contributed to the deaths of five engineers in the last 12 years. This was pretty strong persuasion and at the very next meeting they were given a raise—bringing their salaries to $175 a month.

The Dartmouth Natal Day Committee was given a grant of $450 in 1929. At the following session of the House of Assembly a bylaw was passed: "The Dartmouth Ferry Commission may pay annually to the Natal Day Committee of the Town a sum not exceeding Five Hundred Dollars

77. *Dartmouth ferry terminal, 1931.*

($500) to be used solely for the purpose of assisting in the proper celebration of Natal Day."

The following year, 1931, $50 a year for the MicMac Club and $100 a year for Banook Canoe Club were voted by the commissioners to help pay for the clubs' expenses in hiring bands. Further generosity was evidenced in 1932 when an annual grant of $300 was given to the Victorian Order of Nurses.

Other bylaws were drafted by the solicitor about this time in regard to the carrying of gasoline on the ferries, on the advisability of all motorists turning their engines off while the ferry was under way, and to say that smoking would be permitted in the gentlemen's cabin only. By 1936, public attitudes had sufficiently changed to the point where commissioner Regan urged that a smoking compartment for ladies should be given consideration.

Captain Hunter's letter of resignation was received with regret, in April 1933. Although there was no pension scheme even by 1933, he was granted a yearly allowance of $1,000, to be paid in quarterly installments. His successor was appointed at the same meeting—former Chief Engineer Charles E. Pearce, whose salary was to begin at $2,400. By coincidence, these two men died within two weeks of each other—Captain Hunter at Hantsport, December 28, 1955, and C. E. Pearce in Dartmouth, January 4, 1956.

With their charitable donations, Captain Hunter's allowance, salary increases and expensive wharf repairs, the April 1933 announcement that net earnings were down by $17,492 from the previous year, probably came as no surprise.

A special committee reported that the cost of living was also down and employees should take ten per cent reductions in their salaries, a common occurrence in these Depression years. Employees still had no pension plan and 40 per cent of them were over 60 years of age.

Earlier, in 1920, it was reported that "a committee of Halifax and Dartmouth residents has been formed for a bridge." The ferry commissioners gave hearty endorsement to this project. L. H. Wheaton, a consulting engineer, reported to the Engineering Institute of Canada, Halifax Branch, that a low level bridge could be constructed at the Narrows for approximately $2.5 million or a suspension bridge from the Dockyard to Black Point in Dartmouth for $10 million. Wheaton recommended the Narrows location since, he claimed, the upkeep of the suspension bridge further south, in addition to its greater original cost, would be far beyond the means of the communities to support. Nothing came of this report.

In 1928, a new "Bridge Association" was formed, of enthusiastic citizens and politicians. N. G. Jackson, chairman of the Kennebec, Maine, Bridge Association gave a "splendid address" to a "monster meeting" on January 17, 1928. As a result "The Halifax-Dartmouth Bridge Company Limited" was incorporated.

Monsarrat and Pratley, a well known consulting engineering firm of Montreal, drew up plans for a bridge to be located precisely where the present Angus L. Macdonald bridge spans the harbour. Enthusiasm was keen, but financial difficulties intervened.

Vehicle traffic was increasing, the **Dartmouth** was becoming a heavy burden to maintain, and the still small Town of Dartmouth struggled to provide a ferry service for the town, the City of Halifax, and the County.

A meeting of representatives of the Dartmouth Ferry Commission, the Halifax City Council and the County Council was held in March 1927. H. O'C. Baker, representing the ferry commission, stated the problem and asked for help in solving it. It was resolved to meet with the Halifax County members of the House of Assembly and ask that an expert on transportation be appointed to deal with the situation.

Dartmouth citizens began to press for better ferry service. Dr. M. A. B. Smith, W. H. Covert (soon to be appointed Lieutenant-Governor of Nova Scotia) and Joseph Weeks, three influential citizens, made representation to the commission and pleaded for a new third boat to be larger than, and as a replacement for the old paddlewheeler, **Dartmouth**.

In spite of the poor financial state of the commission it became evident that something drastic would have to be done to improve the service. A new boat was discussed at the meeting of March 4, 1932. Superintendent C. E. Pearce reported that the **Dartmouth** was not suitable for service and that it was impossible to maintain a regular schedule with her. Her hull, he said, was saturated with water and dirt.

A. C. Pettipas, a commissioner appointed in 1929, wisely suggested that the style of a new ferry should be governed by whether or not a bridge would be constructed in the near future, and further that the location of such a bridge would be another point to consider. Two possible sites had been suggested, he pointed out, at North Street or at the Narrows.

As a result of this advice, a telegram was sent to Senator W. H. Dennis in Ottawa, seeking guidance with respect to the latest bridge plans. The Senator's telegraphed reply expressed doubt that the building of a bridge would be sanctioned that year. When this proved to be the case, and when 1933 also passed with no definite plans for bridge construction, the commission was made to realize that it had to take some action.

An aspect of the perspective of the ferries' role in the Greater Halifax scene was highlighted in a newspaper article in 1933. "Including the weight of vehicles, the Dartmouth Ferry handles more tonnage than crosses Harbour Commission piers with little horn blowing and less overhead."

It would be interesting to calculate the traffic carried by the ferries in terms of passenger/miles per year. The numbers would probably be similar to those achieved by a medium-sized ocean liner.

A more romantic viewpoint was expressed by H. M. Hatt who described a crossing—the upper deck promenaders, the beautiful sunsets and the courting couples. The "new business methods of 1921 (when C. H. Williston was manager) did instantly improve the financial position. The commission then owed a quarter of a million dollars for which loans and debentures had been issued." The article closed by pointing out the importance of the ferry as a Dartmouth business, and the employment opportunities it offered.

As on many occasions in the past, the old dilemma had reared its ugly head. A new boat was desperately needed in order to maintain a reasonable service, but the commission was losing money and the problems associated with the financing of new construction seemed enormous. Various naval architects and builders, hungry for work in those Depression years, wooed the commission with plans and offers to build the ideal boat, but it was not until 1934 that a report on the **Dartmouth** was sought from experts. Captain Neill Hall, Port Warden, and Thomas McConkey advised that borings from the hull of the old steamer showed her to be in a badly decayed condition. Thus, the die was cast. The commissioners at once passed a resolution to procure a new ferry boat.

XXVI.
War Clouds Again

In 1934, the ferry commission had a new chairman, Walter A. Topple. For any newly installed mayor the position was a difficult one—not only was he the chief magistrate of the Town of Dartmouth, but he was also, ex-officio, the active head of one of the town's largest business concerns, the ferry commission. Mayor Topple had several senior commissioners working with him, and depending on the personalities, this could be an asset or a liability. That particular year the other commissioners were Ivan Haley, A. C. Pettipas, C. A. MacLean, J. Whebby, Colonel I. W. Vidito, and M. S. Regan. Clara Walker was still the commission's secretary, and W. E. Moseley its solicitor.

Chairman Topple's first task was to deal with the need for a new boat. Early in the year the Montreal firm of naval architects, Lambert and German, were commissioned to prepare plans for a new ferry. This was done with dispatch, and in late June they issued tender calls which were picked up by four Canadian and 12 British shipbuilders. When these were opened and reviewed in July, the firm chosen to build the ferry was the Davie Shipbuilding and Repairing Company Ltd. of Lauzon, Quebec. The tendered price for the new boat was $122,650, almost twice the cost of the Scottish-built **Halifax** in 1911. The contract was signed on July 30, 1934, by ferry commissioners and Davie representatives.

It was decided to name the new vessel for the old ship she was replacing, the Yarmouth-built paddlewheeler **Dartmouth**. To prevent confusion, the old lady was renamed **Old Veteran.**

Mayor Topple and Superintendent Pearce travelled to Quebec for the launching and trials of the new **Dartmouth**. It can be said that her design, contract negotiations, construction, launching, trials, delivery and lifetime performance, were unparalleled in the over 200-year history of the ferry service. From gestation to retirement, this **Dartmouth** appeared to have been especially blessed.

Her launching took place on November 12, 1934, only three months after the signing of the contract. Mayor Topple himself christened her with the traditional champagne bottle as she glided down the ways. **Dartmouth** was 578 tons, 139 feet in length, 50 feet in beam, and with a 13 foot hold. She was registered to carry 550 passengers and 18 to 20 vehicles. Except for her wooden seats and linoleum tile decks she was entirely of steel construction.

Instead of having radiators down the centre of the length of the cabins (on which in the old boats, explosion victims had struck their heads) the radiators were along the sides of the cabins. Unlike the single upper decks of the older boats, the **Dartmouth's** upper decks were divided. She had two narrow "promenade" decks over each cabin, from which a couple of open companion ways led up to the larger centre deck over the vehicle lanes. It was a fine deck arrangement, providing many corners where little groups of passengers and couples could gather and feel more or less alone and separate from the main crowd, even for the 15-minute trip.

She was equipped with steam steering gear, and like her predecessor, the **Halifax**, she had Scottish-built Aitchison and Blair engines. The following partial description of her machinery will be of interest to technically oriented readers:

78. *Signing of contract for new* Dartmouth, *1934. Standing: (left to right) M. S. Regan, W. E. Moseley, C. E. Pearce. Seated: Mayor Topple, Clara Walker, secretary.*

> The propelling machinery, built by Aitchison and Blair, Clydebank, Scotland, consists of two sets of compound surface condensing engines, with cylinders 12 and 24 in. diameter, with a stroke of 18 in. and developing about 440 i.h.p. at 130 r.p.m. There is one condenser, and a reversing engine common to both main engines, which are coupled together on one shaft, driving a propeller at each end. Steam is supplied by two navy type boilers, 18 ft. by 7½ ft. diameter, with a working pressure of 120 lb. per sq. in. The pumps, which are independent, include one vertical single acting twin beam type air pump 7½ x 12 x 8 in., one main centrifugal circulating pump 5½ in., one feed pump 4 x 6 in., a general service pump 7½ x 5¼ x 10 in. duplex, a sanitary pump 3 x 2¾ x 3 in., a boiler circulating pump 3½ x 2¼ x 4 in. duplex. The dynamo is of 7½ kilowatt capacity. All the machinery was built under Lloyds survey, and to requirements of British Board of Trade and Canadian steamship inspection. The propellers are of cast steel sectional type. The electric installation includes main switchboard, distributing panels and fixtures . . . .

The contract for the building of the boat was signed July 30, the keel was laid Sept. 7, the main engines, the last of the machinery equipment, were received November 6, and as the boat was launched November 12, and the official trials were ran November 15, what was probably a record in Canadian shipbuilding was made.

The **Sir C. Ogle** was the only other ferry built with comparable efficiency and lack of mechanical or labour problems.

On the Saturday following the Monday, November 12 launching, **Dartmouth** left Quebec, pilotted by Captain J. B. Lesleuriers, and steamed for her home port. It was a pleasant and uneventful trip, with stops at Gaspe, Port Hastings and Mulgrave. Seventy tons of coal and 45 gallons of oil were used on the 800-mile trip. The chief engineer was Joseph Lepage, who was assisted by two other engineers, three oilers and three firemen, all employees of the builders. The **Dartmouth** logged 10½ knots on the leg from Gaspe to Mulgrave, and was known to be capable of doing 12 knots.

She arrived at Dartmouth at eight o'clock in the evening. Superintendent Pearce and Captain MacDonald had gone out to the mouth of the harbour in a motorboat to meet her. Among the first to board her when she reached her dock were Captain William Myrer, Commissioner Mike Regan, H. Young, and Police Chief John Lawlor. It was reported in a newspaper that everything was done in an orderly manner—there was no crowding or pushing as had occurred at the time of the **Annex 2** arrival.

Two days later the local trials took place, and she was described as "perfect" (an unusual adjective to appear in the traditionally conservative maritime scene). She was officially taken over by the commission on the same day. The public inspected her on December 5, when hundreds of people went on board at the dock. On December 7, there was an evening excursion for invited guests, and on December 17 she was placed on regular service, just in time for the heavy Christmas traffic.

Colonel Vidito, a commissioner since 1927 was very ill that autumn, and died early in December without seeing the new boat. A resolution of sympathy expressing the loss felt by the commissioners was sent to Mrs. Vidito. This was the second major change that year in the commission, since the secretary, Clara Walker had resigned due to illness in July. She was succeeded by Guy M. Mitchell.

To fill the vacancy left by Colonel Vidito's death, John Paterson of the Dartmouth Slips (Halifax Shipyards), was appointed by the Executive Council. Paterson's appointment brought a knowledgeable and practical voice to commission meetings, and even after he resigned due to the pressure of business in 1938, he continued to contribute time and expertise to the hard-pressed ferry officials.

A ghost from the past appeared at commission meetings in 1937—the Reading Room. It had been started up again, this time more along public library lines, and was located in the top floor of the Post Office. Undoubtedly the citizens responsible for its reincarnation were aware that the ferry commission was now in a better financial position, since it was able to rebate $10,000 of operating surplus to the Town treasury in 1936. Then in 1937, and again in '38 and '39, a delegate from the Reading Room came to ferry commission meetings to request assistance. For the first two years, $100 grants were made. When a lady delegate came to make the annual appeal, the grant was upped to $150.

While the new **Dartmouth** was beginning her career with the ferry commission, the **Old Veteran** was slowly fading away. The last reference to her in the engineer's log book was on December 19, 1934, when it was recorded that "John Moir, machinist, was removing packing from the main piston and auxiliary steam glands of the **Old Veteran.**"

A. C. Pettipas, who had previously served as commissioner, offered $400 for salvage from her, and she was subsequently stripped at Bishop's wharf, just south of the Dartmouth ferry dock. Superintendent Pearce wrote in his log book: "Nov. 20, 1935: **Old Veteran** being stripped off this day. Jan. 9. 1936: **Old Veteran** hung up on top of Bishop's wharf and listed badly as tide falls."

A newspaper report in early December said that "the work of dismantling the ferry steamer **Old Veteran** is now well advanced. The superstructure has been removed and much of the fittings in the engine room has been taken away. Since the work was started quite a demand has been made for doors, windows and other equipment. The 45- (actually 47) year old boat will soon be a thing of the past but history will always contain a record of the great service she rendered."

Various citizens today still have assorted souvenirs from

the vessel—a lamp here, a window there, a door somewhere else. A. C. Pettipas, the public-spirited citizen who paid $400 for salvage, had the benches from the deck installed in various green areas about the town. Like the **Ogle**, it is sad that the **Old Veteran** could not have been preserved, if only as a tourist attraction. However the effects of the depression were still around in 1935, and expenditures for such projects would have been regarded as bordering on the frivolous.

Pettipas resold the bare hull for use as a sand barge. It was later reported that it was wrecked at Eastern Passage.

Meanwhile the **Chebucto** and **Halifax** continued their steady service with few interruptions. In July of 1936, **Chebucto** struck the float in Halifax dock with such force that two cars were damaged.

The new steam steering gear on the **Dartmouth** so impressed the captains that the commission seriously considered having it installed in the **Halifax**. However there was no provision in the 1937 budget for it. It was installed in 1938 for $1,055 by T. Hogan and Company and first used on December 10, 1938. It had been supplied by Marine Industries Ltd.

A veteran captain, William Myrer, celebrated 45 years with the ferry service on March 10, 1936. He was presented with a case of pipes, and in the following year, November 1937, he retired and was given a superannuation of $50 a month.

The commissioners passed a resolution that same year expressing faith and pride in the captains and mates of the permanent staff for the transporting of over one million passengers annually without a serious mishap. In a time of economic depression, these words of appreciation must have been good for the morale of the deck officers.

Captain C. H. MacDonald, a cheerful Pictonian, who wore both his cap and smile at a jaunty angle, was given leave of absence to attend 28 days of naval training at the dockyard in November of 1938. Before another year was up he was called to active service with the Navy on September 1, 1939, two days before the declaration of war by Britain and ten days before Canada's.

The two station houses had to be kept in repair and altered

79.   Old Veteran (Dartmouth) *being scrapped, 1935.*

as the need arose. An exceptionally high tide in December 1934 flooded the Halifax waiting room and put the furnace out. Another indignity arose when an exterminator had to be retained to rid the building of "a large quantity of cockroaches"—not altogether unusual in a waterfront location. New ticket booths were installed in both stations in 1938.

A Dartmouth civil engineer, W. P. Morrison, drew up plans for improvements to the Halifax docks in 1936. His fee was $450. A year later the design was implemented, and the new dock used for the first time on May 28, 1937. While the alterations were being done, the makeshift north dock was used, with vehicular traffic disembarking and passing through two old buildings on Upper Water Street, while the embarking vehicles entered from George Street between the ferry terminal and the Bauld and Gibson building. The commissioners appeared to be pleased with the completed repairs in Halifax and planned major improvements to the Dartmouth docks.

When the **Dartmouth** arrived on the scene in 1934, it became possible once again to use a third boat for excursions. Organizations such as the Trades and Labour Council and the Canadian Medical Association hired the **Dartmouth** for entertainment as part of their conventions. The ferry

80. Old Veteran (Dartmouth) *in lay-up dock, with coal gondola on raised track, early 1930s.*

commission arranged moonlight excursions, and trips to the North West Arm for the benefit of those who wished to see the elimination, four-oared shell races between rival boating clubs—Jubilee, North West Arm Rowing Club, North Star and MicMac. In August 1936, Halifax sponsored a Venetian Night on the Arm, in which hundreds of boats took part. Many of them were beautifully decorated and illuminated, and the **Dartmouth** carried 675 passengers to watch the event.

Each year, Dartmouth Natal Day attracted more and more Haligonians. As time went on, the ferry commission counted on this day to improve its revenue position. Income from this source reached its peak in 1936, and the following figures published in a Halifax newspaper indicate just how busy the ferries were on that day:

YEAR	PASSENGERS	VEHICLES	RECEIPTS
1933	14,473	1241	$1220.74
1934	16,028	1377	1413.19
1935	11,758	1441	1224.52
1936	17,852	1420	1706.97

159

1937	17,174	1432	1559.82
1938	17,613	1277	1489.87
1939	18,024	1330	1621.48

In Superintendent Pearce's log book are recorded many glimpses of special events which occurred during these pre-World War II years. In 1935, King George V and Queen Mary celebrated their Silver Jubilee. The ferries were decorated with flags and bunting for the occasion. On January 20, 1936, there was a brief note in the log that the King had died, and it was later recorded that "(this is the) Coronation Day of King George VI." When George VI and Queen Elizabeth visited Halifax on June 15, 1939, school children were given free passage on the ferry, as they went with their respective classes to take their allotted spaces on Citadel Hill to greet the visiting Royal couple.

Other entries were earthier. Pearce may have been an unwilling father confessor for an in-law of one of his employees. An anonymous and pathetic little note was found within the pages of the log book, beseeching him to speak to Mr. XXXX, who was ill-treating his wife. "Night after night he has been hanging around the ferry buildings with another woman in dark corners misconducting, knowing you would not be around at that time at night."

Another event noted in the Pearce log book was the Moose River Mine disaster in April 1936, when three men were trapped for 11 days in an abandoned gold mine in Halifax County. The ferry carried supplies across the harbour which were required for the rescue operation. The commissioners later agreed to send no bills for this service.

American warships **Arkansas** and **Wyoming**, accompanied by two destroyers were in the harbour in September 1935, and were mentioned in the log book. They made an impressive sight as they steamed out of the harbour. (One author recalls that the junior officers of the **Arkansas** challenged the junior members of the Royal Nova Scotia Yacht Squadron to a sailing race in their whaleboats, of which they had at least four. The whaleboat in which this writer served as a crew member, crossed the finish line among the bottom three.)

Pearce's neighbour, Captain William Crowell, left from a wharf adjoining the ferry docks on July 16, 1936, with his dog as his only crew, to sail around the world in his "home made" yacht, **Queen Mary**.

When there was no bridge or all night ferry service, the citizens of Dartmouth were, from time to time, concerned about the possibility of medical emergencies occurring in the middle of the night, there being no suitably staffed hospital in Dartmouth at the time. If such an emergency did occur the usual action was to drive the 17 miles around Bedford Basin to a Halifax hospital.

On one occasion at least, the ferry ran a special trip. This was noted in the log on August 5, 1937. It was for the patient of a Dr. Mader, who required hospital care at 2.00 a.m.

The log noted that the dial telephone system came into service on July 17, 1936, and observations were made about two spectacular fires. The first was in the old Reform Club Hall on King Street in Dartmouth, which burned to the ground on December 5, 1938. At the time of the fire it was the Royal Theatre, one of Dartmouth's first movie theatres, but it had formerly seen many controversial meetings in connection with town events, including the Citizens' Committee for a People's Ferry, the cause so ardently supported by Benjamin Russell in 1890.

Ferry passengers had a terrifying view of the second fire which destroyed the old Queen Hotel on Halifax's Hollis Street early in March 1939. Many lives were lost in that conflagration and the cries of people trapped or injured could be heard by the passengers as the ferry approached the Halifax dock.

As the threat of war loomed closer, Superintendent Pearce received orders to have the **Dartmouth** stand by for military purposes. Anti-aircraft guns and other heavy equipment were carried across the harbour when defense units were hastily installed at strategic points around the area. Shortly after war was declared, the first blackout drill was held on September 11, 1939, and the ferries were required to remain in their docks.

Halifax and Dartmouth were by this time in the throes of another war, and the ferries were heavily involved.

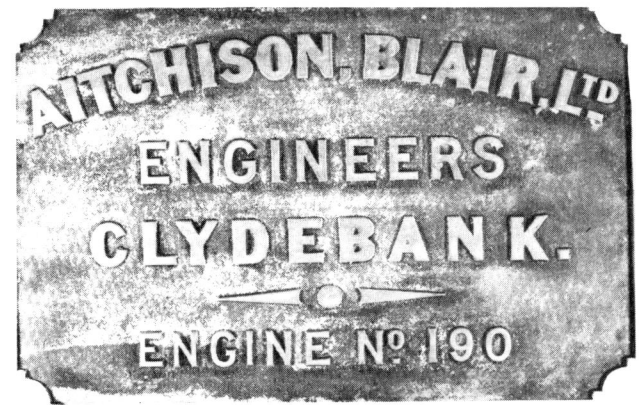

81. Dartmouth, *early 1950s.*

82. Dartmouth *engine builder's nameplate, 1934.*

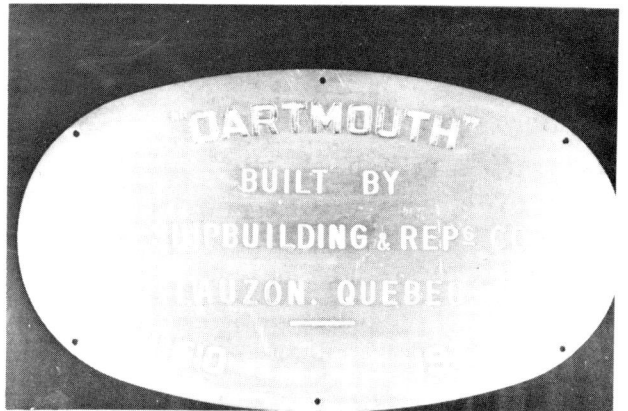

83. Dartmouth *builder's nameplate, 1934.*

XXVII.
GOVERNOR CORNWALLIS

Even before the beginnings of World War II there was some discussion about the next new ferry boat. **Chebucto** and **Halifax** were still serving well in 1938, although some considered them past their prime. In addition, vehicular traffic had increased drastically to the point where there was traffic congestion on both sides of the harbour caused by long lines of waiting cars, trucks and horse-drawn wagons. In Halifax, the line was a single lane back from the ferry gates up George Street and around the corner in a southerly direction down Lower Water Street. On the Dartmouth side, vehicles were lined up two or three abreast on Ferry Hill, and the rest of those waiting passage continued in a single line south on Commercial Street. Traffic constables hired by the ferry commission directed the vehicles in an orderly manner to the gates. Whenever possible, three boats were operated during peak hours.

In August 1939, the commissioners once again asked the Town Council to apply to the Legislature for approval of a $175,000 loan. Lambert, German and Milne produced revised plans for another steel boat, but when the commissioners received an estimate from the Halifax Shipyards for such a vessel, it was found to be prohibitively costly.

Superintendent Pearce suggested that he contact his neighbour, William J. Roue, designer of the **Bluenose**, with the view to sounding him out on designing a new ferry, which was to be of timber construction and with three lanes. Roue was agreeable and said that his fee would be 3 per cent of the total construction cost, or 5 per cent if he was to oversee the construction. Meanwhile, a committee visited various yards in Nova Scotia which had substantial experience in the construction of wooden ships. These included yards in Mahone Bay, Lunenburg and Shelburne. Six tenders were received, the contract being awarded to

84. *Platform guests at launching of* Governor Cornwallis, *1941 (left to right) Hugh Weagle, William Roue, Premier A. S. MacMillan.*

Hugh D. Weagle of Dartmouth. His tender was for $93,551. This caused a stir of excitement in the town - a ferry boat designed and built by Dartmouthians! The first **Chebucto**, launched in 1864, was the last locally built ferry boat. Weagle began at once.

Quite quickly after the declaration of war, the military establishment increased in the area. New Army, Navy and Air Force bases and barracks were built to accommodate the swelling service population. With so many high spirited young men travelling on the ferries, in a part of the country that was new to them, and with uncertain futures lying ahead, it might have been expected that property damage to the ferries would have been part of the scene. In March of 1940, celebrating sailors broke windows on ferries and threw

the watchman's clock into the main dock. The clock was later recovered by a diver, but in the meantime, military police began a regular patrol on the ferries. In spite of their presence, an RCA gunner fell overboard and was drowned in December 1941. Rescue attempts were hopeless in the icy cold water on that black December midnight.

Again, as in World War I, with ships anchored in the ferry lanes, and in a heavy July fog, the **Halifax** collided with the **S. S. Trewellard**. Very little damage was done.

By February 1941, all windows on the ferries were required to be covered as an "air raid precaution" which made harbour pilotage even more precarious. In January 1942, the **Halifax** and **Dartmouth** had to pass between two ships, and at the same time keep clear of each other. A second accident occurred. The ferries collided in mid-harbour at 11:45 p.m., on a clear evening, causing a panic among the passengers. There was some damage to the rails and stanchions, and a few passengers suffered minor injuries when they were knocked to the cabin deck. A letter of protest was fired off to the Hon. Angus L. Macdonald, Minister of Naval Affairs in Ottawa. He replied that the commission should contact Rear Admiral G. C. Jones of Halifax. A result of this exchange was that naval patrol boats were to advise the ferry captains of any obstructions in the ferry lanes, particularly in foggy weather.

Financially, the ferry service was doing very well indeed. In March 1941, $1,000 was donated to the War Services Fund and in June of the same year, $1,000 was presented towards the completion of a canteen for servicemen in Dartmouth. This canteen was staffed by lady volunteers, mainly from various I.O.D.E. chapters in Dartmouth.

The commission set aside $40,000 in July for wartime contingencies, and the usual $500 towards the Natal Day expenses was donated.

In 1942, $35,000 was invested in the Third Victory Loan bonds. The employees invested $8,600. Meanwhile the V.O.N. had been receiving its $500 annual grant, and the Reading Room donation was upped from $150 to $300 in 1944.

Each year traffic was heavier and by the end of January

85. (top) *Artist's conception of engine room*, Governor Cornwallis.
86. (bottom) *Early stage of construction*, Governor Cornwallis.

1945, a surplus of $150,000 was reported. The peak year for ferry travel was reached in 1944, during which six million passengers and over half a million vehicles were transported.

An all night ferry service was begun during the war years, starting on New Year's Eve, 1942. It was not in itself financially successful, but was subsidized by the heavy daytime traffic. Permanent residents and transients alike appreciated the service, especially since gas rationing and tire shortage made a late night drive around Bedford Basin even less attractive.

Crew members came and went during these years, but were amazingly stable considering the turmoil in the area. Captain Reuben Findlay, a 15-year veteran of the service, died in April 1940. Captain William Myrer, who had retired in 1937, died in 1943, and William Case, an engineer for 30

years died in 1944 after a year of retirement. Bertram Ord was appointed to the permanent engineering staff in January 1940. One captain who had only been two months with the commission was fired for crashing the **Chebucto** into the Dartmouth dock. In his defense, the captain said that the **Chebucto** was difficult to handle, "like a car without brakes." There may have been some truth in this statement, since during a gale the previous February, the **Chebucto** had gone aground on the shoal by Cunard's wharf at the foot of Ochterloney Street. On this occasion, the passengers were removed by a small boat, and the **Chebucto** floated off at high tide with no damage.

Percy Wallace was appointed in January 1941, to be in full charge of all ticket collectors. Another administrative appointment was made in August when Robert T. Lynch was made assistant general superintendent.

The employees finally approved a group insurance plan in June 1940. Fifty-seven people benefitted from this scheme. In April 1941, crews received a pay increase and a cost-of-living bonus due to increased responsibility in wartime. For married men the increase was $2.40 a week, and the single men received $1.50. There were six crews employed by June 1941. Their hourly pay scale was:

Captains	82 cents	Engineers	82 cents
Mates	73 cents	Oilers	58 cents
Deckhands	57 cents	Firemen	58 cents

The Unemployment Insurance Act came into effect that summer, so between this, the employees' insurance plan and the cost-of-living bonus, the ferry commission must have been considered a fairly secure place of employment.

While these changes were taking place at the foot of Ferry Hill, Hugh Weagle's boatyard in Mill Cove was buzzing with activity as the new three-lane ferry boat was beginning to take form.

Mr Weagle is determined that a first class job shall be delivered, that not only the ferry commissioners, but the ratepayers of Dartmouth and the patrons of the ferry who must pay the price, will be pleased and satisfied when the boat is in operation. Experienced shipbuilders from all parts of the province have been engaged and it is surprising the progress they have made. Large quantities of materials have been delivered on the job—the best obtainable.

As evidence of his determination to deliver to the ferry the best wooden boat they ever had, Mr. Weagle, at his own expense laid the keel in American oak, far superior in quality than the keel specified because it was believed that American oak could not be obtained.

Huge timbers are being used, a great deal of which is the finest Douglas fir grown in B.C. The boat is now taking definite shape with the sides nearing completion, upper deck with passenger accommodation partly built, while the first deck is laid and the three traffic lanes are about completed. The workmanship is of the best and so is the material.

Shortly after the contract had been awarded, Pearce had recommended diesel electric engines for the new boat—a radical departure from a long history of steam propulsion for the Dartmouth ferries. John Paterson of the Dartmouth Marine Slips, Professor Montgomery of the Nova Scotia Technical College, and Ross Barteaux, a professional engineer, were retained to advise the commission on the matter and they agreed with Pearce. Thus Wm. Stairs Son and Morrow's tender to supply diesel electric machinery was accepted. The machinery offered comprised two General Electric 500 H.P., D.C. propulsion motors, four Caterpillar 100 K.W. main diesel generator units and two Caterpillar 30 K.W. auxiliary diesel generators. Control equipment and various other pieces of auxiliary machinery were included. The engines were due to arrive in September, and installation was expected to take three months. (Readers will recall from the previous chapter that with the **Dartmouth**, the elapsed time from keel-laying to trials was only two and a half months.)

Schoolchildren were asked to submit suggestions for names for the new ferry, and they did so with great enthusiasm—some 70 names appeared. Some of these were

Churchill, Victory, Nova Scotian, and even Duke of Kent (who had recently been the first member of the Royal Family to visit this region by air). Twelve names were culled from the lengthy list and sent to the Registrar of Shipping. The name **Governor Cornwallis** was chosen.

The launching was scheduled for 8:30 a.m., November 20, 1941. Being a memorable event in Dartmouth history, the schoolchildren were given a half holiday. Every vantage point near Mill Cove was crowded with old and young—an estimated 5,000 people. Every part of the ceremony went off smoothly. The Mayor (and ferry commission chairman) L. J. Isnor welcomed the crowd over the public address system at precisely 8:30. Hon. A. S. MacMillan, Premier of Nova Scotia, was a special guest, along with W. C. MacDonald, M.P., the Mayor of Halifax, ferry commissioners, builder Hugh Weagle, designer William J. Roue and Ross Barteaux, engineer in charge of machinery, who comprised the platform dignitaries.

The new boat was christened by Miss Edith Isnor, daughter of Mayor L. J. Isnor. The bottle of champagne was smashed against the rudder post of the boat the second that the boat began to move on the ways, although it was 15 minutes later or more before the boat began to gather real momentum. Cheers from the crowd followed the christening which was carried out gracefully and with dignity.

Following the christening Miss Isnor was presented with a bouquet of roses by Premier MacMillan . . . .

Immediately after the opening remarks by the Mayor the contractor sounded a whistle and 50 expert workmen started with hammers to release the boat, then huge jacks were brought into play and after a delay of 15 minutes the boat showed some signs of moving, hardly perceptible to the naked eye, while the thousands of people along the shore line waited with close interest.

The contractor moved quietly among his workmen directing every detail, but it was not until nearly nine o'clock that the boat began to show encouraging signs of sliding down the ways. With jacks and hammers and the use of manual power the boat was finally got on her way and to the roar of more than 5,000 throats slid down the ways and into the harbour waters "like a swan." It was beautiful and impressive . . . .

Less than half a dozen persons were on the boat when she was launched. Among them was Captain J. Murphy of the permanent ferry staff, C. E. Zink, ex-councillor, and a few workmen looking after details.

All streets leading to the shipyards were blocked with traffic. People began arriving on the scene at 7:30 and by 8:30 the shore line was crowded. Hundreds witnessed the launching from steamers under repairs at the Dartmouth Shipyards.

After the boat was launched Mr. Weagle was personally congratulated by the Premier and many others. Asked what he thought of the launching Mr. Weagle said, "It was perfect, it could not have been better." Mr. Weagle showed his delight and pleasure with a smile.

The new ferry was moved to the south ferry dock in Dartmouth, and work began immediately on her fitting out.

Roue and Weagle had played their parts well, and the **Governor Cornwallis** was as much a triumph as the **Ogle** had been more than a hundred years before. The novelty of the **Ogle's** steam engine and its operators' lack of knowledge and experience in its management had drawn the wrath of the travelling public, when she first went "on the ferry." Readers will recall that she seemed to spend as much time in her dock as in working the harbour crossings.

History was about to repeat itself. The **Cornwallis'** trials took place a year later, on Bedford Basin, after which she was open for public inspection on December 6, 1942, from 2 to 5 in the afternoon, and was heartily approved by all (at dockside). Her glassed-in cabin on the upper deck was a novelty which added much extra seating capacity; the three car lanes received favourable reaction as well. It was hoped that this feature would cut down the long waits on Ferry Hill.

87. Governor Cornwallis ca. 1943. Capt. Urquhart and crew.

Since 1934, the Quebec-built ferry **Dartmouth** had been running smoothly and efficiently—the good child of the ferry fleet. The **Governor Cornwallis**, on the other hand, was soon to resemble the very worst kind of problem child. She was no sooner put on the service than the troubles began. Some of the problems are summarized here, having been abstracted from Superintendent Pearce's log book. Non-technically minded readers will find it incredible that so many things could go wrong in such a short space of time.

December 31, 1942:
Steering gear trouble.
January 7, 1943:
Complaints about engine vibrations.
January 16, 1943:
Steering gear trouble.
February 19, 1943:
Stairs, Son & Morrow lifting engines and fitting rubber vibration absorbers. Hugh Weagle lining lower cabin windows with felt.
March 5, 1943:
Broke down in harbour. Tug called.
March 16, 1943:
Steering gear ram cylinder blew out.
March 29, 1943:
Steering gear ram cylinder blew out.
March 31, 1943:
Oil pipe in #4 main generator set broke off.
April 2, 1943:
Feed pipe to #4 diesel generating set given out.
April 28, 1943: Steering gear trouble. Nail driven through oil pipe.
May 4, 1943:
Laid up—steering gear. John Paterson overseeing.
May 17, 1943:
Capt. Potts, Hughes Owens consulted re steering gear.
June 8, 1943:
Blew fuse on main control panel. Struck north bridge.

June 9, 1943:
John Paterson to supervise locking rudders in mid position.
June 12 & 14:
Hare and Harrison turning locking pins.
June 28, 1943:
Cornwallis back in service.
July 15, 1943:
Guildford and Sons covering exhaust pipes.
July 19, 1943:
Hugh Weagle building air ducts to engine room.
October 7, 1943:
Trouble with #4 circulating pump.
November 9, 1943:
Trouble with forward propulsion motor.
December 14, 1943:
Fan installed on furnace pipe.
February 2, 1944:
Turning and polishing commutator #1 propulsion motor. Reduced diameter about ½ inch. J. P. Dunn insulating heater pipes to pilot houses.
February 8, 1944:
Exhaust fans in engine rooms.
March 18, 1944:
Carpenters tacking up Cellutex on ceiling of engine room.
March 31, 1944:
Steering gear trouble.
April 4, 1944:
Steering gear trouble.
May 16, 1944:

Trouble with #1 propulsion motor

May 29, 1944:
Relays "kicked off"—no power.

June 12, 1944:
Magnetic switch demagnetized.

August 10, 1944:
Contact points on generator alarm stuck. **Cornwallis** off service 45 minutes.

September 18, 1944:
Steering gear, locking pin trouble.

October 3, 1944:
Repairs to steering gear and hydraulic pump.

October 29, 1944:
#2 main motor out. **Cornwallis** replaced by **Halifax**.

October 30, 1944:
#2 main generator crank shaft broke.

October 31, 1944:
Stripped down and repaired while in service.

November 1, 1944:
One hour off service. Door on switch box #2 main generator had been opened.

November 2, 1944:
Removed crank shaft from #2 engine and taken to shop.

November 15, 1944:
New crank shaft placed on board.

November 16, 1944:
Crashed into dock.

December 3, 1944:
Crank shaft repairs to #1 auxiliary generator.

A terribly sad chronology.

The commission, with presumably good advice, had embarked on a new chapter, for them, in marine propulsion technology. But it was not altogether new and ought to have been workable in the **Cornwallis**. Reading only slightly between the lines from the log, one gets the feeling that the **Cornwallis** and her machinery were being abused. But by whom? Was it involuntary or deliberate? Having the wrong kind of people in the engine room, that is marine engineers with only steam training and experience, might have been one kind of involuntary abuse. Did the particular machinery vendors have a reasonable background in marine diesel-electric propulsion? If not, then perhaps this was more involuntary abuse. One point that did not ever receive much public attention, was that **Cornwallis** was the commission's first ferry with almost total wheelhouse control. Gone was the jangling engine room telegraph frequently heard during docking and departure.

This was a technological change that, rightly or wrongly, was highly resented by marine engineers of the time, and thus the attitudes of engine room staff under these conditions might have been something less than that of total dedication to their jobs.

In any event, it seems likely that some better combination of machinery vendors experienced in like applications, engine room staff with training and experience in diesel-electric propulsion, and owners with full-time relevant engineering staff competence, might have made some difference in the outcome of the story of the **Governor Cornwallis**.

The sad tale concluded most ingloriously.

At 4:05 p.m., December 22, 1944, the **Governor Cornwallis** left the Halifax dock with about 20 motor vehicles and between 300 and 400 passengers. Almost immediately the engine room crew discovered a fire in the ceiling of the engine room. It was located between the false ceiling of Cellutex and the deckhead. Rather than raise a general alarm the two men fought the fire with extinguishers as the boat kept on across the harbour, the captain unaware of events below. All vehicles and passengers had actually disembarked at Dartmouth before it was generally known that there was a fire on board.

By the time Dartmouth fire engines arrived on the scene within a few minutes of the boat's docking, the engine room crew had been ordered to leave their posts. The fire was out of control. Tugs and fire boats rushed across the harbour and the ill-fated ferry, spectacularly ablaze, was towed down to George's Island and beached there. She was a total loss.

Dartmouthians were aghast at this fiery ending to the controversial ferry. Great relief was felt that a terrible tragedy had been avoided and perhaps there was even a hint of a "good riddance" attitude. Rumours of sabotage were heard, but an investigation called by the provincial Fire Marshall, on January 12, 1945, concluded that the

88.   *A sad ending, December 22, 1944.*

cause was due to poor installation of the heating furnace's smoke pipe.

"This pipe, in the opinion of the Fire Marshall, was installed without regard to the principles of basic safety. A fire simply had to occur in the vicinity of this smoke pipe at some time. It came when the radiated heat from the pipe exceeded the ignition point of the adjacent combustible materials [especially the Cellutex acoustic tiles]. As a safety factor the installation of the asbestos board was useless. It is quite true that asbestos board will not in itself burn, but it does conduct heat."

The Fire Marshall gave special mention to Engineer Carmichael and Oiler Horobin. "The conduct of these men is brought to the attention of the Minister of Labour because it was outstanding in character. These two men, without regard for their own personal safety, held this fire in check until and after the ship was docked. In their hands rested the safety of the passengers carried on that voyage.

By their efforts they did control this fire and that action probably resulted in the saving of hundreds of lives. They did not leave their posts until ordered to do so."

On January 11, 1945, Alex Hart, at a commission meeting, moved that the insurers be given notice of abandonment of the **Governor Cornwallis** as a constructive total loss. A cheque for $65,000 was sent to the commission by the underwriters, but two months later they received a letter from Rainnie and Company Ltd., saying that the underwriters were "considerably perturbed by the fact that no notice had been given them of the Cellutex installation."

In retrospect it seems to have been a dreadful waste of the enthusiastic work of designer Roue and builder Weagle. As for the **Cornwallis**, as if not wanting any more of this world, she slid off the beach at George's Island and quietly sank in deep water near by.

XXVIII.
End of World War II

By 1944 the Dartmouth Ferry Commission was a big business. This was the year of peak traffic and consequently of peak revenue. Immediately before the disaster of the **Governor Cornwallis** occurred, its affluence was such that one of the commissioners has suggested that it might be a worthwhile and public-spirited venture to improve the recreational facilities of the town. With the war drawing to a close, North Americans were becoming conscious of town planning in their hopes for a better world in peacetime. Dartmouth ferry commissioners looked to improving the shores of Lake Banook for a beginning, and hoped to create a park-like circumference or green belt around the popular lake. The Hon. Geoffrey Stevens, MLA, introduced a private memeber's Bill to the Legislature at the 1944 spring session which read, in part:

The Dartmouth Ferry Commission shall have power

for the purpose of stimulating post-war traffic and developing the tourist trade, to do all things deemed necessary for the purpose of improving Lake Banook in and adjoining the Town of Dartmouth and making such Lake and the surrounding locality more suitable for a sporting and recreation centre and resort; and without limiting the generality of the foregoing, the said Commission shall have power for the said purpose to purchase, acquire, subdivide, improve, lease and sell real estate, lay out roads, construct buildings, parks and amusement and recreational facilities, operate the same or any of them, own, lease and operate ferries to or from any place in Lake Banook or in any of the Dartmouth Lakes, lease concessions and engage in any business that might reasonably be carried on in connection with the powers hereinbefore set out, and to charge tolls in and to any of the same.

(2) The said Commission shall have power to expend

89. *"Gateway to the City," 1943. Drawing by Robert W. Chambers.*

from time to time within five years from the passing of this Act a total sum on capital account not to exceed $50,000 for the purposes set out in this section.

Thus, in May 1944, the commissioners as their first step to develop lakeside property, voted to purchase an ice house (one of the many that had long been familiar landmarks on the Dartmouth scene) next to the MicMac Club on Prince Albert Road, for the sum of $3,000. A committee was formed in conjunction with service clubs plus ten private citizens, whose first task was to seek out other available lands adjoining the lake. Shortly thereafter the "chairman stated that several letters had been received from owners of desirable locations on Lake Banook—i.e. S. Chittick, H. R. Silver, Dr. S. R. Johnston, J. E. Rutledge and the Nova Scotia Power Commission."

The development of this area was not only for summer sports, but for horse racing in the winter as well. At the junction of the first two lakes in the chain, were two channel markers—large heavy steel plate cylinders, filled with rocks, a location known as "The Tittle." An emergency meeting in October 1945, held in connection with the Lake Banook development, decided to make this channel 110 feet wide from Lake Banook into Lake MicMac, four feet deep at low water and eight feet deep at high water. It was felt that this would be an improvement for shell racing in the summer and horse racing in the winter.

The Lake Banook development seemed totally unrelated to the business of operating a ferry service. Perhaps fortunately for this story, it was a short-lived adventure in relation to the more than 200-year history of the Dartmouth ferries. In April 1947, one of the "developed" properties was leased to the MicMac Amateur Athletic Club for $1 a year for 25 years. The last item relating to Lake Banook real estate appears in June 1956 when the commission transferred this property to the Town of Dartmouth for $1.

Future researchers into this period of the Dartmouth Ferry Commission's history may be intrigued by the apparent relationships between some of the incumbent commissioners and those who seem to have just purchased lakeside property only to resell immediately to the commission.

The most pressing business in the new year of 1945 was the mounting traffic problem. Unsatisfactory as she had been, the **Governor Cornwallis** at least had carried large loads of vehicles while she was operating, and there had always been the hope that her deficiencies would be overcome. Now, with her gone, the situation was worse than it had ever been. Not only was traffic heavier, there was an increasing awareness of the fact that the **Chebucto** and **Halifax** were on the verge of old age, and soon wanting retirement. The **Dartmouth**, serenely and steadily plied her way, the ideal ferry boat, except for her limited vehicle accommodation. Commissioner M. S. Regan noted that the situation was so bad, even for foot passengers, that the ladies had to stand, while men sat in the ladies cabin.

At the January 11, 1945 meeting, the naval architects firm of German and Milne (formerly Lambert and German the designers of the **Dartmouth**) presented plans for a new boat, but warned the commissioners that even if a start was made as soon as possible, a new boat would probably not be ready for service until the spring of 1946. Mayor Isnor, Commissioners Hartlen and MacLean, and Superintendent Charles Pearce visited the Montreal firm in late February. At a meeting it was decided to abandon diesel engines and return to steam, but with oil-fired boilers.

Back in Dartmouth, a delegation of VIPs attended the commission meeting of March 28, 1945—Minister of Trade and Industry Harold Connolly, Attorney General J. H. MacQuarrie and Professor Montgomery of the Nova Scotia Technical College. They spoke strongly in favor of having the new ferry built in Nova Scotia and recommended Pictou Foundry and Machine Company, which had tendered a price of $404,000. It is not clear that this delegation was invited by the commissioners to attend their meeting, but this uncertainty along with the fact that the minutes did not mention any other tenders (which must have been received) is quite astonishing. Only the most naive citizen

90. *Ships in Bedford Basin awaiting convoy during World War II.*

would not recognize this as possible political interference in the affairs of the town.

In any event, Pictou Foundry and Machine Company were awarded the contract to build the new ferry. Another Nova Scotia firm, Robb Engineering of Amherst was to manufacture the boiler. A Skinner "Unaflow" engine, the final development of the steam reciprocating engine, was ordered from Vickers of Montreal.

The contract for the new ferry was signed on April 17, 1945, in the board room of the ferry commission; W. H. Milne represented the architects, and Mr. Ferguson was there for the Pictou Foundry.

173

While the **Governor Cornwallis** and her subsequent replacement took much of the discussion time at commission meetings, and the new Lake Banook development scheme was also begun, other items of business were receiving attention as well. On May 22, 1944, the commission decided to remodel the Dartmouth offices of the ferry terminal, with particular attention to the board room. A Mr. Skerry (presumably descended from the original ferry operator, John Skerry) tendered for the plastering job.

Montreal engineer O. J. MacCulloch met with the commission in January 1945, and shortly afterward T. C. Gorman Company was awarded a contract for new docks on the Dartmouth side. The Gorman tender was for $264,999.

Superintendent Pearce wrote joyously in his log on May 7, 1945, that whistles and horns announced the end of war in Europe at 10:45 a.m. City and Town officials rushed to put into operation plans to celebrate the victory on the following day, but the preparations took time—bunting had to be hung, bands assembled, loudspeakers arranged and wooden platforms built. The people, both civilian and armed forces, were in no mood to wait for festivities. They took matters in their own hands, and celebrations which started with an air of elation soon turned into ugly riots, after crowds had broken into the government liquor stores. When it was all over, a Royal Commission under Mr. Justice R. L. Kellock released a report which said:

> There was no trouble of any kind in Dartmouth throughout the day or night of May 7th . . . .
> About 2:00 p.m. on May 8th, word reached the Chief of Police (Lawlor) that trouble had broken out in Halifax. He immediately made arrangements to tie up the ferry service between the two places should that later prove necessary . . . .
> About 4:00 p.m. the Chief was returning to his office, after having made the above arrangement, and, as he passed the ferry terminus, he noticed that there were coming off the ferry quite a number of civilians and service personnel considerably under the influence of liquor.

About 5:30 p.m. a crowd of naval ratings began to gather in front of the liquor store in Dartmouth. The manager of the store, who was alone at the time, telephoned the town police and the two city policemen who were there on duty at the time were sent and all town police (10) were called for duty. The Chief also notified the RCMP, the shore patrol and the army provost. Before any of the police arrived at the liquor store, it was attacked by the crowd and the manager observed that the attack was led by eight sailors and two airmen who used a battering ram. The lower part of the door was pushed in but before entry was gained, the two civil police, six or eight shore patrol, and the same number of army provost arrived and were able to stay the attack temporarily. The "crowd" at that time was estimated by the manager at about 35, mostly naval ratings. In a very few minutes the attack was renewed and one door was pulled off its hinges by sailors. By this time a large crowd had gathered. One observer said it was composed 30 per cent to 40 per cent navy, 10 per cent army and air force, and the rest civilians. Rocks, sticks and bottles were thrown in the door and the crowd entered on the heels of the service men and looting of the liquor stocks began. This went on for about an hour, notwithstanding the presence of six army provost, five municipal police and eight or ten shore patrol. The store was emptied of 439 cases of beer, 141 cases of wine and 818 cases of spirits . . . . A very small quantity was ultimately recovered.

While the raid on the liquor store was in progress, the Chief of Police endeavoured to get Lieutenant Commander Wood, or a commissioned officer of the shore patrol, and later Admiral Murray on the telephone, but was unsuccessful. He then telephoned the Attorney General, who referred him to Brigadier White. The latter said that assistance could be procured from Colonel Meighen, the Officer Commanding A-23 Training Centre. Colonel Meighen, on being applied to, agreed to send soldiers. It was then in the neighbourhood of 6:00 o'clock. A wholesale grocery store near the liquor store had also been broken into at that time.

The next development was the breaking of windows

in business premises on Commercial Street, which runs along the waterfront and which, with Portland Street, are the two business streets of the town, Portland Street being the principal business street.

It was then decided to stop the ferry service and this was done shortly before 7:00 p.m. . . . .

The report went on and told of further damage done by the mob up and down Portland Street. "Ultimately a detachment of approximately 125 men arrived from A-23 and about the same time 50 air force men arrived from the airport. These, together with the ten town constables, seven or eight shore patrol and three RCMP, were used as one body, and with two parties of sailors from ships in the harbour totalling 60 men, and the additional shore patrol when they arrived, began a sweep of the streets and by 10:30 p.m. succeeded in dispersing the crowds. The example of Halifax was followed, a curfew and a declaration of the ending of V-E Day being broadcast about 9:00 p.m. Ferry service was resumed shortly after midnight."

Pearce kept his own record of events in his log:
"Tues., May 8, 1945:
V-E Day. Riot started 6 p.m. Portland St. suffered heavy damage. **Chebucto** at Shipyards Wharf, **Dartmouth** tied to tanker at Government Buoy, **Halifax** to Marine and Fisheries Wharf. One boat service after 1 a.m.
Wed., May 9, 1945:
Martial law. **Chebucto** at Shipyards. **Halifax** at Marine and Fisheries Wharf.
Thurs., May 10, 1945:
Curfew law in Dartmouth.
Sun. May 13, 1945:
Curfew law lifted."

Business resumed as usual, only to be literally shattered once more from explosions at the Bedford naval magazine on the night of July 19, 1945. Systematic ammunition storage there had not kept pace with the unloading of the large fleet of Canadian warships no longer involved in the Battle of the Atlantic.

Pearce recorded: "July 19, 1945: Explosions at armament depot (Bedford Magazine). Ferry staff greatly reduced. Only **Dartmouth** on. All north end residents evacuated. July 20, 1945: Back to normal."

Only one resident was killed in these explosions, but memories of the 1917 Explosion, and the more recent riots had made citizens extremely nervous. In the light of these experiences, ferry crews who deserted their posts might well be excused, and those who remained on duty ought to have been especially commended.

V-J Day finally came on August 14, 1945, and the regular ferry commission meeting was scheduled for that night. However, "due to the announcement of the Declaration of Peace, the noise of horns made it impossible to transact business," wrote secretary Guy M. Mitchell.

The meeting, adjourned until August 17, received a letter from Commander C. H. MacDonald, R.C.N.R., the first ferry employee called up for war service in 1939. He was seeking reinstatement as Captain and Assistant Superintendent. About this time, after a long and dedicated career with the commission, Superintendent Pearce decided to resign. Captain Charles H. MacDonald was appointed General Superintendent at the October 29 meeting.

Incredibly, there was still no pension scheme for ferry employees. Two different plans had been offered to them and both were rejected. The commissioners decided to grant Pearce $50 a month, he to be retained in an advisory capacity, and when a pension plan was adopted he was to be included. Pearce wrote his last entry in the neatly kept log book on October 31, 1945.

Now, like a fresh breeze from the Atlantic, and with post-war optimism, Captain MacDonald took command as Superintendent. Assistant Superintendent Robert T. Lynch was assigned the task of keeping the log book. His easy flowing style was symbolic of the new administration at the ferry terminal. The mood of operations changed as abruptly as did the writing in the contrasting logs. The more precise, old-world administration of Charles E. Pearce had ended, and the hectic era which followed World War II had begun.

XXIX.

The Last Years of the Car Ferries

With peace came a period of readjustment. Servicemen were demobilized and brought back into useful productive activity. Factories commandeered to produce instruments of war returned to their normal economic role in society in time to meet the upsurge of consumerism (a word unknown in 1945).

L. J. Isnor began his last term as Mayor of Dartmouth in 1946. He had been 14 years on the ferry commission, 12 of them as chairman. Many well-known citizens of Dartmouth had served with him: J. P. Otto, Fred M. Lahey, Charles MacLean, John Paterson, M. S. Regan, Walter Mosher, A. C. Pettipas, R. T. Lynch, A. R. Publicover, W. M. Austin, W. L. Matthews, L.R. Hartlen, J. J. MacIntosh, J. A. Harris, R. J. Ferguson, W. T. Kilroy, Alex Hart, J. A. West, H. J. Cann, F. J. Keohan and A. I. Ross.

The commission's solicitor, W. E. Moseley resigned in June 1948, when he was appointed prothonotary, and was succeeded by Walter DeW. Barss.

Moseley's family had varied connections with Dartmouth's ferries. Ebenezer Moseley was consulted on the condition of the first **Halifax (Annex 2)** in 1893. Henry Moseley, also a boat builder, served as one of the early commissioners in 1897. His brother, W. P. Moseley, a commissioner for about six years from 1915, was the father of solicitor W. Everett Moseley, who was especially interested in the commission because of these former family connections.

The **Dartmouth** was a new ferry when Mayor Isnor joined the commission, the **Governor Cornwallis** had her brief and troubled career, and now another new ferry was about to arrive on the scene.

Once again school children suggested names for the latest addition to the fleet. Some related to the times: Churchill, Roosevelt and Victory. Others were the old familiar ones:

Cornwallis II, Scotian, Micmac, Joseph Howe, Harbour Queen and Chebucto. Awareness of Superintendent Pearce's impending retirement resulted in the suggestion, Charles E. Pearce. On October 29, 1945, the name **Scotian** was selected.

All the commissioners except M. R. Regan went to Pictou on November 26 to review progress on the new vessel, and just before Christmas, on December 20, they made the journey again for the launching. The weather had been frightfully cold for a week, and the day of the launching was stormy and with high winds. There was the appropriate ceremony and the boat was christened by Miss Nita Harris, daughter of ferry commissioner Arthur Harris.

Unfortunately, the grease on the ways had hardened from the low temperatures, and for the first time since the **Ogle's** launching, a ferry was reluctant to take to the water. The **Scotian** became stuck after having moved about half way down, and even the icebreaker **Sorel** could not tow her off her cradle. Later, at high tide, the launch was completed.

Photographs in the local papers show that the superstructure of the **Scotian** was hardly begun at the time of launching and it was not until almost seven months later, in July, that Superintendent C. H. MacDonald and Mechanical Superintendent Arthur T. Hare attended the preliminary trials at Pictou. Sea trials took place two weeks later, and on August 3, the **Scotian** left Pictou for Dartmouth, Captain Trefry of Pictou in command. Lemuel Freeman, Chief Engineer of the ferry commission represented his employers on the trip. A rough one it was. Dense fog and heavy seas delayed the **Scotian's** arrival in Dartmouth. She came by way of Mulgrave, Canso and Whitehead, Guysborough County, where she laid up until the weather was more agreeable, finally arriving at the commission's south dock at 12:15 a.m. August 10, 1946.

The fireboat **Rouille** had been offered to the commission to allow a welcoming party to meet the **Scotian.** The **Rouille** left Halifax at 8 p.m. with Mayor Isnor, commissioners Kilroy and Regan, Mac Hiltz, A. C. Pettipas, Walter Regan, Cyril Kane, Norman Weagle and Captain Joseph Murphy on

91.   (top) Scotian *full astern, entering Dartmouth dock, late 1940s.*

92.   (bottom) *Dartmouth ferry commissioners at Pictou, 1945. Left to right: Ralph Ferguson, Ted Kilroy, Arthur Harris, L. J. Isnor, Lorne Hartlen, C. A. MacLean.*

177

board. After a long wait at the mouth of the harbour which was blanketed by fog, they decided to return to the dock. Word finally came from Camperdown that the **Scotian** had been sighted. **Rouille** set off once more, and the on-board guests were thrilled when the fog lifted as suddenly as it had earlier descended, the moon shone through the clouds, and the **Scotian** appeared.

Invitations had been issued for an excursion trip on Monday, August 5. Due to the delay because of the bad weather, the excursion was postponed to the 10th, the evening of the very day the **Scotian** tied up in Dartmouth. Three hundred guests were entertained by a two-hour cruise around the harbour.

Like a theme with variations, history repeated itself. The **Scotian** went into service on August 12 at 11:15 a.m. It would be pleasant to record that this new ferry, a product of a Nova Scotia yard, was a huge success. Alas, not so. **Scotian's** performance, especially during her early years, created as many if not more problems for the commission than the unfortunate **Governor Cornwallis.**

It may suffice to note that for two years she was off the service as much as she was on it. Like the **Governor Cornwallis**, ventilation in the engine room was inadequate, and more than once, engineers, oilers and firemen walked off and refused to operate her. Temperatures of 115 to 130 degrees fahrenheit were reported. Dissatisfaction with the ventilation continued in spite of attempts by Pictou Foundry workers, and a visit from Mr. Milne, of German and Milne. Another attempt was made in 1949 to ease the situation by adding extensions to the ventilators.

Another problem which occurred frequently was the loss of vacuum when the engine was called to reverse. This would happen about one in ten times, and the cause could not be identified. On one occasion when this happened, the **Scotian** crashed into the main Halifax dock, pushing the

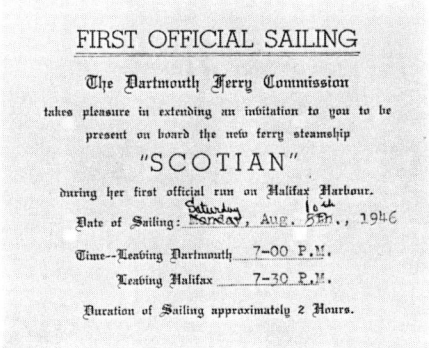

FIRST OFFICIAL SAILING

The Dartmouth Ferry Commission

takes pleasure in extending an invitation to you to be present on board the new ferry steamship

"SCOTIAN"

during her first official run on Halifax Harbour.

Date of Sailing: Saturday, Aug. 10th., 1946

Time--Leaving Dartmouth ____ 7-00 P.M.

Leaving Halifax ____ 7-30 P.M.

Duration of Sailing approximately 2 Hours.

93. Invitation, 1946.

floating bridge about ten feet into the fixed dock. The crash was heard for blocks around. The air pump (the pump that withdraws the condensed exhaust steam from the condenser discharge) was dismantled and it was found that a quantity of hard metal had scored the cylinder walls.

Mr. Beresford of Canadian Vickers was consulted and after a trial run, he found the water in the condenser at a much higher temperature than it should have been. "The condenser was badly choked with foreign substance sufficient to contribute to the major part of the trouble causing the steamer to lose her vacuum. The condenser was given a thorough cleaning and put in operation. Since then it has been operating satisfactorily."

It may have been satisfactory for a few days, but then the loss of vacuum recurred, which had the effect of considerably reducing the power of the engine and causing difficulties in starting when stopped for manoeuvring. On August 19, 1947, commissioners were advised that the engine had failed to function once more and crews were told that the speed must be kept down until the situation was corrected. An irate delegation of taxpayers attended the September meeting in 1947 to complain of the poor service given by the **Scotian**, and they insisted that the blame for her poor performance be fixed. There was internal squabbling and dissension among crews, largely due to their intense dislike of working on the **Scotian.**

This was the point at which Milne of German and Milne arrived on the scene, and also Engineer Munn, a representative of the Skinner Engine Company of Erie, Penn. When the latter was told that the engine would lose its vacuum after three hours of operation he asserted that this was the first time there had been any difficulty with Skinner Unaflow engines. As a result of the visiting experts' investigations, the **Scotian**, to the ratepayers' further rage,

94. Scotian *in mid-harbour, 1955.*

was once again taken off the service to have another "new bucket...fitted in the air pump and the circulating pump to be overhauled." The air pump was rebored and the bucket "fitted."

From this point on the loss of vacuum problem was cured, but complaints about the temperature in the engine room continued throughout the **Scotian's** career.

One of the last and major activities during Mayor Isnor's term of office was the appointment of two firms to make an in-depth study of all aspects of ferry operations, in an effort to improve the dwindling income and to recommend areas where economies might be made. The firms appointed were H. R. Doane and Company, chartered accountants, and Engineering Service Company, consulting engineers.

Mayor Isnor felt that fares should be increased and said that although "revenue from vehicles was 32 per cent of all revenue," vehicular traffic was "responsible for at least the reverse in cost." Whether to continue the all-night ferry service was another question, and the last major consideration was whether to keep the 48-year old **Chebucto** in service.

A Board of Public Utilities hearing was held in September 1946, to review these questions. A. C. Pettipas said that it

had cost $100,000 to keep the ferry **Chebucto** suitable for service in the past five years, and that she should be sunk or junked. To this, John Kaye of Engineering Service Company replied that because the commission had recently purchased a new ferry at a cost of about $245,000, the **Chebucto** should be kept on.

As if to agree with Kaye, the **Chebucto** showed her mettle on Hallowe'en that year, when she was the only boat on the service. The **Dartmouth** was in for refit, the generator on the **Halifax** had burned out, and the **Scotian** in one of her tantrums, had to be withdrawn from service for two hours for "certain adjustments." The reliable old **Chebucto** showed that she was not yet ready for the scrap heap.

It was not until late 1951 that she did retire. In November 1951, she was sold to the Loudee Steel Corporation of Montreal, for $5,000, after having served faithfully for 53 years. A Foundation Maritime tug towed her to Montreal, and there were many sad faces who watched her depart from the harbour.

It was later learned that she was used as a floating machine shop during the construction of the St. Lawrence Seaway, and was therefore contributing a useful service as late as 1956.

Returning to 1946 and Mayor Isnor's request for higher fares, a rate increase application prepared by H. R. Doane and Company was presented at a Public Utilities Board hearing. The Board approved the following fare schedule which came into effect December 1, 1946:

		At night
Children between 5 and 12	.05	.10
Over 12	.10	.20
Commuters— 20 tickets	$1.25	
52 tickets	$2.00	
104 tickets	$3.50	
Automobiles	.35	

H. R. Doane also recommended that all vouchers should be signed by two commissioners, department heads and the superintendent.

The all-night ferry service was a thorny problem. It was

expensive to operate, and not heavily used, but every time there were rumours of it being stopped, a public outcry was heard. The loudest voice was that of the Airport Transportation Company. Scheduled airlines, mainly TransCanada Airlines, in 1946 used the military airport at Shearwater in Eastern Passage. Passengers disembarking for Halifax either had to be taken across on the ferry by taxi, or driven around Bedford Basin. Bernard McGarva of the Airport Transportation Company said that the all-night ferry was essential for airport traffic since sometimes in winter the road around the Basin was impassable. This was true in the case of hospital emergiencies as well. The Dartmouth-Bedford highway was not paved until 1952.

So the all-night service was maintained for a short while longer, but finally, on November 13, 1948, it was discontinued. An emergency service was advertised as being available between 1:30 and 6:00 a.m. at $25 a trip, but was little used.

During World War II many public buildings and private homes were still heated by coal. The two consulting firms investigating ferry operations recommended that both ferry buildings and the boats themselves be converted to oil. "Conversion from coal to oil would save $15,000 a year," reported John R. Kaye of Engineering Service Company. "The thermal efficiency of the boilers is not very high and this is aggravated by the use of coal," added the representative of the Doane firm, a perceptive observation coming from an accountant. "It would cost somewhere from $25,000 to $30,000 to convert each ship to oil." With the ever-present expectation of a bridge, this was never done. However in 1953, a new oil heating furnace was installed in the Dartmouth terminal.

Before leaving the ferry commission, Mayor Isnor, on October 14, 1947, had the pleasant task of presenting Gordon H. Wright, a yard employee, with a lifesaving certificate from the Royal Humane Society. Wright had jumped late at night into the cold waters of the harbour a year earlier and assisted with the rescue of Norman Weagle, foreman carpenter, who had fallen overboard.

In February 1948, A. C Pettipas was elected Mayor of Dartmouth. During his term of office there were several changes of personnel. In 1949, Miss Minnie Boutilier, who had once masqueraded as a Mate, retired after 43 years. Freeman Conrad, oiler, and a 35-year veteran, died in 1948, and Captain Fred Williams, 33 years service, died the following month.

Although the all-night service had stopped, excursions and picnics were once again a source of revenue. The **Dartmouth** was now the favourite picnic boat, and among such trips were the ones of the Halifax and Dartmouth Shipyards' personnel to McNab's Island on August 29, 1948, and the Loyal True Blue Grand Lodge on an excursion up the North West Arm, August 31. The price for the latter was $245—quite a change from 1891 when the **Ogle** could be had for $50.

What might have been a serious accident occurred in February 1946, between the **Halifax** and the naval tug **Glenevis**. It was an extraordinarily foggy morning, and the **Halifax,** with Captain Urquhart, had just left the Halifax dock at 8:30 a.m. Knowing there was a freighter anchored in the vicinity, Urquhart proceeded at a very slow speed, and at the time of the collision was at a standstill. **Glenevis**, with Captain Browdidge, was travelling from the Dockyard to King's Wharf. The women's cabin of the **Halifax** was damaged, a door knocked down and one large window broken, but fortunately there were no fatalities or injuries.

In February 1949, the **Dartmouth** crashed into the Halifax dock and an engineer admitted responsibility. She suffered $3,000 worth of damage, and her boilers were shifted three inches. In March 1949, after many such crashes of varying magnitude, William P. Morrison of Dartmouth was asked to supervise the construction of new docks in Halifax. The Foundation Maritime crane **Shipshaw** moved in and rapidly demolished the south dock in April.

From time to time babies were born on the ferries as maternity cases were being "rushed" across to Halifax hospitals. Usually such births took place in passenger cars, but one unfortunate lady, a pedestrian passenger, delivered herself of an unpaying customer on the trip across. This extra passenger was born in the ladies cabin on August 17,

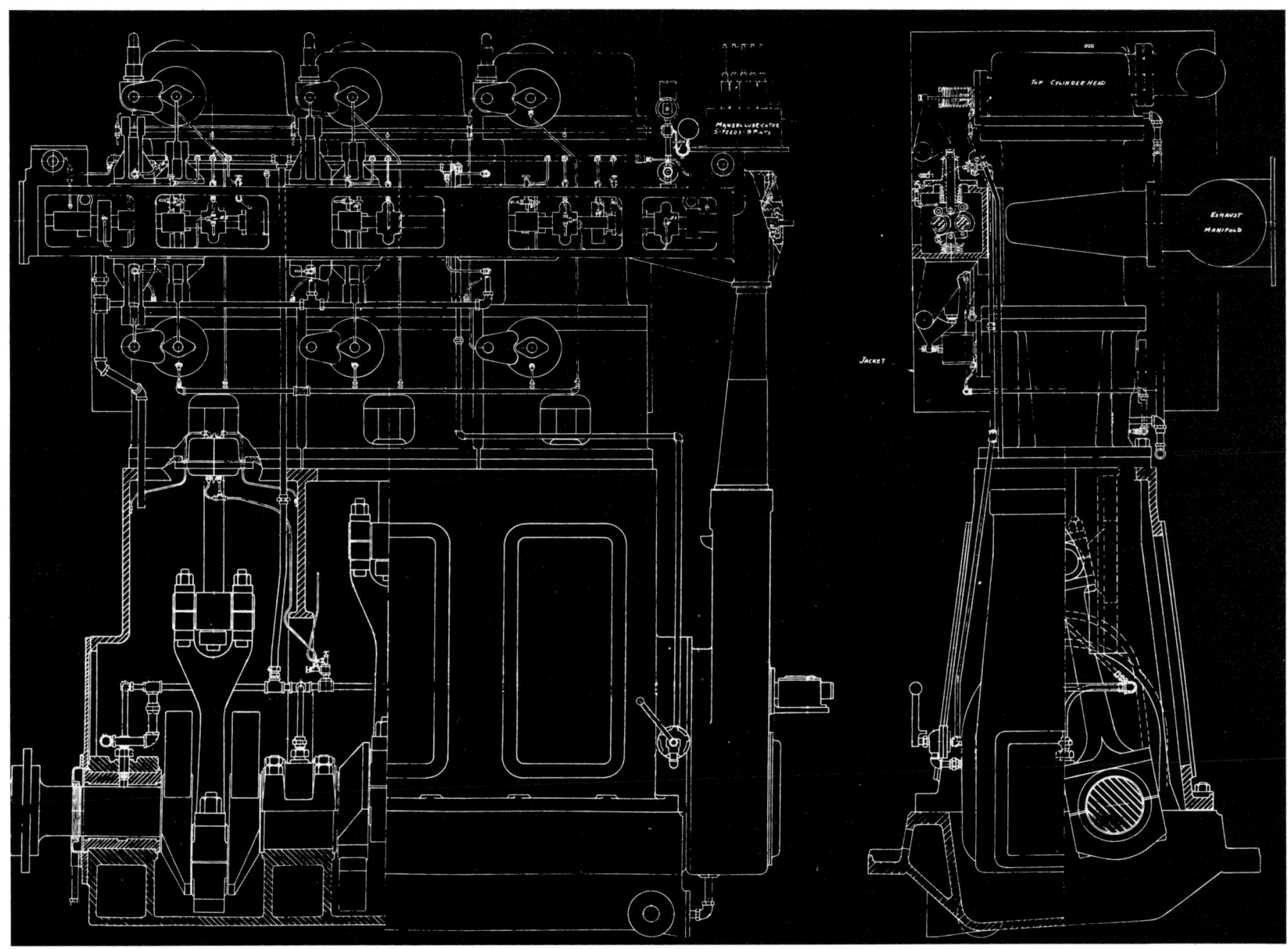

95. Scotian's *Skinner "Unaflow"* engine.

1949, at 8:45 a.m. A nurse among the passengers assisted, and the boat was delayed in the Halifax dock until an ambulance came to remove the mother and new baby. Alas, the intrepid pair was not identified by name in either log book or newspaper.

An associate of one of the authors claims he was born on a Dartmouth ferry, but is reticent when queried about the clinical details. We can only conclude he has a bad memory.

At the half century, 1950, Claude H. Morris, a Dartmouth druggist, became mayor. His drugstore was, for many years, located in the building which had once been John Skerry's Ferry Inn. As mayor, and later as commissioner, Morris served the ferry for eight years. During his mayoralty significant changes took place, the greatest of which was the beginning of construction of the first harbour bridge.

Three boats operated efficiently during Mayor Morris' term. One of his commissioners, Mike Driscoll suggested a study into the effect the bridge would have on traffic, and the types of ferries that would be needed. His fellow commissioners perversely refused to consider this idea.

New commissioners during Mayor Morris' term of office were David T. Marsh, Harry N. Wrathall, Gilbert Sprague, James L. Harrison, C. W. Merson, W. H. Chisholm, Grafton Carter and Ralph A. Logan.

At the January 23, 1951 meeting, Superintendent C. H. MacDonald's report contained the following statistics:

Year	Vehicles Carried	Passengers Carried	Vehicle Revenue	Passenger Revenue
1939	329,090	2,457,558	91,814.15	117,155.90
1944	517,349	6,029,308	160,219.10	329,960.17
1945	476,572	5,629,809	142,260.00	304,426.38
1946	504,272	4,894,354	151,642.60	257,989.17
1947	536,092	4,355,684	175,193.59	285,137.74
1948	526,897	4,212,905	200,964.63	262,098.86
1949	513,863	4,476,101	227,142.40	291,791.90
1950	561,076	4,526,519	242,039.10	291,629.34

It is interesting to note that 1944 was clearly the peak year

96. *Mayor A. C. Pettipas in wheelhouse with crew: Capt. C. H. MacDonald, Mate Joseph Murphy and Deckhand Albert Findlay, ca. 1938.*

for passengers, a year when Halifax and Dartmouth were thronged with wartime residents.

In January 1952, J. P. Martin, later to be recognized as Dartmouth's official historian, came to a ferry commission meeting to ask that recognition be given to the 200th anniversary of the ferry crossing, its bicentennial year. Martin gave an excellent paper to the Nova Scotia Historical Society on the Halifax-Dartmouth ferry service to mark the occasion.

Vincent Massey, the first native-born Governor General of Canada, visited Dartmouth and Halifax in August of that bicentennial year. He arrived at Shearwater airport and was taken by the **Scotian,** Captain Joseph Murphy, to Halifax.

He paid an official visit to Dartmouth the following day, also crossing on board the **Scotian,** suitably decorated for both occasions with flags and bunting.

Early in February 1954, the Superintendent wrote the last entry in his log book. After a short illness, he died on February 17, in his 60th year. Captain MacDonald had served in World War I on minesweepers, before joining the ferry service in 1919 as a mate. During World War II he was called back to naval duty, returning as Superintendent of the ferry commission in 1945. One of his most outstanding contributions in his later years was his close involvement with the modernization of the docks and ferry property.

Later that year, Dartmouth had a brief visit from the Duchess of Kent and her daughter, Princess Alexandra. Unlike Governor General Massey, they were driven from Shearwater directly around Bedford Basin, and left the following day by train from Halifax. Thus the ferry was not involved in their visit. It is presumed that they were shown the site of the 18th century Duke of Kent's Lodge and the Rotunda at Rockingham, this being the reason for the motor drive around the Basin.

In the same month, September 1954, Hurricane Edna arrived on Nova Scotia's shores with great force. For the first time in years ferry service was temporarily suspended. The **Scotian** was removed from service at 6 p.m. The **Halifax** struggled on alone, but at 8 p.m. suffered a mechanical failure. She managed to get halfway on to the Dartmouth Marine Slip, and there passengers had to wait for three hours before they could be removed (the Dartmouth Marine Slip faces roughly southwest and thus is a lee shore for the prevailing winds of the fall gales). One of the passengers was the newly appointed Superintendent on the ferry commission, Captain Robert Armstrong, an Englishman, and not previously connected with the ferries.

At 11 o'clock the passengers were disembarked, and at midnight the chartered buses took passengers from the Dartmouth terminal around the Basin to Halifax, and brought Dartmouth people back.

In November 1954, the most dreaded kind of ferry accident occurred—a collision resulting in loss of life. It happened at 7:52 a.m., November 8. Once again fog was very thick on the harbour. As the **Scotian** left the Halifax dock it was under the command of Captain Perry Thomas, a veteran with 11-year's experience as master. Captain Thomas was leaning out of an open wheelhouse window, while Mate E. A. Codner was at the wheel. Suddenly, close by the Furness Withy wharf, they came practically on top of another vessel, a 46-ft. R.C.N. yard craft, on its way from the Dockyard to Shearwater. There was no chance of avoiding the collision, and the yard craft was swamped when the big ferry hit it. Three people were killed and six injured.

The casualties were: Albert Webster, stores man at Shearwater; Pat Powers, crane operator; and Petty Officer Walter Neilson.

Among the survivors were: Sub-Lieut. T. A. Squire; Ldg. Seaman George MacAllister; John F. Payne, Master of the yard craft; and crewmen L. B. Clattenburg and B. F. Drysdale.

It was the first serious loss of life since the **Annex 2** disaster of 1890, all in all not a bad record. This particular accident, however, was a shock to the whole community. An inquiry was held under Captain C. L. Waterhouse, Superintendent of Pilots, in the Customs House. At the next ferry commission meeting, Grafton Carter and Albert Nichols moved a resolution of regret, and sympathy was extended to the families of those who had lost their lives.

Following the accident, the Captains and Mates Association called for improvements so the boats would be better equipped to meet such emergencies. The association recommended that ship-to-shore communication, search lights, boat hooks and rescue ladders be installed on each vessel.

It was a sad note on which to end 1954, the last year in which the ferry was the major route across the harbour. The Angus L. Macdonald bridge was rapidly approaching completion, and although most commuters looked forward with eagerness to the novelty of being able to drive across the harbour on the new spans, ferry officials were acutely aware that big changes lay ahead for the 200-year old ferry service.

XXX.

The End of the Dartmouth Ferry Commission

Another major turning point in ferry history occurred in 1955. As the time of the opening of the new bridge drew closer, speculation on the effect it would have on the ferry operations was a common topic of conversation. Since 1890 the ferry commission had been a vital component in the life of Dartmouth, and it was difficult to imagine that it would suddenly become a much less significant part of the lives of Dartmouthians. But it did.

The name chosen for the bridge was an obvious one. The popular Liberal Premier of Nova Scotia, Angus L. Macdonald, one of the leading advocates of a harbour bridge, died shortly before it was completed. The opening ceremonies were held on the Dartmouth side on April 2, 1955, and were attended by dignitaries from all levels of government, as well as hundreds of private citizens. Ironically, for the last time, an extra ferry boat was put on the service to accommodate vehicular traffic travelling to

97.   Tickets, 1930s to 1950s.

Dartmouth to take part in the ceremonial procession across the bridge. What was a joyous parade for the bridge was a funeral procession for the car ferries.

From that day on, both vehicular and pedestrian traffic on the ferries dropped dramatically, as these figures indicate:

	Pedestrians	Vehicles
Monday, March 28, 1955	9610	1830
Monday, April 4, 1955	8000	727
Friday, April 8, 1955	3268	224

Immediately, the ferry commission took strong measures to cut its losses. A committee of Mayor Morris and commissioners Paterson and Nichols was formed to look into staff reductions, and arranged a meeting with the Agent of the International Union of Marine and Shipbuilding Workers of Canada as well as with individual employees. Superintendent Captain Robert Armstrong said that any crew reductions would be done according to seniority. In the meantime, one janitor, the Ferry Hill traffic constables, and a few labourers and painters were given notice. It must have been a devastating experience for ferry employees, especially the older ones, to witness the collapse of the once thriving car ferry system.

Two ex-employees died that year, and so were spared the sad demise witnessed by their fellow employees. Assistant Superintendent Robert T. Lynch, who had retired due to ill health about three years before, died in June. Captain Abraham Young, with the service for 30 years, first as a captain, and later as a ticket taker, died in November.

Ex-Mayor and ferry commission chairman A. C. Pettipas prepared a long article for a newspaper urging citizens to keep an optimistic outlook about the ferries. He quoted past statistics, but his report gave the impression that he, along with many others, were refusing to face facts, and could not visualize the end of the once powerful commission. Sample payroll figures from his report are interesting and give some idea of the importance of the commission as an employer in Dartmouth, given the size of the community on the dates shown and the decline in the value of dollars over the period:

Payroll Of The Dartmouth Ferry Commission

1930	$ 81,602.94
1940	$ 99,800.28
1945	$196,276.66

Laurie W. Granfield, who had been running the ferry newsstand in Halifax for a number of years, was at this time president of the Dartmouth Chamber of Commerce. To show his faith in the ferries' future, he took over the Dartmouth ferry newsstand as well, saying that ferries could and must pay their way.

Despite Pettipas' and Granfield's faith, losses mounted, and the situation grew more desperate each day. Superintendent Armstrong apparently did not share their optimism since he handed his resignation to the commission on May 12, to become effective on June 30, 1955. He gave no reason for his resignation to the press, at the time, but soon after joined Northumberland Ferries Ltd.

Captain Dalton S. Randall was appointed Acting Superintendent in June 1955, and his appointment was confirmed the following February.

Commissioners clutched at any straws that might improve the situation, and when two of the boats were engaged for excursions at $80 an hour it was suggested that this was one way the boats could be made a paying proposition again. However, there was not a continuing demand and the short summer season in Nova Scotia is one of the risks in the tourist or excursion business, thus this hope was short-lived.

Consequently, brokers all over North America were sent photos and plans of the car ferries, and discussion turned to pedestrian-only boats. Mr. Rowland of Milne, Gilmore and German, the Montreal naval architectural firm with the ever-changing name, came to a commission meeting to talk about designs for such ferries—such as the ones used between Ogdensburg, N.Y., and Prescott, Ont. Ferry commissioners were almost persuaded that these pedestrian ferries were the only alternative to a complete shutdown of the system.

Before a final decision was made, a firm of consulting

engineers, with a specialty in traffic studies, was retained to make a potential pedestrian-use survey. The firm was DeLeuw Cather of Chicago and Toronto, with Herbert Baker as its representative.

By the middle of June, the ferry commission was operating "in the red." It was estimated that 76 per cent of the vehicular and 45 per cent of passenger revenue had been lost. A newspaper reported that ratepayers were of three opinions:

1. The ferries should be given up entirely.
2. The ferries should be maintained at any cost.
3. The majority did not care what happened to the ferries.

The final decision was made at the August 9, 1955, ferry commission meeting. It was moved by commissioner Gordon Waterfield, and seconded by commissioner Ralph Ferguson, that the ferry commission convert to an all-pedestrian service, and that purchase of two small ferry boats be approved by the Town Council and that legislation be sought to borrow a maximum of $100,000 if needed, to convert to the new service.

In June the **Scotian** was laid off the service, since the remaining boats were more than adequate to keep it operating. Although she was widely advertised, there were few inquiries from potential buyers. This, according to commissioner John Paterson, was due to the fact that most ferries were diesel at this time, and the steam ferries were outdated. Reluctantly, the commission accepted an offer from Black Ball Ferries of Vancouver for $50,000, a far cry from the $430,000 the commission had paid for her in 1946. Commissioners rationalized that sometimes it was necessary to take such a loss to avoid the even greater loss that would be entailed in advertising and rental of docking facilities while hoping for a more advantageous offer.

On October 18, 1955, the **Scotian** went to the Dartmouth Shipyard to be prepared for the long voyage down the Atlantic Coast, through the Panama Canal, and up the Pacific Coast to Vancouver. The preparations were estimated to cost between $12,000 and $14,000. Unlike the Scottish ferries, **Chebucto** and **Halifax,** the **Scotian** did not intend to undertake her lengthy journey under her own steam. She was to be towed by a Panamanian registered tug, **Grenadier.** Four men were on board the **Scotian,** Captain Frank Shaw, Engineer Roland Gaudet, Deckhand Robert Williams and Cook Buddy Purcell. Well-stocked with food, and equipped with two-way radios, **Scotian** and her tug left Halifax Harbour on December 22, but only got as far as Shelburne where they tied up for three weeks, waiting for better weather. The Captain of the **Grenadier** was Dartmouthian Sidney Chapman. He had a crew of 22, most of whom were Jamaicans. His engineer was Frank Greene, and chief officer was Sid Evans.

When they left, they hoped to have the **Scotian** in Vancouver in 40-55 days, but because of the storms in the Atlantic end of the trip, it took 103 days. Tugs were changed at Panama, and the **Superior Straits** took over the tow from there. Record time was made on the passage from Panama to Vancouver, 22 days. After cosmetic work at Burrard Drydock, the **Scotian** was ready to go to work again, but under another name, **Smokwa.**

Later again **Smokwa** was sold to J. H. Todd and Sons Ltd., and used as a floating fishing camp either at Rivers Inlet or on the west coast of Vancouver Island.

Tenders for the new ferries were opened at the end of October. The commissioners were shocked at the prices quoted, all from Maritime shipyards. They had expected prices in the vicinity of $125,000 each, but the tenders came in around $200,000. In dismay, the commission sought guidance from the Town Council.

The editor of the Dartmouth "Free Press" was critical of the secret "in committee" meetings of the ferry commission, not an original point-of-view among editors. "Let's have open discussion and public hearings where leading citizens with some know-how can express their views," trumpeted editor Kelly Morton.

About this time, two novel propositions were put forth by an American company, Sunrise Ferries Inc., of New York. One scheme was to lease and operate three diesel passenger ferries to the commission, using existing termini and facilities, with the cost of modifications to be borne by the

FERRY TO HALIFAX

98. *(top)* Halifax II, *1969.* 99. *(right) Launching of pedestrian ferry, Lunenburg, 1956.*

commission. Sunrise Ferries forecast a gross income of $180,000 a year, with $20,000 in rental fees going to the commission.

The second scheme was for the commission to lease the three Sunrise Ferries for ten years with an option to buy at the end of that time for $79,000. Under this plan the commission would pay heavily for rental, and still have all the headaches of the operation of the boats.

Both these propositions were seriously considered, but finally, taking into account the 25 per cent duty on American-built boats, the commission decided against the Sunrise Ferries Inc. proposals.

The commission and Town Council then considered a third

alternative, that of having the new ferries built of wood rather than steel. Wood had been definitely out of favour after the fire which destroyed the **Governor Cornwallis** in 1944. Now, in spite of the many prophets of doom who warned against this decision, a contract to build two small passenger ferries was awarded to Smith and Rhuland, of Lunenburg. The contract was signed on December 30, 1955, with Mayor Morris and secretary Percy A. Wallace representing the commission.

Local boatbuilder Hugh D. Weagle had been contacted with respect to these ferries, but was not interested at that particular time, because he had several other contracts under way in his yard.

The plans for the steel ferries had been drawn up by Milne, Gilmore and German. The boats now to be constructed would use only part of those plans as "a basis for the engine room, and mechanical equipment to be used or installed in the wooden hull." The amended drawings and specifications for the wooden boats had been the work of W. J. Roue. Engines for the boats were to be Cummins diesels. The contract price for each boat was $142,500.

One final move in that traumatic year of 1955 was to strike new commutation rates, which were to come into effect on January 1. There were to be no more monthly books of tickets for $2.50 (50 tickets); instead, 25 tickets which could be used any time by any person could be purchased for the same price. This was another way of saying that passage was ten cents for adults, either in coin or by ticket. Children could still cross for five cents.

The new commission met on January 9, 1956, under a new chairman, Mayor I. W. Akerley. Like his predecessor, he took firm hold of the difficult situation and announced plans for further economies.

Turnstiles were ordered, and ticket collectors told that their services would not be required after April 30.

The turnstiles were installed in both terminals, two for adults and one for children. An employee was retained at each terminal just to provide change. Tickets became a thing of the past, but the commission offered to redeem all outstanding tickets up until May 31. Commission-owned

bonds to the amount of $83,500 were sold in order that initial payments could be made on the new boats. There would be no grant to the Natal Day Committee for the first time in many years, nor would boats be available for excursions.

Superintendent Randall and Chief Engineer Hare were appointed to supervise the construction of the new boats. There were many interested "inspectors" as the little craft neared completion, and curious Dartmouthians made the pleasant drive to Lunenburg to observe their progress. Commissioner John Paterson reported that the new boats exceeded their specifications in workmanship and the materials used in their construction.

On July 24 and July 27, 1956, the two boats were launched, first the **Dartmouth Ii**, at which ceremony Archdeacon Ryder of Dartmouth asked the blessing. Mrs. I. W. Akerley christened her and Premier Henry Hicks spoke at the ceremony. Because **Halifax II** was further up the same ways, the second launching was reported to be more spectacular. Mrs. Dalton Randall christened the little ship, and Rev. G. B. Murphy asked the blessing.

There was not total agreement in regard to the dimensions of these 1956 ferries. Herewith are several versions and their sources:

	Mail-Star July 28	Milne, Gilmore & German Spec'ns.	Roue Spec'ns.
Length	82 feet	66 feet	75 feet
Beam	36 feet	36 feet	35 feet
Depth hold	9 feet	9 feet 4 inches	6 feet 6 inches
Engines	262 H.P.	260 H.P.	260 H.P.

The hulls of the boats were of American white oak, and interior finishing was done with marine plywood, with rubber tile decks, popular in all construction at that time. Heating of the cabins was by forced hot air oil furnaces.

After dockside and sea trials, the new ferries, referred to as "rubber ducks" by one writer, arrived at their Dartmouth docks, and were once more blessed at the inauguration ceremony held on August 31, 1956. The fireboat played streams of water high in the air behind them as Mayor

Akerley, Hon. Geoffrey Stevens, MLA, Dartmouth historian John P. Martin and Rev. W. Grant MacDonald officiated. The Pipe Band of the Somme Branch, Royal Canadian Legion added festive notes to the proceedings, and the 5th Dartmouth Boy Scout Troop assisted in the ceremony. Thousands inspected the little ferries and Robert Chambers noted the event in an astutely pertinent cartoon depicting the two bridge towers, leaning together and commenting about the perky little vessels.

Captain Levi Clark, on September 3, 1956, was the first man to take the **Dartmouth II** on regular service, but the honour was short-lived. She developed engine trouble after only four hours. Fortunately this was soon corrected, and the story of these new ferries did not repeat the sad histories of the **Governor Cornwallis** and the **Scotian.**

The design life of the **Dartmouth II** and **Halifax II** was 20 years. Now in 1979 they are still shuttling back and forth across the harbour.

Once the pedestrian ferries were established, and the minor problems which seem to accompany new machinery had been ironed out, the remaining car ferries were sold. The Scottish-built **Halifax** went to Dartmouth Scrapyard for $2,710 in October 1956. She reappeared the following May, through a newspaper photograph showing her being stripped down at Foundation Maritime wharf, where she was being converted into a barge for her new owners, Construction Equipment Company.

The **Dartmouth** was sold to the firm of Pawlick and Gough in July 1957, for $5,475. She was broken up for scrap at Pier 9.

Soon all evidence of the coal-fired steamers had disappeared. The coaling truck was sold for $275, and the rail siding with its ramp and unloading trestle was removed. Now that cars could no longer cross on the ferries, space was needed for parking near the terminal. Along with the railway siding, the removal of some of the smaller outbuildings provided additional space for vehicles.

John Paterson, Superintendent of the Dartmouth Shipyards, having served the commission for many years, retired in 1957. He was presented with a combination weather instrument inscribed "To John Paterson from the Town of Dartmouth," in appreciation of his outstanding service during the war years, and the critical changeover period between car and pedestrian ferries. Paterson volunteered to act in an advisory capacity in the future, and no doubt his knowledge and experience was frequently sought.

Newcomers to the commission in 1957 were Captain W. H. Crook, a harbour pilot, and Roland J. Thornhill.

In February, discussion took place as to which persons should have the privilege of free parking at the terminal. It was decided at the May meeting that only employees and commissioners would be permitted free parking, others would pay a fee. Even so, this was a great convenience to those commuters who worked in downtown Halifax, where parking, on a daily basis, was expensive. In addition this provided another source of revenue for the commission.

Because the passenger ferries were quicker to load and unload than the car ferries had been, at the recommendation of Herbert Baker of the consulting firm DeLeuw Cather, a ten-minute-each-way service was tried for a short period.

It put the whole system, boats and crews alike, under too much pressure, and was therefore a short-lived experiment.

An advertisement for radar had raised the interest of the commissioners, but Captain Fergus Cross of Gabriel Aero-Marine Instruments attended a "demonstration of this equipment in Montreal...and decided that it would be unwise to go ahead and fit this equipment due to it not being suitable for use in harbour work."

A $4,470 contract for revisions to both Halifax and Dartmouth docks was awarded to Walker and Hall at the July 1957 meeting. Probably this expenditure, a necessary one, discouraged the commissioners from delving further into radar possibilities.

A major change which was to lead to another turning point in this chronicle was proposed by Chairman Akerley in his annual report of January 1958. He suggested that the ferry commission be abolished and that the operation of the ferry system be vested in the Town of Dartmouth. The commissioners unanimously agreed with the concept, and

100. John Paterson,
O.B.E. 1887-1973.

101. Crew of tug Grenadier. Left to right: Engineer Evans, Captain S. Chapman and Mate Greene, 1955.

subsequently an Act was passed in the Legislature on May 3, 1958:

CHAPTER 92

An Act Relating to Dartmouth Ferry Commission

Be it enacted by the Governor and Assembly as follows:

1. In this Act "Commission" means the Dartmouth Ferry Commission and "Town" means the Town of Dartmouth.

2. (1) The Commission may enter into and consummate an agreement with the Town to transfer and convey all its assets to the Town in consideration of the Town assuming all the liabilities of the Commission.

(2) Upon such agreement being executed and all the assets of the Commission being conveyed to the Town the Commission shall be dissolved and cease to be a body politic and corporate as constituted under Chapter 83 of the Acts of 1890, an Act to provide for the establishment and operation of a Public Ferry between Dartmouth and Halifax, and amending Acts.

At the September meeting, the following resolution, proposed by Captain W. H. Crook, was passed:

RESOLVED that the Dartmouth Ferry Commission enter into and consummate an agreement with the Town of Dartmouth to transfer and convey all of its assets to the Town of Dartmouth in consideration of the Town assuming all the liabilities of the Commission;

FURTHER RESOLVED that when such agreement is executed and all the assets of the Dartmouth Ferry Commission have been conveyed to the Town of Dartmouth the Commission shall dissolve and cease to be a body politic and corporate as constituted under chapter 83 of the Acts of 1890, an Act to provide for the establishment and operation of a Public Ferry between Dartmouth and Halifax, and amending Acts;

FURTHER RESOLVED that the Chairman and Secretary be and they are hereby authorized to execute agreements and other documents on behalf of the Dartmouth Ferry Commission.

FURTHER RESOLVED that the said Transfer is to take place on December 31st., 1958.

Signed: W. H. Crook

I. W. Akerley   W. H. Chisholm
Chairman

102. Dartmouth II, *1976.*

Well, there it was. At the end of December the Dartmouth Ferry Commission was made to disappear by statutory fiat. What about Benjamin Russell? What about the "People's Ferry"? Their successors, the Dartmouth Ferry Commission served the people of the town for 68 years through many ups and downs. Russell, with his progressive and keen mind, would no doubt have been overjoyed to see a bridge at last, and would have been willing to accept as fact that the ferry now had a secondary role in cross-harbour transportation.

XXXI.
The North Ferries

The nomenclature "North Ferry" has meanings which differ, depending on the time frame in which it was used. In the early 19th century, "North Ferry" referred to the Upper or Skerry's Ferry at the foot of Ochterloney Street, as opposed to the South or Lower Ferry, which was Creighton's or Findlay's Ferry.

One hundred and fifty years later this may have been confusing. In the mid-19th century, the Steam Boat Company purchased a dock at the foot of Cornwallis Street in Halifax, and for a brief time the ferries alternated between the Market Slip dock and the more northerly one. At that time, then, the ferry which docked at Cornwallis Street, was called the North Ferry.

It was mentioned in an earlier chapter that in 1845 an unusual ferry ran on Sundays only at the Narrows—the **Archimedes,** the handcranked, propeller driven boat which mainly carried picnickers and excursionists from Halifax to the rural outskirts of northern Dartmouth.

At this time in its history, Dartmouth was something of a shipbuilding centre. Along its shoreline were small shipyards, and industries associated with shipbuilding established in their neighbourhoods—nail factories, barrel works, tanneries, grist mills and saw mills. The Stairs family established the Dartmouth Ropewalk Company, and built a substantial wharf to which hemp was delivered by lighters and taken thence by teams to the factory. This wharf was close by Albro's Nail Factory and was variously known as Stairs', Albro's or the Ropeworks wharf.

A little further north, Oland's Brewery was built in 1868, close by a Micmac Indian Reserve, at Turtle Grove. The brewery also had its own wharf and lighter service, at which its raw materials were landed and from which its famous brew was shipped.

For a time there were many large and beautiful estates in North Dartmouth—Falconer's, Dawson's and Sinclair's, to name a few. Joseph Howe lived at Fairfield for three years,

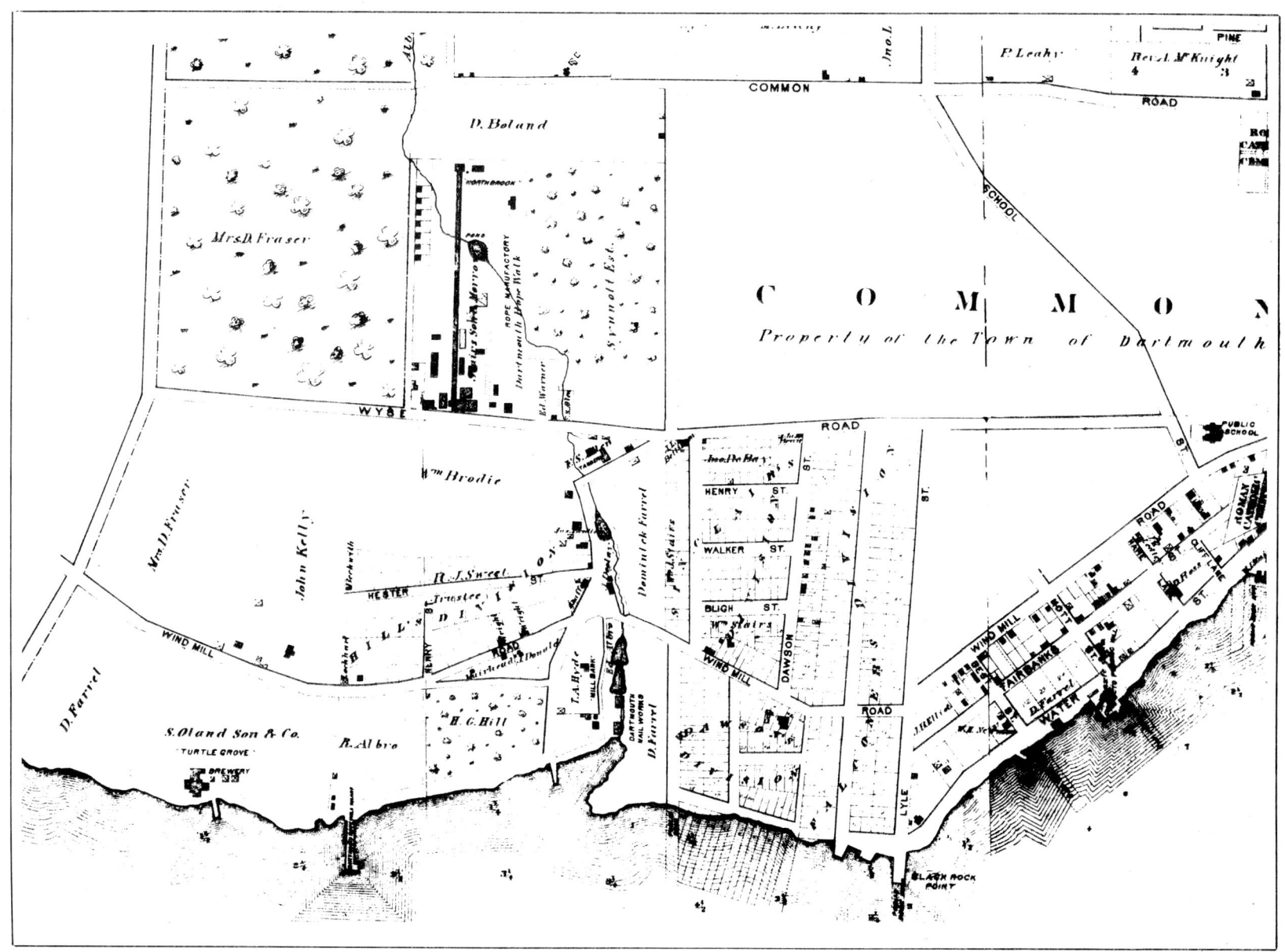

103. *Part plan, Town of Dartmouth, by Hopkins, 1878.*

near the present Naval Armament Depot. However, as factories were built in the area, the estates were sold and subdivided to provide housing for the factory workmen. The north end of Dartmouth became almost a separate little village, divided from the older town centre by the hill on which the Dartmouth Park, grazing lands, and cemeteries were located. A need was felt, and indeed expressed, for transportation across the harbour at the Narrows, and from time to time row boats provided such a service.

In 1907 citizens from both Dartmouth and Halifax, presented a petition to the Legislature which stated their case: "For many years, and at irregular periods, private parties have conducted a row boat ferry across the harbour, which has been altogether inadequate and uncertain, it not being maintained during the winter months, and but for a short time each day in the summer, and even then without any regular hours of sailing."

Accounts of these North Ferry companies, with one exception, are scanty, but some details have been uncovered and are recorded here, since they are very much a part of the history of the Halifax Harbour ferries:

1871:   William Heffler ran a ferry service between Stairs Wharf near the brewery across to Richmond. Fare was five cents.

1876-1885:   James Keans ran a ferry from Albro's Nail Factory Wharf to the foot of Young Street in Halifax from 6 a.m. until 9:30 p.m. In 1886 this ferry was taken over by others, as evidenced by the following: "James H. Keans has disposed of his interest in the North Ferry. The service has been taken over by the Lovett brothers who will operate three row boats this summer. The Halifax dock is at Young Street."

1881:   While Kean's ferry was running from Young Street to Albro's Wharf, the steamer **Siena** was on another route "between Smith's Wharf, foot of Round Church Hill and Dartmouth, calling at Young Street."

1897: Two ferries were operating. One service was run by a Mr. Evans who had two (row) boats, which carried workmen between their Dartmouth homes and the dry-dock. Evans' unnamed competitor ran a steamboat, the **Lenora,**

104.   *Capt. C. Wesley Dauphinee on* Dartmouth II, *1972.*

from the foot of Russell Street to the landing at the foot of Jamieson Street in Dartmouth. Trips were scheduled every 15 minutes.

Heffler (1871) was listed in McAlpine's City Directory of 1871-72 as a "ballastman", and as living on Windmill Road, Dartmouth.

Evans (1897) lived on Russell Street in Halifax, and was listed in the City Directory as "ballaster". The Oxford Dictionary defines both these terms as meaning a "seller of ballast material for ships."

The petition of 1907, applying for a North Ferry subsidy, was signed by 100 citizens from both sides of the harbour. Five of the signatures were made with "X"s, their owners apparently being unable to write. The subsidy requested was $100 a month, not only to accommodate them and ensure their transportation, but to encourage the "building up and development of the north end of Halifax and Dartmouth." Ronald Blakeney was recommended as a suitable operator. It is doubtful whether Blakeney ever did run a north end ferry, since he is listed in the City Directory of 1907-08 as an employee of the Halifax Brewery, and in

1912, as captain of the **Pastime.** It is possible that this was the name of a North Ferry.

1912:   The next ferry, mentioned in newspaper accounts, was run by the firm of Duggan and Son. William Duggan first lived on Barrington Street, but later moved across the harbour to Turtle Grove Cottage in Dartmouth. Many Haligonians used this ferry to cross to North Dartmouth camps, picnic grounds or swimming places. A pleasant family outing was to be had by making an afternoon tour, crossing the main ferry and returning on the North Ferry. The Duggan ferry could be summoned by a bell, rung by commuters at either terminal. Shortly before the Halifax Explosion in the same area served by the North End Ferry, the Duggans had added an engine-powered Lunenburg schooner to their fleet, but this, along with most of their property, was destroyed in the explosion.

Mrs. Charles Wheeler (Helen Duggan) said that at the time of the explosion, "Charles Duggan and **Gray Starling** was blown clear out of the harbour, and the boat, with Charlie in it, still alive but unconscious, ended up in a north Dartmouth field. It was some hours before Charlie Duggan recovered consciousness and lived to tell of his experiences

105.   *North Ferry fleet with* Gray Starling *on far right, ca. 1930.*

106.   *North Ferry No. 155, ca. 1930.*

107.   *Haldart, 1942.*

as a harbour ferryman."

1917: George Holmes of Tufts Cove was also operating his motor ferry on that day, December 6, 1917. The last thing he remembered was heading for the burning **Mont Blanc** to pick up passengers or crew from the ship. It was not until Christmas Day that he regained consciousness, finding himself on board the U. S. Hospital Ship **Old Colony,** and with not the slightest recollection about how he came to be there. He had been gathered up with other casualties and placed in a morgue, where an acquaintance, looking for her husband's body, was startled by a groan! Recognizing Holmes, she immediately advised the staff who quickly arranged for transfer and hospital care. In all, Holmes spent months in hospitals, and when he had recovered, seemed to have no desire to return to ferry work.

1921: J. H. Dauphinee took over the Duggan operation, or what was left of it, and ran his ferries with the help of his two sons, Wesley and Dewey, until 1956. The Dauphinees had a sizeable fleet—three 40-passenger boats, and one 90-passenger vessel. These boats provided quick, reliable transportation, and the Dauphinees were justifiably proud of their fine record, keeping up their service throughout World War II, the V-E Day riots, and the hurricane in September 1954, which forced the large car ferries to stop.

There are probably many people in the Halifax-Dartmouth area today, one-time commuters on the Dauphinee North Ferry, who will recall the sight and sound of one of the Dauphinees handcranking the Lister diesel, at the beginning of the trip to "the other side."

The terminals for the Dauphinee boats were at the foot of Grove Street in Dartmouth (a small reminder of "Turtle Grove") and the bottom of Russell Street in Halifax. There, a steep flight of wooden steps climbed between the fences of the Halifax Shipyards and the Naval Dockyard up to Barrington Street.

A coincidence, substantially abetted by the foggy conditions prevailing at the time, occurred in February 1949. On the day and hour in which the **Halifax** collided with the naval tug **Glenevis**, one of Dauphinee's boats, **Haldart**, collided with a Dockyard harbour craft. Captain J. H.

Dauphinee was knocked into the water, but was able to swim to the harbour craft and was taken to hospital, briefly, for examination along with three of his passengers. Fortunately no one was drowned or injured. According to a newspaper report, damage amounted to $2,000. Accidents on both routes were blamed on the extremely thick fog, and all naval yard craft were recalled until the fog had abated.

The North Ferry ceased operations, as did the larger car ferries of the ferry commission, with the opening of the Angus L. Macdonald Bridge in 1955. Later, Captain Dauphinee's son, Captain Wesley Dauphinee worked for the Dartmouth Ferry Commission, and was promoted to Superintendent in March 1960. He held this post until his retirement in August 1973. Another son, Captain Dewey Dauphinee, also worked for a short time with the ferry commission.

The Angus L. Macdonald Bridge contributed to substantial new industrial and residential growth in Dartmouth and reached its capacity sooner than the planners had anticipated. A second bridge at the narrows was opened in July 1970, and is now also carrying heavy cross-harbour traffic.

In spite of the two bridges, a brisk ferry service, not mentioned before, is carried on by naval yard craft which carry DND employees to their various places of employment on the waterfront. These ferries provide quick, free transportation for civil servants and military personnel, and reduce the need for vast parking lots in crowded government establishments.

Other north end residents of both cities now cross the harbour on either of the two bridges, by private automobile or public transit. But it is not, and cannot be, the same. Even the most blase ferry commuter, when pressed, will admit that the 12-15 minute harbour crossing, on the water, is not a bad way to begin and end the working day.

XXXII.
The Present Day

108. *Ferry tokens, 1960s and 1970s.*

The once powerful Dartmouth Ferry Commission had disappeared and the management of ferry affairs was taken over by a committee of the Town Council and the town administration. Dartmouth Ferry Committee (also "D.F.C.") meetings were now held in the Town Hall instead of the board room in the ferry building. The old Mechanics Institute, which had served as a Town Hall for almost a century, had been torn down, and a new Town Hall built on the crest of Windmill Road, overlooking Halifax Harbour, was built in 1957.

Dartmouth was experiencing substantial population and industrial growth. People much preferred to travel in private automobiles from their homes, over a bridge, and directly to their destinations. Not only was this more convenient but it was frequently cheaper. A regional transit system has been a long time in coming to the area, and lack of integration between buses on the Dartmouth side (which until very

197

109.   Dartmouth II, *on the rocks, 1977.*

recently were privately owned and operated) the ferries and Halifax Transit, has been a serious drawback to users of all three systems in the downtown areas.

During 1958 the ferry deficit was $14,000. Economy measures were continually being sought, and one resulted in the resignation of Superintendent Randall, early in 1959. He had been asked to take a shift on the boats in addition to his administrative duties, and found this arrangement a bit heavy. Captain Heather was appointed to succeed him in February 1959, but unfortunately died a year later. In the meantime Percy Wallace was appointed office manager, and he relieved the superintendent of many administrative duties.

One of the ferry captains at the time of Captain Heather's death was the former North Ferry operator, C. Wesley Dauphinee. He was a logical candidate to fill the vacancy and was appointed superintendent in March 1960. His brother Dewey Dauphinee, was working on the boats as

captain also, but at this time it was decided to reduce the number of crews from five to four, Captain Dewey Dauphinee being low on the seniority totem pole was in the fifth crew.

The demise of the ferry commission was a relatively small change compared to the outcome of a later proposal by Mayor I. W. Akerley. Dartmouth and environs were booming as a partial result of the new bridge and the postwar economy. Mayor Akerley felt it would be advantageous, from many viewpoints, if the old town annexed its suburban areas and reincorporated as a city. The annexation involved an area some five times the size of the town's area at the time. This historic turning point took place in 1961. Once again a new administration building was necessary to house the ever-increasing departments of civic government. The present City Hall was built and occupied in 1967. The proposal contained in a letter to the editor of the "Atlantic Weekly," 1893, had been realized. "My idea had

198

been that the Town Hall should be nearer the ferry and all the clerical work of the town, (ferry and water works included) be done from there.''

Passengers on the ferry approaching Dartmouth are now confronted by Dartmouth's impressive City Hall as they near the dock.

Administrations at City Hall have changed since the ferry commission was abolished. Mayors after I. W. Akerley have been Joseph Zatzman, Roland Thornhill, Eileen Stubbs and Daniel Brownlow. None of these will ever be as strongly identified with ferry operations as were their predecessors from 1890 onwards. However, these more recent mayors will certainly carry with them strong and lasting impressions of the ferries and Dartmouth terminal, since the attractive office of Dartmouth's chief magistrate overlooks the terminal at close range. From this vantage point one can follow the small craft as they shuttle back and forth across the harbour.

For the most part, the little wooden ferries have plied steadily and unobtrusively on their service in the harbour, but there was one unfortunate exception. In thick fog, two days before Christmas in 1963, Captain Joseph Murphy, on the **Halifax II,** left the Dartmouth dock and carefully began to feel his way across the harbour. On his first trip that morning he had grazed the cable ship **Lord Kelvin** while about to enter the Halifax dock, so he was now being especially cautious. Suddenly and without warning the **Dartmouth II** loomed out of the fog, with Captain Lockie Carter at the wheel. Captain Murphy reversed his engine in vain, but the passengers had no warning when the two ferries crashed together, 300 feet from the Dartmouth dock. Three passengers were hurt, but did not require hospitalization. They were Gordon Lowe, Melvin Bateman and a Mr. MacDonald. The **Halifax II** fared worse than her passengers; with a gaping hole in her forward end, she had to be laid up in the north dock for repairs. The **Dartmouth II** suffered slight damage to the women's cabin but was repaired while she continued in service.

Once again the captains raised the question of radar installations. However it was not until 1972 that

110. (top) Dartmouth terminal, 1976.

111. (bottom) Halifax II, collision damage, 1963.

radio-telephones were fitted, and radar was finally obtained in 1973.

Superintendent Wesley Dauphinee retired on Natal Day in 1973. After having operated his small North Ferry through V-E Day riots and hurricanes, he had firm ideas on the sort of service a ferry system should give to the public. When the city authorities decided to economize still further and ceased ferry operations on Sundays and holidays, Captain Dauphinee became disenchanted with his role as superintendent.

Successor to Dauphinee is the youngest man ever to act as superintendent of the Dartmouth ferries. He is Captain John Robert Keddy, who took the job in 1973 at 29 years of age, after an exciting career on ocean-going ships. He had sailed on the Lunenburg-built replica of the famous **Bounty,** which was used for the film "Mutiny on the Bounty", made near Tahiti; he was a crew member of the **Bluenose II,** a replica of the famed fishing schooner; he also served on an ocean-going tug. Captain Keddy's youth and enthusiasm have been assets in his demanding position as Captain-Superintendent of the Dartmouth ferries. Serving with him are four crews of three men each. An extra crew is hired in the summer, when in addition to extra tourist traffic, vacation arrangements must be looked after. A janitor and part-time mechanic (seconded from the City Works Department when required), today make up the total complement of the once much larger and more complex operation.

One veteran captain retired at the end of August 1978. Captain Cyril Urquhart had been with the service for 38 years, and served on the large car ferries during the busy days of World War II. Mayor Daniel Brownlow presented Captain Urquhart with cuff links and a cheque, and thanked him on behalf of all ferry travellers.

In the summer of 1976, the Angus L. Macdonald bridge was closed for repairs and ferry traffic increased substantially as a result. Many newer citizens enjoyed the novelty of ferry commuting, and when the novelty was gone, such was the enthusiasm for this mode of travel that they did not return to the bridge when it reopened. About the same time, the price of gasoline began to escalate rapidly. This enhanced the appeal of the ferries. Commuters either walked to the ferry and crossed to Halifax without making use of their cars at all, or rented ferry parking spaces on the Dartmouth side. In 1977, about 60,000 more passenger trips were recorded than in 1976, and officials hope that this may indicate a trend which will become even more pronounced when the harbour ferry crossing is fully integrated with Dartmouth and Halifax transit systems.

The **Dartmouth II** had a design life of 20 years which was reached in 1976. A bit of excitement in January 1977 demonstrated that at least one of the little boats was still able to take a beating and come through unscathed. On a very cold and windy January 29 Saturday morning, **Dartmouth II** broke away from her north dock berth and was blown up the harbour shoreline until she came aground just north of the foot of Ochterloney Street. This was likely quite close to the same place where previous ferries (such as Skerry's overloaded rowboat of 1831 with its drunken operator, Costley) had met the same fate. The 1977 grounding occurred on a bitter day during which the wind shifted from a very strong southerly around to north-westerly. **Dartmouth II's** lines were snapped from the force of the southerly wind on the ship's side and she was carried in a northerly direction. It must have been just moments later that the wind shifted to the northwest and pushed her onto the rocky shore and held her there. In short order, lines were got off to the Eastern Canada Towing tug **Point Valiant,** who maintained a cautious tension until the flood tide eventually enabled **Dartmouth II** to be towed off. She was drydocked for a hull inspection, presumably a requirement of their underwriters, and was found undamaged. **Dartmouth II** was soon back on her cross-harbour shuttle, carrying her customary complement of passengers.

Meanwhile, developments had been taking place which would lead to the eventual retirement and replacement of **Dartmouth II** and **Halifax II.**

XXXIII.
Of Things to Come

In May 1976, the Waterfront Development Corporation was founded. It is a provincial Crown corporation, funded by the federal Department of Regional Economic Expansion (DREE) and the provincial Department of Development. The once thriving downtown areas of both Dartmouth and Halifax have grown shabby and neglected with the advent of shopping centres and suburban growth. The purpose of the Waterfront Development Corporation is to restore and revitalize the waterfront areas commercially, aesthetically and to add recreational elements.

Dartmouth's components of the restoration will be two new passenger ferries, new docking facilities and terminal buildings, a marina, and waterfront parks and walks. In January 1977, the Dartmouth City Council approved the design and construction of all these facilities at a projected cost of more than $5.6 million.

The parks and walks were almost completed in the summer of 1978, and citizens and tourists alike were pleased to have new access to our historic waterfront, enhanced by amenities such as benches, attractive landscaping and, at night, pleasantly subdued lighting.

The ferries are to be a side-loading type, and once again it is hoped to have a ten-minute service. Veteran captains are sceptical about this. One pointed out, for example, the case where several naval ships may be crossing the ferry lane, and the ferry may be requested to stand off until they have passed. This would add three or four minutes to the ten. Another delay factor is the turnstile, and the human element involved. The same captain feels that the only way to eliminate this problem is to make the ferries free. He also says that the present system is the best for the harbour and its prevailing winds—double-ended boats, **end** loaded. The docks are protected from drift ice in their present configuration, at least more so than a side-loading dock would be.

An ex-superintendent explained how ferries between

112. *Captain Lockie Carter, 1979.*   113. *Captain Almont Baltzer, 1979.*   114. *Supt. Captain J. Robert Keddy, 1979.*

Vancouver and North Vancouver are side-loading, but they tie up between two docks. While passengers are disembarking on one side, the other side is opened for those who are boarding, thus there is a more or less continuous flow of passengers on and off at the same time.

Explaining how the loading operation will be expedited in the proposed system here, Dartmouth City Planner Donald Bayer says that neither the present Halifax nor Dartmouth terminal buildings could be used in the new passenger traffic system. "The new terminals will make it more like an airport...You pay your fare first and then go to a holding area until the ferry arrives. It helps the turnaround time and makes the ferry a more efficient way to travel." This statement may quell some of the fears expressed by ferry personnel regarding loading procedures.

A contract to build the new ferries was awarded in December 1977, to Ferguson Industries Limited of Pictou, N.S., the firm that built the **Scotian.** Its tender for the two

boats was $2,112,566. The only other bidder was Breton Industrial and Marine of Port Hawkesbury, N.S. which tendered a price of $2,397,700.

The two boats were launched less than a year after the signing of the contract, in October and November of 1978, and the fitting out was done during the winter months of 1979. The official christening was scheduled for the early summer.

Designed by Evans, Yeatman and Endal (Associates) Limited, the boats will carry 400 passengers, and the side-loading ramp will be covered into the terminal buildings, protecting passengers from the elements. The terminals were designed by Sperry Associates Limited. The Dartmouth terminal will have three floors—the top one to be used by the city for offices, the second floor to be leased, perhaps as a restaurant. From the third floor a covered ramp will lead over the railway tracks to the bus terminal, now on the site of Dominick Farrell's store (later Simmond's

115. *One of the new ferries by W. G. Scott, Marine Artist and Ship Illustrator.*

Hardware). The Halifax terminal will be two stories and will have a covered passage into the new law courts building.

Considerable opposition to the planned demolition of the old terminal buildings was expressed at public meetings by historical and preservation-minded groups. However, since both were structurally unsound, and not truly "old" (Dartmouth, 1906; Halifax, 1913), the decision was made to tear them down.

A great deal of nostalgia will be felt when they disappear from their respective locations, but in fact it would require an exorbitant amount to make them sound, attractive and serviceable. The dirt and odours accumulated through past decades make the interiors most unappealing, while storm driven high tides have on several occasions flooded the interior of the Halifax terminal.

The contract for the second phase of the new operation—the ferry docks, and foundations of the terminals —was awarded in June 1978 to Robert McAlpine Limited for $2.9 million. Other firms bidding were Lundrigans Limited; McNamara Marine Limited; Beaver Maritime

Limited; Woodlawn Construction Limited; D. C. Menchions Construction Limited; Dineen Construction limited; and R. A. Douglas.

Associated with the McAlpine firm is Beasy Nicoll Engineering Limited, Halifax. Halifax Metal Workers, a steel fabrication company, is building the two large landing pontoons for the docks. These are being built on the north Dartmouth side of the harbour in a unique way. A dam was constructed across the mouth of a small cove, and the pontoons are being manufactured in the drained area formed by the dam. When the pontoons are finished the dam will be bulldozed and water reentering the cove will float the pontoons, which will then be towed to the ferry terminals.

The new ferries and their terminals will some day evoke feelings of nostalgia in future generations. Perhaps then others may be inclined to add more chapters to this story of the harbour crossing.

As old documents and newspapers were researched, the importance of the ferry to generations of Dartmouthians became increasingly clear. It was a livelihood, a means of transportation, and to many the ferries themselves were old friends. A great many of today's Dartmouthians had anecdotes or "ferry tales" to relate. Perhaps these will be collected in another volume.

For almost two and a quarter centuries the ferries have been woven into the fabric of Dartmouth lives. Courting couples enjoyed the 15-minute interlude, tense businessmen sorted out problems while they walked the decks, and school children finished up last minute homework.

There are many stories of the embarrassed commuter who, engrossed in conversation with a fellow passenger, walked off with him, up George Street, only to recall that he had **driven** onto the boat. On turning back to the ferry he observed a perspiring crew pushing his car off the boat. Others have been known to have become so deeply engrossed in conversation that they were completely unaware that the boat had docked, and when conversation lagged they discovered that the ferry on which they were still passengers was on its return journey.

During the two wars, wives, sweethearts and sisters sometimes travelled back and forth on the upper deck while a convoy was leaving the harbour, hoping for a last glimpse of their loved ones.

Children, canvassing for good causes, such as Boy Scout apple day, vied for the ferry for their territory, since it was usually one of the most rewarding in terms of contributions and fun. On a rough day, however, the canvassers would sometimes feel a bit queasy after 20 or 30 trips.

One Halifax lady recalls a picnic on the ferry. She was the guest of a family which made this an annual affair, which even included the spreading of a tablecloth on the upper deck.

Various tales are told of people rushing to catch the ferry, including some who in desperation jumped across the ever-widening gap as a boat was leaving the dock. In a variation of this, one gentleman, to his chagrin, leaped across this gap in his haste to get to Halifax, only to find that the boat was coming in!

—and there are many other such stories yet to be retold.

Since the late 1920s we have had a close and continuous association with these ferries. In recent years we have been able to watch them from our dining room window, as they shuttle back and forth. Having assembled the elements of this story, it emerges that the whole is perhaps a view from the harbour of the growth of its shores, and in spite of being twice bridged, it seems likely that the ferries of Halifax Harbour have a future as well as a history.

The Ferries -An Outline

	SHERBROOKE	SIR C. OGLE	BOXER	MICMAC
OFFICIAL NUMBER		75841		75842
BUILT (LAUNCHED)	Dartmouth (Sept. 1816)	Alexander Lyle, Dartmouth, N.S. (Jan. 1830) Reg'd. 1878	Alexander Lyle, Dartmouth, N.S. (Feb.1838)	Alexander Lyle, Dartmouth, N.S. (June 1844) Reg'd 1878
PROPULSION TYPE N.H.P. BUILDER	Centre paddle, 8 Horses	Side paddlewheels, Side-lever engine 30" Diam. 3' stroke 30. Edward Bury, Liverpool	Side paddlewheels, Side-lever engine 28" Diam. 3' stroke 25. Rigby, North Wales, 1835	Side paddlewheels, Side-lever engine, 35" Diam. 3' stroke 40, Thomas Wingate, Glasgow, 1844
DIMENSIONS	Keel—59' Breadth—10' (one hull) Depth hold—4'-5"	L.O.A.—98' Breadth—19'-5" Depth hold—9'-6"		L.O.A.—99' Breadth—21' Depth hold—9'
DISPLACEMENT (N.R.T.)		(76.9)		(102.3)
DISPOSITION (Length of Service)	Sold at auction, 85 pounds, 1830 (14 years)	Sold, $200, 1894 (64 years)	Sold less engine, 1864, re-sold, re-christened HOPE, burned at McKay wharf 1872 (26 years)	Scrapped 1901, hull burned near Imperial Oil refinery (57 years)

	CHEBUCTO[1]	DARTMOUTH [Old Veteran]	ARCADIA	ANNEX 2 [Halifax]
OFFICIAL NUMBER	75843	90889	85555	96794
BUILT (LAUNCHED)	Cameron, Dartmouth, N.S. (January 1865) Reg'd 1878	Burrell Johnson Iron Co., Ltd. Yarmouth, N.S. (June 1888)	Harry G. Poole, Arcadia, Yarmouth Co. (April 1884) Purchased 1890	William H. Baldwin, New Baltimore, N.Y., 1878. Purchased by D.F.C. in 1890.
PROPULSION TYPE N.H.P. BUILDER	Side paddlewheels, Engine ex BOXER I	Side paddlewheels, compound, surface condensing, direct inclined, 22" & 42" x 60", 75, Burrell-Johnson, Yarmouth, N.S.	Screw propellor, compound, surface condensing, 18" & 19" x 14", 30. Burrell-Johnson, Yarmouth, N.S.	Side paddlewheels, Beam engine, 36" x 9', 43, McEntee & Dillon, Roundout, N.Y. (Ex STATES RIGHTS—1858)
DIMENSIONS	L.O.A.—86' Breadth—20' Depth hold—9'	L.O.A.—136" Breadth—28' Depth hold—11'	L.O.A.—68' Breadth—16' Depth hold—6'-4"	L.O.A.—117' Breadth—38' Depth hold—10'
DISPLACEMENT (N.R.T.)	65.3	196	42	228 (169)
DISPOSITION (Length of Service)	Sold, 1892, $275 (27 years)	Scrapped, Dartmouth 1935 (47 years)	Sold, $3500, Feb. 1891 (one year)	Burned at Dartmouth Dock, arson suspect Dec. 1909. Sold to Charles Brister (19 years)

	CHEBUCTO [2]	HALIFAX	DARTMOUTH	GOVERNOR CORNWALLIS
OFFICIAL NUMBER	108683 (Glasgow) Re-registered Halifax, May 1906	129590 (Glasgow)	158089	174894
BUILT (LAUNCHED)	John Shearer & Son, Kelvinhaugh Slip, Glasgow, (1897)	Napier and Miller Ltd. Old Kirkpatrick (1911)	Davie Shipbuilding and Repair Co., Lauzon, Quebec. (1934)	Hugh Weagle, Dartmouth, N.S. (1941)
PROPULSION TYPE N.H.P. BUILDER	Fore and aft screw propellors, tandem compound inverted cylinders, 2—24'' 2—12'' x 18'' McKie & Baxter, Copeland Works, Govan	Fore and aft screw propellors, tandem compound inverted cylinders, 420 I.H.P. Aitchison, Blair Ltd. Clydebank 2—12'', 2—24'' x 18''	Fore and aft screw propellors, tandem compound inverted cylinders, 2—12'' 2—24'' x 18'' Aitchison Blair, Ltd. Clydebank	Fore and aft screw propellors, electric motor drive, 2—500 HP at 350 rpm, from 4—100 KW Caterpillar diesel generators
DIMENSIONS	L.O.A.—125' Breadth—48' Depth hold—12'	L.B.P.—125' Breadth—48' Depth hold—14'	L.B.P.—125' Beam—50' Depth hold—12'	L.B.P.—135' Beam—51' Depth hold—10.7
DISPLACEMENT (N.R.T.)	(184) (260)	(267)	(247)	485 (246)
DISPOSITION (Length of Service)	Sold to Loudee Steel Corp., Montreal, 1951, $5000. (52 years)	Sold to Dartmouth Scrapyard, 1956, $2710 (45 years)	Sold to Pawlick & Gough, 1957, $5,475 (23 years)	Destroyed by fire while in service, 1944. (3 years)

	SCOTIAN	DARTMOUTH II	HALIFAX II
OFFICIAL NUMBER	175498	189027	189028
BUILT (LAUNCHED)	Pictou Foundry & Machinery Co., Ltd. (1946)	Smith & Rhuland, Lunenburg, N.S. (1956)	Smith & Rhuland, Lunenburg, N.S. (1956)
PROPULSION TYPE N.H.P. BUILDER	Fore and aft screw propellors, Skinner "Unaflow" engine, 3 cylinders, 17'' x 14'' 550 I.H.P. at 205 rpm. Canadian Vickers Ltd., Montreal.	Fore and aft screw propellors, Cummins four-stroke diesels, 260 HP (each, of two)	Fore and aft screw propellors, Cummins four-stroke diesels, 260 HP (each, of two)
DIMENSIONS	L.B.P.—149.7' Beam—52' Depth hold—12.5'	L.B.P.—64.6' Beam—34.9' Depth hold—9.5'	L.B.P.—64.6' Beam—34.9' Depth hold—9.5'
DISPLACEMENT (N.R.T.)	(480)	(171)	(174)
DISPOSITION (Length of Service)	Sold to Black Ball Ferries, Vancouver, 1955, $50,000 (10 years)	Still in service, 1979. (23 years)	Still in service, 1979. (23 years)

Acknowledgements

We gratefully acknowledge the help and encouragement of many individuals and institutions in writing this history: the Dartmouth Museum Society and the staff of the Dartmouth Heritage Museum, the Public Archives of Nova Scotia, the Nova Scotia Museum, Dalhousie Archives, Public Archives of Canada, Dartmouth Regional Library, Provincial Library, Nova Scotia Legislative Library, Nova Scotia Technical College Library and National Library of Canada.

In the United States: James Wilson and Harry Cotterell, Jr. of the Steamship Historical Society of America; the Mariners Museum, Newport News, Virginia.

In the United Kingdom: B. W. Bathe and Mrs. Cole of the Science Museum, South Kensington; Christopher Terrell of the National Maritime Museum, Greenwich; M. Stammers, Merseyside County Museums, Liverpool; West Room staff, Public Records Office, London; Mr. Storrer of the Royal Scottish Museum, Edinburgh; J. P. Shaw, Glasgow Museums and Art Galleries; J. A. Fisher, Mitchell Library, Glasgow; William Lind, Secretary, Business Archives Council of Scotland; A. G. Veysey, Archivist, Clwyd County Council, Wales.

The following people gave us personal interviews which provided us with material unavailable elsewhere: Mrs. W. H. Chisholm, Dr. Helen Creighton, Capt. C. Wesley Dauphinee, Ronald Findlay, Mrs. George Holmes, Mrs. W. A. Johns, Supt. Capt. J. Robert Keddy, Mrs. C. H. MacDonald, C. H. Morris, W. Everett Moseley, Mrs. R. H. Murray, Miss Theresa O'Regan, Mrs. John Paterson, Miss Isobel Paterson, William Robar, Engr., Capt. Cyril Urquhart.

C. A. Moir, City Administrator, Dartmouth, arranged for access to ferry related archival material.

Our employers, the Dartmouth Board of School Commissioners and Canadian British Consultants Limited, provided various forms of assistance and encouragement.

Lastly, to Dr. Phyllis Blakeley, Associate Archivist, Public Archives of Nova Scotia, we are grateful for her assistance in reading our manuscript and providing us with helpful comments.

J.M.P. & L.J.P.
Dartmouth, N.S., 1979

References

CHAPTER 1
Page 1, line 26—Public Record Office, London, CO217.33 ff, Colonial Office Papers, Letter—Governor Cornwallis to Board of Trade, August 19, 1750; *p. 2, l. 7*—City of Dartmouth, *Urban Renewal Study*, Canadian British Engineering Consultants and Norman Pearson, Town and Country Planner, 1964; *p.2, l.22*—PANS, RGI, Vol. 209, July 14, 1749—October 26, 1753, Minutes of His Majesty's Council (Halifax). (February 3, 1752); *p.2 l.49*—Murdoch, Beamish, *A History of Nova Scotia*, Vol. II, p,219; *p.2 l.50*—Blakeley, Dr. Phyllis R., *The Story of Nova Scotia*. p. 73; *p.2 l.70*—Lawson, Mrs. William, *History of the Townships of Dartmouth, Preston and Lawrencetown*, p. 42; *p.2 l.75*—As line 22 above, (March 8, 1753); *p.4 l.21*—PANS, RGI, Vol. 210, January 1756; *p.5 l.12*—Akins, Dr. T. B., *History of Halifax City*, p. 88.

CHAPTER II
Page 8, line 28—PANS, RG5 Series S. Vol. 6, *Statues of Nova Scotia*, 1785 Cap. V.; *p.8 l.34*— Lawson, Mrs. William, *History of the Townships of Dartmouth, Preston and Lawrencetown*, p. 125.

CHAPTER III
Page 9, line 23—Croil, James, *Steam Navigation*, pub. William Briggs, Toronto, 1898; Facs. Ed. pub. Coles Publishing Co., Toronto, 1973; *p. 10 l.5*—PANS, MG3 Vol. 367, *Minutes*, Halifax Steamboat Co., 1815-1836; *p.10 l.71*—Akins, Dr. T. B. *History of Halifax City*, pub. N.S. Historical Society, 1895; Facs. Ed., pub Mika Publishing, Belleville, Ont., 1973.

CHAPTER IV
Page 19, line 12—D.H.M., original correspondence; *p.19 l.27*—D.H.M. original deed; *p.19 l.42*— *Acadian Recorder*, October 5, 1816; *p.19 l.68*—PANS, MG3, Vol. 367, *Minutes*, Halifax Steam Boat Co., August 26, 1816; *p.19 l.77*—Akins, Dr. T. B., *History of Halifax City*, p. 168, Mika Ed.

CHAPTER V
Page 21, line 26—Akins, Dr. T. B., op. cit., p. 168; *p.21 l.48*—PANS *Journal of the House of Assembly*, February 26, 1818, p. 33; *p.21 l. 73*—Schult, Joachim., *Curious Boating Inventions*, Paul Elek, London, 1974; *p.22 l.4*—*Acadian Recorder*, "Occasional" Column, March 24, 1917; *p.22 l.12*—PANS, MG3, Vol. 367, Halifax Steam Boat Company, *Minutes*, September 1818; *p.23 l.40*—Akins, Dr. T. B., op. cit., p. 189; *p.24 l.28*—Croil, James, *Steam Navigation*, originally published by William Briggs, Toronto. 1898. Facsimile edition, Coles Publishing Co. Toronto, 1973; *p.25 l.14*—PANS, RG5, Series P, Vol. 119, Halifax Steam Boat Company, *Assembly Petition*, February 1820; *p.25 l.23*—*Evening Mail*, October 16, 1897; *p.25 l.32*—Akins, Dr. T. B., op. cit., p. 168.

CHAPTER VI
Page 26, line 10—PANS, MG3 Vol. 367, Halifax Steam Boat Company, *Minutes*, March 1821, et seq.; *p.28 l.32*—Original Letters, DHM; *p.28 l. 51*—Martin, Dr. J. P., op. cit. p. 212; *p.28 l. 57*—Original Documents, DHM; *p.29 l. 55*—PANS, MG3 Vol. 367, Halifax Steam Boat Company, *Minutes*, September 21, 1829; *p.29 l.63*—*Novascotian*, September 3o, 1830; *p.30 l.23*—*Novascotian*, August 17, 1831; *p.30 l.42*—Martin, Dr. J. P. op. cit. p. 193; *p.30 l.64*—*The Mirror*, August 1,

1848.

CHAPTER VII
Page 32, line 29—PANS, MG3, Vol. 367, *Minutes,* Halifax Steam Boat Co., May 1828; *p.32 l.37*—PANS, MG3, Vol. 367,*Minutes,* Halifax Steam Boat Company, August 1828; *p.34 l.17*—Croil, James, op. cit. p. 56; *p.34 l.36*—N.S. Statues, Cap. XLVII, 1829; *p.34 l.78*—D.H.M., original document; *p.35 l.28*—D.H.M., original document; *p.35 l.64*—*Novascotian,* June 4, 1829; *p.37 l.4*—*Nova Scotia Royal Gazette,* January 13, 1830; *p.37 l.50*—*Nova Scotia Royal Gazette,* January 13, 1830; *p.37 l.59*—*Nova Scotia Royal Gazette,* June 9, 1830.

CHAPTER VIII
Page 38, line 33—*Nova Scotia Royal Gazette,* January 6, 1830; *p.40 l.6*—*Acadian Recorder,* February 2, 1918; *p.40 l.21*—*Nova Scotia Royal Gazette,* January 2, 1830; *p.41 l.7*—*Nova Scotia Royal Gazette,* January 13, 1830; *p.41 l.23*—Martin, Dr. J. P. *The Story of Dartmouth,* p. 221; *p.41 l.33*—*Novascotian,* January 6, 1830; *p.41 l.56*—*Acadian Recorder,* February 2, 1918; *p.41 l.53*—*Acadian Recorder,* February 6, 1830; *p.41 l.55*—*Nova Scotia Royal Gazette,* February 3, 1830; *p.41 l.73*—*Nova Scotia Royal Gazette,* February 17, 1830; *p.41 l.78*—*Acadian Recorder,* February 20, 1830; *p.42 l.13*—PANS, MG3 Vol. 367, Halifax Steam Boat Company *Minutes,* various, 1830; *p.42 l.22*—*Acadian Recorder,* May 12, 1831; *p.42 l.52*—PANS, MG3 Vol. 367, Halifax Steam Boat Company *Minutes,* June 1833; *p42 l.81*—Martin, Dr. J. P., *The Story of Dartmouth,* p. 194; *p.43 l.20*—*Acadian Recorder,* February 20, 1830; *p.43 l.24*—*Novascotian,* February 18, 1830; *p.43 l.31*—*Acadian Recorder,* August 28, 1830; *p. 43 l.44*—*Novascotian,* January 6, 1830; *p.43 l.54*—Vide ref. (1), Chapter IV.

CHAPTER IX
Page 44, line 13—PANS, MG3 Vol. 367; Halifax Steam Boat Company *Minutes,* January 20, 1830; *p.44 l.24*—idem, April 29, 1830; *p.44 l.26*—idem; *p.46 l.2*—idem, January 14, 1830; *p.46 l.19*—idem, April 29, 1830; *p.46 l.50*—idem, May 18, 1830; *p.46 l.53*—*Novascotian,* April 7, 1830; *p.46 l.65*—Martin, Dr. J. P., *The Story of Dartmouth,* p. 171; *p.47 l.1*—NSHS, Collections, Vol. XXXIV, Jefferson, H.B., *Mount Rundell, Stellarton and Albion Railway of 1839;* *p.47 l.3*—Lawson, Mrs. William, *Townships of Dartmouth, Preston and Lawrencetown,* footnote, p. 53, Mika Ed.; *p.47 l.6*—*Novascotian,* May 5, 1830; *p.47 l.18*—PANS, MG3 Vol. 367; Halifax Steam Boat Company *Minutes,* October 12, 1830; *p.48 l.22*—idem, March 7, 1831; *p.48 l.27*—idem, May 17, 1831; *p.48 l.53*—idem June and July, 1831; *p.48 l.57*—idem. August 1831; *p.48 l.72*—Croil, James, *Steam Navigation,* p. 56; *p.48 l.75*—Wood, William, *The Record-Making ROYAL WILLIAM Canadian Geographical Journal,* Vol. 7, No. 2, August 1933, pp. 52-63; *p.50 l.53*—PANS, MG3 Vol. 368; Halifax Steam Boat Company *Minutes,* February 4, 1836.

CHAPTER X
Page 53, line 17—D.H.M. original document; *p.53 l.34*—*Nova Scotia Royal Gazette,* February 21, 1838; *p.54 l.4*—D.H.M., original document; *p.54 l.22*—*Novascotian,* July 23, 1829; *p.54 l.43*—*Dartmouth Patriot,* June 14, 1902; *p.54 l.75*—*Novascotian,* August 20, 1840; *p.55 l.6*—Croil, James, *Steam Navigation,* Mika Ed., p. 71; *p.55 l.29*—PANS, MG3—368, *Minutes,* Halifax Steam Boat Company, August 26, 1839; *p.55 l.37*—Raddall, Thomas, *Halifax Warden of the North,* p. 191; *p.55 l.53*—*Novascotian,* July 23, 1840; *p.55 l.55*—*Novascotian,* July 30, 1840; *p.56 l.12*—*Novascotian,* 1840; *p.56 l.33*—D.H.M., original document.

CHAPTER XI
Page 57, line 12—PANS, MG3-368, *Minutes,* Halifax Steam Boat Company, April 17, 1840; *p.58 l.52*—D.H.M., original document; *p.60 l.10*—D.H.M., original document; *p.60 l.15*—D.H.M. original document; *p.60 l.21*—Glasgow Art Gallery and Museum—*Ship Models,* p. 39; *p.60 l.56*—Martin, Dr. J. P., *The Story of Dartmouth,* p. 256; *p.60 l.61*—*Morning Chronicle,* February 2, 1844; *p.60 l.66*—*Morning Chronicle,* March 15, 1844; *p.60 l.75*—Martin, Dr. J. P., *The Story of Dartmouth,* p. 277; *p.62 l.37*—Rolt, L. T. C., *Victorian Engineering,* Allen Lane, The Penguin Press, 1970; *p.62 l.51*—*Acadian Recorder,* June 21, 1845; *p.62 l.59*—*Acadian Recorder,* June 21, 1845; *p.62 l.63*—*Acadian Recorder,* July 22, 1845.

CHAPTER XII
Page 63, line 34—D.H.M., *Minutes,* Halifax Steamboat Company, November 2, 1880; *p.64 l.25*—*Acadian Recorder,* May 6, 1848; *p.65 l.6*—*Acadian Recorder,* May 6, 1848; *p.65 l.49*—*Acadian Recorder,* several, summer 1850; *p.65 l.55*—*The Mirror,* June 13, 1848; *p.66 l.2*—*Columbia Encyclopaedia,* 2nd Ed. Columbia University Press, 1950; *p.66 l.7*—*Acadian Recorder,* October 12, 1850; *p.66 l.13*—*Acadian Recorder,* November 23, 1850; *p.67 l.13*—D.H.M., Agent's Report, February 10, 1851; *p.67 l.30*—*Acadian Recorder,* February 15, 1851; *p.67 l.49*—D.H.M., Agent's Report, December 31, 1853; *p.67 l.64*—D.H.M., Agent's Report, December 31, 1856.

CHAPTER XIII
Page 68, line 13—*Halifax Sun,* December 24, 1850; *p.70 l.12*—Blakeley, Dr. Phyllis R., *Glimpses of Halifax,* p. 145; *p.70 l.30*—D.H.M., Agent's Report, December 31, 1854; *p.70 l.42*—D.H.M., Agent's Report, December 31, 1855; *p.70 l.61*—*Halifax Sun,* February 8, 1855; *p.70 l.66*—*Halifax Sun,* February 14, 1855; *p.70 l.75*—D.H.M., Agent's Report, December 31, 1853; *p.71 l.7*—D.H.M., Agent's Report, December 31, 1856; *p.72 l.49*—D.H.M., Agent's Reports, as dated; *p.72 l.68*—PANS, MG3-368, *Minutes,* Halifax Steam Boat Company, December 4, 1861.

CHAPTER XIV
Page 73, line 24—*Acadian Recorder,* July 14, 28, August 4, 1860; *p.74 l.8*—*Acadian Recorder,* July 7, August 25, 1860; *p.74 l.21*—*Acadian Recorder,* August 25, 1860; *p.74 l.50*—*Acadian Recorder,* August 3, 1864; *p.74 l.70*—*Novascotian,* September 30, 1867; *p.76 l.6*—*Acadian Recorder,* August 13, 1864; *p.76 l.32*—*Acadian Recorder,* May 8, 1865; *p.76 l.36*—*Morning Chronicle,* November 2, 1872; *p.76 l.43*—*Herald,* September 28, 1907; *p.76 l.48*—*Mail,* October 16, 1897; *p.76 l.51*—Lawson, Mrs. William, *History of the Townships of Dartmouth,* etc., Ed. note, p. 54; *p.76 l.57*—D.H.M., Agent's Report, 1863; *p.76 l.69*—*Acadian Recorder,* January 25, 1865; *p.76 l.73*—*Acadian Recorder,* May 8, 1865; *p.76 l.79*—*Acadian Recorder,* September 2, 1922; *p.78 l.4*—Martin, Dr. J. P., *The Story of Dartmouth,* p. 392; *p.78 l.6*—*British Colonist,* March 4, 1872; *p.78 l.18*—D.H.M., *Minutes,* 1874; *p.79 l.12*—*Acadian Recorder,* March 25, 1848; *p.79 l.16*—*Acadian Recorder,* August 27, 1864; *p.79 l.22*—*British Colonist,* February 25, 1871; *p.79 l.34*—*Chronicle,* January 28, 1876 (and *Minutes*); *p.79 l.70*—*Acadian Recorder,* December 18, 1872; *p.80 l.9*—*Acadian Recorder,* August 13, 1873; *p.80 l.12*—D.H.M., *Minutes,* December 7, 1875; *p.80 l.22*—*Acadian Recorder,* December 13 & 18, 1875; *p.80 l.36*—*Chronicle,* July 22, 1881; *p.80 l.64*—*Royal Nova Scotia Gazette,* November 30, 1831; *p.81 l.8*—*Acadian Recorder,* June 5, 1865; *p.81 l.35*—D.H.M., *Minutes,* April 15, 1873; *p.81 l.42*—*Acadian Recorder,* May 14, 1870; *p.81 l.47*—*Acadian Recorder,* June 23, 1870; *p.81 l.52*—*Chronicle,* July 6, 1881.

CHAPTER XV
(In addition to specific references, most of the substance of this chapter was derived from the Company minutes.) *Page 82, line 33*—*Novascotian,* March 13, 1828; *p.83 l.8*—*Nova Scotia Medical Bulletin,* February 1948, Vol. 27, No. 12, p. 56; *p.83 l.14*—PANS, MG3-367 &368, *Minutes,* Halifax Steam Boat Company; *p.83 l.44*—Parker, William Frederick, *Daniel McNeill Parker, M.D., His Ancestry and a Memoir of His Life,* pub. William Briggs, Toronto, 1910; *p.84 l.22*—*Herald,* September 24, 1878; *p.84 l.64*—PANS, RG 32 "C" Box 340; *p.85 l.19*—Various accounts: *Herald,* January 25, January 28, 1881 and *Chronicle,* January 25, January 31, April 4, 1881; *p.85 l.29*—D.H.M., *Minutes,* December 2, 1879; *p.86 l.8*—*Chronicle,* December 24, 1886; *p.86 l.20*—Martin, Dr. J. P., *The Story of Dartmouth,* p.367; *p.87 l.76*—D.H.M., *Minutes,* 1885; *p.88 l.6*—*Herald,* September 28, 1907; *p.88 l.12*—D.H.M., *Minutes,* March 4, 1879; *p.88 l.20*—D.H.M., *Minutes,* December 2, 1879.

CHAPTER XVI
(In this chapter also, much of the substance was derived from the Company minutes.) *Page 89, line 33*—D.H.M., *Minutes,* June 3, 1884; *p.90 l.14*—D.H.M., *Minutes,* June 5, 1883; *p.90 l.21*—D.H.M., *Minutes,* August 5, 1884; *p.91 l.21*—D.H.M., *Minutes,* April 2, 1884; *p. 91 l.30*—Lawson, Mrs. William, *History of the Townships of Dartmouth, etc.,* pp. 123 &124; *p.91 l.35*—*Herald,* February 6, 1886; *p.91 l.51*—D.H.M., Original Document, Acc. No. 69.80.13; *p.91 l.52*—D.H.M., *Minutes,* March 2, 1875; *p.92 l.12*—D.H.M., *Minutes,* June 24, 1881; *p.92 l.14*—Blakeley, Dr. Phyllis, *Glimpses of Halifax,* p. 35; *p.92 l.23*—D.H.M., *Minutes,* July 4, 1882; *p.92 l.39*—*Acadian Recorder,* January 8, 1886; *p.93 l.24*—*Herald,*

February 11, 1886; *p.94 l.10*—D.H.M., *Minutes*, April 10, 1886; *p.94 l.21*—Parker, William Frederick, *Daniel McNeill Parker, M.D., His Ancestry and a Memoir of His Life,* pub. William Briggs, Toronto, 1910; *p.94 l.53*—Charles E. Creighton, *Reminiscences of Charles E. Creighton in His 86th Year as Told to his Daughter Helen, in 1942.* (Typewritten note in author's collection of related documents.)

CHAPTER XVII
Page 95, line 26—*Acadian Recorder,* January 30, 1886; *p.96 l.41*—*Herald,* July 24, 1886; *p.96 l.53*—*Yarmouth Herald,* May 9, 1888; *p.98 l.19*—*Yarmouth Herald,* May 9, 1888; *p.98 l.21*—*Chronicle,* May 15, 1888; *p.98 l.34*—*Yarmouth Herald,* May 30, 1888; *p.98 l.40*—*Herald,* June 14, 1888; *p.99 l.4*—Charles E. Creighton, *Reminiscences of Charles E. Creighton in his 86th Year as Told to his Daughter Helen, in 1942.* (Typewritten note in Authors' collection of related documents.); *p.99 l.10*—*Chronicle,* June 14 and 16, 1888; *p.99 l.14*—*Chronicle,* June 16, 1888; *p.99 l.22*—*Herald,* June 18, 1888; *p.99 l.26*—*Acadian Recorder,* June 20, 1888; *p.99 l.38*—*Novascotian,* August 10, 1889; *p.100 l.3*—Russell, Benjamin, *Autobiography,* p. 227 Royal Print & Litho, Halifax, N.S. 1932; *p.100 l.19*—PANS, MG3 Vol. 368, *Minutes,* Halifax Steam Boat Company.

CHAPTER XVIII
Page 101, line 11—*Herald,* January 22, 1890; *p.101 l.24*—*Herald,* February 11, 1890; *p.102 l.4*—*Chronicle,* March 7, 1890; *p.102 l.12*—*Chronicle,* March 7, 1890; *p.102 l.14*—*Herald,* March 19, 1890; *p.102 l.26*—*Chronicle,* March 28, 1890; *p.102 l.30*—*Chronicle,* March 29, 1890; *p.102 l.34*—Russell, Benjamin, *Autobiography,* p. 230; *p.103 l.5*—*Herald,* March 29, 1890; *p.103 l.8*—*Herald,* March 29, 1890; *p.103 l.18*—*Chronicle,* March 31, 1890; *p.104 l.3*—*Chronicle,* June 11, 1888; *p.104 l.15*—*Chronicle,* March 31, 1890; *Reminiscences of Charles E. Creighton*—vide ref. p. 99 line 4; *p.104 l.34*—*Chronicle,* April 1, 1890; *p.104 l.58*—*Chronicle,* April 4, 1890; *p.104 l.60*—*Chronicle,* April 11, 1890; *p.104 l.72*—*Chronicle,* April 4, 1890; *p.105 l.3*—*Chronicle,* April 8, 1890; *p.105 l.6*—*Herald,* April 15, 1890; *p.105 l.35*—*Chronicle,* April 24, 1890; *p.105 l.37*— Russell, Benjamin, *Autobiography,* p. 229-230; *p.106 l.6*—D.H.M., *Minutes,* April 24, 1890.

CHAPTER XIX
Page 109, line 8—*Herald,* July 11, 1890; *p.109 l.28*—*Herald,* July 12, 1890; *p.110 l.21*—*Mail,* July 12, 1890; *p.110 l.36*—*Chronicle,* July 12, 1890; *p.110, l.78*—*Mail,* July 12, 1890; *p.112 l.25*—*Acadian Recorder,* July 14, 1890 (ex *Saint John Gazette*]; *p.112 l.48*—*Acadian Recorder,* July 14, 1890 (ex *Saint John Sun*]; *p.112 l.51*—*Acadian Recorder,* July 14, 1890 (ex *Quebec Chronicle*]; *p.112 l.54*—*Acadian Recorder,* July 14, 1890 (ex *Boston Globe*].

CHAPTER XX
Page 113, line 20—*Atlantic Weekly,* April 15, 1893; *p.114 l.14*—*Acadian Recorder,* January 30, 1893; *p.114 l.22*—D.H.M., *Minutes,* June 30, July 24, 1890; *p.114 l.61*—*Atlantic Weekly,* April 22, 1893; *p.116 l.5*—*Acadian Recorder,* February 29, 1892; *p.116 l.14*—*Atlantic Weekly,* February 17, 1894; *p.116 l.26*—*Acadian Recorder,* January 23, 1893; *p.116 l.35*—*Atlantic Weekly,* February 17, 1894; *p.116 l.38*—*Acadian Recorder,* February 6, 1893; *p.116 l.50*—*Atlantic Weekly,* April 15, 1893; *p.116 l.69*—*Atlantic Weekly,* June 10, 1893; *p.116 l.77*—D.H.M., *Minutes,* June 16, 1893; *p.116 l.78*—*Atlantic Weekly,* June 24, 1893; *p.116 l.80*—D.H.M., *Minutes,* February 11, 1895; *p.118 l.9*—*Atlantic Weekly,* March 31, 1894; *p.118 l.16*—*Atlantic Weekly,* June 24, 1893; *p.118 l.20*—D.H.M. *Minutes,* July 3, 1893; *p.118 l.29*—D.H.M., *Minutes,* November 9, 1891; *p.118 l.31*—D.H.M., *Minutes,* February 19, 1892; *p.118 l.44*—Martin, Dr. J. P., *The Story of Dartmouth,* p. 53; *p.118 l.50*—*Acadian Recorder,* January 15, 1886; *p.118 l.64*—*Acadian Recorder,* January 2, 1892; *p.118 l.71*—Martin, Dr. J. P., *The Story of Dartmouth,* p.54; *p.119 l.5*—*Atlantic Weekly,* May 27, 1893; *p.119 l.20*—*Atlantic Weekly,* August 26, 1893; *p.119 l.36*—*Atlantic Weekly,* May 20, 1893; *p.119 l.61*—*Atlantic Weekly,* August 14, 1897.

CHAPTER XXI
Page 120, line 23—D.H.M., 77.48.69, Correspondence Book, p. 316; *p.120 l.30*—D.H.M., Ferry Display *p.121 l.4*—*Atlantic Weekly,* October 17, 1896; *p.121 l.7*—D.H.M., *Minutes,* November 16, 1896; *p.121 l.14*—*The Engineer,* October 8, 1897; *p.121 l.27*—D.H.M., 77.48.69, Correspondence Book, p. 320; *p.121 l.38*—*The Marine Engineer,* December 1, 1897; *p.122 l.7*—D.H.M., *Minutes,* June 14 1897; *p.122 l.11*—*Atlantic Weekly,* August 7, 1897; *p.123 l.72*—*The Glasgow Herald,* August 13, 1897; *p.124 l.29*—*Atlantic Weekly,* Feb. 8, 1898; *p.126 l.9*—*Atlantic Weekly,* July 23, 1898; *p.127 l.8*—*Atlantic Weekly,* August 6, 1898; *p.127 l.31*—*Atlantic Weekly,* September 10, 1898.

CHAPTER XXII
(Most of the material for this chapter, if not specifically referenced, was derived from the Dartmouth Ferry Commission minutes of meetings.)
Page 129, line 16—D.H.M., *Minutes,* December 12, 1904, and March 5, 1906; *p.129 l.39*—*The Evening Mail,* September 12, 1911; *p.129 l.42*—D.H.M., *Minutes,* January 15, 1912; *p.129 l.55*—D.H.M., *Minutes,* November 10, 1913; *p.133 l.3*—D.H.M., *Log Book,* Chief Engineer Murray.

CHAPTER XXIII
Page 136, line 8—*Atlantic Weekly,* December 15, 1900;*p. 136 l.11*—*Dartmouth Patriot,* December 18, 1909; *p. 137 l. 44*—*Marine Engineer and Naval Architect,* August 11, 1911; *p. 137 l. 44*—*Chronicle,* September 11, 1911; *p. 137 l. 65*—*Marine Engineer and Naval Architect,* August, 11, 1911; *p. 139 l. 39*—*Chronicle,* September 11, 1911; *p. 139 l. 43*—*Dartmouth Patriot,* September 2, 1911; *p. 139 l. 50*—*The Evening Mail,* September 20, 1911; *p. 139 l. 54*—*Dartmouth Patriot,* September 2, 1911; *p. 139 l.*

70—*Dartmouth Patriot,* November 15, 1913.

CHAPTER XXIV
Page 142, line 4—*The Evening Mail,* June 25, 1908; *p.142 l.17*—D.H.M., *Minutes,* September 11, 1911; *p.142 l.22*—D.H.M., *Minutes,* December 11, 1911; *p.142 l.32*—*Acadian Recorder,* May 17, 1912; *p.142 l.56*—*Halifax Mail,* December 12, 1946; *p.142 l.60*—D.H.M., *Minutes,* July 8, 1912; *p.142 l.72*—*The Evening Mail,* June 27, 1908; *p143 l.7*—D.H.M., Correspondence, August 15, 1916; *p.143 l.22*—D.H.M., *Minutes,* March 8, 1915; *p.143 l.39*—*Acadian Recorder,* August 26, 1915; *p.143 l.51*—*Acadian Recorder,* September 7, 1915; *p.143 l.52*—D.H.M., *Log Book,* Chief Engineer Pearce; *p.143 l.74*—D.H.M., *Minutes,* March 20, 1916; *p.144 l.3*—Oral Reminiscences, Mrs. R. H. Murray, 1977; *p.144 l.39*—*The Evening Mail,* September 9, 1916; *p.144 l.46*—D.H.M., *Log Book,* Chief Engineer Pearce; *p.147 l.27*—D.H.M., *Minutes,* March 1918.

CHAPTER XXV
Page 148, line 6—D.H.M., *Minutes,* October 2, 1918; *p.148 l.8*—D.H.M. *Minutes,* September 9, 1918; *p.148 l.10*—Martin, Dr. J.P., *The Story of Dartmouth,* p. 524; *p.149 l.3*—*Acadian Recorder,* December 11, 1918; *p.149 l.22*—D.H.M., *Minutes,* March 10, 1919; *p.149 l.49*—*Acadian Recorder,* October 15, 1926; *p.150 l.47*—D.H.M., *Minutes,* November 23, 1917; *p.150 l.56*—D.H.M., *Minutes,* September 11, 1916; *p.150 l.59*—*Halifax Mail,* September 12, 1916; *p.150 l.61*—*Halifax Mail,* September 13, 1916;*p150. l.70*—D.H.M., *Minutes,* June 11, 1918; *p.151 l.19*—D.H.M., *Minutes,* January 11, 1926; *p. 151 l.32*—D.H.M. *Minutes,* April 8, 1918;*p.151 l.36*—D.H.M. *Minutes,* March 12, 1925;*p.151 l.40*—D.H.M. *Minutes,* November 24, 1926; *p.151 l.49*—D.H.M. *Minutes,* April 9, 1928; *p.151 l.75*—D.H.M. *Minutes,* November 13, 1928; *p152. l.2*—D.H.M., Correspondence, July 3, 1930;*p.152 l.13*—D.H.M. *Minutes,* December 8, 1930; *p153 l.2*—D.H.M. *Minutes,* May 11, 1936; *P.153 l.12*—D.H.M., *Log Book,* Superintendent Randall, entries as dated; *p153 l.25*—D.H.M., *Minutes,* February 11, 1920; *p.153 l.34*—D.H.M., Pettipas papers, L. H. Wheaton report as quoted in Pettipas et al report entitled, "Halifax-Dartmouth Harbour Bridge," dated February 27, 1945; *p.153 l.41*—Nova Scotia statutes, Cap. CXLIII, 1928;*p.153 l.65*—D.H.M., *Minutes,* November 16, 1930; *p.153 l.73*—*Halifax Mail,* March 7, 1932; *p.154 l.5*—D.H.M. *Minutes,* March 4, 1932; *p.154 l.14*—*Halifax Mail,* November 30, 1933; *p.154 l.29*—*Port and Province,* January 1934, Article, *Friendly Old Ferry Builds Profit and Population for the Town,* by H. M. Hatt; *p.154 l.42*—D.H.M. *Minutes,* April 9, 1934.

CHAPTER XXVI
Page 156, line 54—*Canadian Railway and Marine World,* December 1934, article, "Passenger and Vehicular Ferry for Dartmouth Ferry Commission," p. 553; *p.157 l.79*—*Halifax Mail,* December 2, 1935; *p.158 l.10*—*The Mail-Star,* January 2, 1964; *p.158 l.43*—D.H.M., *Log Book,* (Engineer's), December 20, 1934;

p.158 l.46—D.H.M. *Log Book*, C. E. Pearce, November 27, 1938; *p.158 l.59*—D.H.M. *Minutes*, December 17, 1938; *p.159 l.5*—D.H.M. *Log Book*, C. E. Pearce, June 15, 1936; *p.160 l.3*—Unidentified newspaper clippings, ca. August 5, 1939; *p.160 l.29*—D.H.M., *Minutes*, May 11, 1936; *p.160 l.72*—D.H.M. *Log Book*, C. E. Pearce, August 27, 1939.

CHAPTER XXVII
Page 163, line 23—*Halifax Mail*, July 18, 1940; *p.163 l.33*—*Halifax Mail*, January 3, 1942; *p.165 l.55*—*Halifax Mail*, August 1941; *p.166 l.60*—*Halifax Mail*, November 20, 1941; *p.170 l.11*—D.H.M. *Fire Report No. 2430*, Department of Labour, Fire Marshall Branch, January 19, 1945.

CHAPTER XXVIII
Page 172, line 3—PANS, J 104. 46, *Acts of Nova Scotia*, 1944, CAP. 56; *p.172 l.15*—D.H.M., *Minutes*, August 22, 1944; *p.172 l.33*—D.H.M. *Minutes*, April 14, 1947; *p.172 l.36*—D.H.M. *Minutes*, June 11, 1956; *P.175 l.19*—Kellock, Hon. Mr. Justice R. L., *Report on the Halifax Disorders*, May 7th-8th, 1945; *p.175 l.32*—D.H.M., *Log Book*, C. E. Pearce; *p.175 l.54*—D.H.M., *Minutes*, August 17, 1945; *p.175 l.66*—D.H.M., *Minutes*, September 19, 1945.

CHAPTER XXIX
Page 178, line 8—*Halifax Mail*, August 10, 1946; *p. 178 l. 31*—*Halifax Mail*, September 24, 1946; *p. 178 l. 33*—*Halifax Mail*, September 30, 1946; *p. 178 l. 33*—*Halifax Mail*, September 17, 1947; *p. 178 l. 35*—D.H.M., *Minutes*, August 8, 1949; *p. 178 l.42*—*Halifax Mail*, September 30, 1946; *p. 178 l 58*—*Halifax Mail*, October 21, 1946; *p.178 l. 58*—D.H.M., *Log Book*, R. T. Lynch, October 15, 19 and 20, 1946; *p. 178 l. 67*— D.H.M., *Minutes*, August 19, 1947; *p. 178 l. 79*—*Halifax Mail*, September 17, 1947; *p. 179 l.3*—*Halifax Mail*, October 15, 1947; *p. 147 l. 4*—D.H.M., *Monthly Report*, C. H. MacDonald, November 8, 1947; *p.179 l. 17*—*Halifax Mail*, September 10, 1946; *p. 179 l. 43*—D.H.M., *Monthly Report*, C. H. MacDonald, November 9, 1951; *p. 179 l. 46*—*Mail-Star*, September 11, 1956; *p. 180 l. 13*—*The Bicentenary of Dartmouth*, Booklet, 1950; *p. 180 l. 32*—D.H.M., *Log Book*, C. H. MacDonald, May 19, 1953; *p. 180 l. 43*— D.H.M., *Monthly Report*, C. H. MacDonald, January 18, 1949; *p. 180 l. 66*—*Mail-Star*, February 7, 1949; *p. 182 l. 5*—*Mail-Star*, August 17, 1949; *p. 183 l. 73*—D.H.M., *Minutes*, December 13, 1954.

CHAPTER XXX
Page 185, line 9—D.H.M. *Log Book*, Robert Armstrong, April 8, 1955; *p.185 l.43*—*Dartmouth Free Press*, May 5, 1955; *p.185 l.48*—*Dartmouth Free Press*, May 12, 1955; *p.185 l.72*—D.H.M. *Log Book*, Dalton Randall, June 23, 1955; *p.186 l.13*—*Dartmouth Free Press*, June 16, 1955; *p.186 l.21*—D.H.M. *Log Book*, Dalton Randall, August 9, 1955; *p.186 l.30*—*Halifax Mail*, December 24, 1946; *p.186 l.43*—*Dartmouth Free Press*, October 20, 1955; *p.186 l.63*—Cadieux, H. L. Griffiths, Garth, *Dogwood Fleet*; *p.186 l.75*—*Dartmouth Free Press*, July 21, 1955; *p.187 l.12*—*Dartmouth Free Press*, November 17, 1955; *p.188 l.18*—D.H.M. *Agreement*, Dartmouth Ferry Commission and Smith & Rhuland Ltd., December 1955; *p.188 l.21*—D.H.M. *Log Book*, Dalton Randall, December 19 and 30, 1955; *p.189 l.27*—*Mail Star*, May 15, 1957; *p.189 l.69*—Correspondence, ex *Minute* Book, December 9, 1957; *p.190 l.21*—PANS, J.104.1-16 *N.S. Laws* 1958.

CHAPTER XXXI
Page 194, line 17—PANS, RG 7, Vol. 137, Provincial Secretary Papers, *Petition for a Subsidy for a North Ferry*, August 6, 1907; *p.194 l.24*—Martin, Dr. J.P., *The Story of Dartmouth*, p. 383; *p.194 l.27*—*Dartmouth Free Press*, "70 Years Ago," June 2, 1955; *p.194 l.32*—*Dartmouth Free Press*, "70 Years Ago," May 3, 1956; *p.194 l.36*—*Chronicle*, July 6, 1881; *p.194 l.43*—*Herald*, May 11, 1897; *p.196 l.1*—*Mail-Star*, "Dartmouth Diary," Wm. McCall, March 31, 1978.

CHAPTER XXXII
Page 199, line 3—*Atlantic Weekly*, April 15, 1893; *p.199 l.40*—*Mail-Star*, December 23, 1963.

CHAPTER XXXIII
Page 201, line 16—*Mail-Star*, January 6, 1977; *p.202 l.13*—*Mail-Star*, 1976; *p.202 l.21*—*Mail-Star*, December 13, 1977; *p.203 l.2*—*Mail-Star*, December 12, 1977; *p.204 l.13*—*Barometer*, January 11, 1979.

Illustrations

Mrs. Raymond Adlington: 100, Atlantic Air Survey Ltd.: 103, Authors: 97, 102, 108, 110, 116, Bank of Nova Scotia: 8, L. G. Billard: 98, 109, City of Dartmouth: 115 Frederick Cole: 60, 66, Miss Isabel Creighton: 5, Dr. Helen Creighton: 51, Dartmouth Heritage Museum: 6, 9, 10, 15, 16, 19, 25, 31, 33, 35, 36, 37, 38, 39, 40, 43, 44, 46, 49, 50, 52, 53, 55, 58, 59, 61, 62, 63, 64, 67, 68, 70, 71, 72, 73, 75, 76, 77, 78, 79, 80, 81, 82, 83, 88, 91, 92, 93, 95, 99, 101, 111, Capt. C. Wesley, Dauphinee: 104, 105, 106, 107, Mrs. C. S. Duncan: 84, 86, Glasgow Museums and Art Galleries: 18, Halifax Herald Ltd.: 20, 89, 94, Nova Scotia Legislative Library: 57, 74, Nova Scotia Museum: 4, 14, 21, 28, 69, Mrs. C. H. MacDonald: 96, Mariners' Museum, Newport News: 26, Public Archives of Canada, Ottawa: Title Page (C-11202), 2(C-2554), 22(C-2419), 23(C-41907) 27, Public Archives of Nova Scotia: 1, 3, 7, 11, 13, 24, 29, 30, 32, 34, 41, 45, 47, 48, 65, 90, Alan R. Payzant: 112, 113, 114, William Peters: 85, United States Patent Office: 12, Capt. Cyril Urquhart: 87, Rev. Mr. Wilkinson: 54, Endpaper I: PANS, Endpaper II: Canadian Hydrographic Service.

Index

Bold numerals indicate an illustration of the subject mentioned.

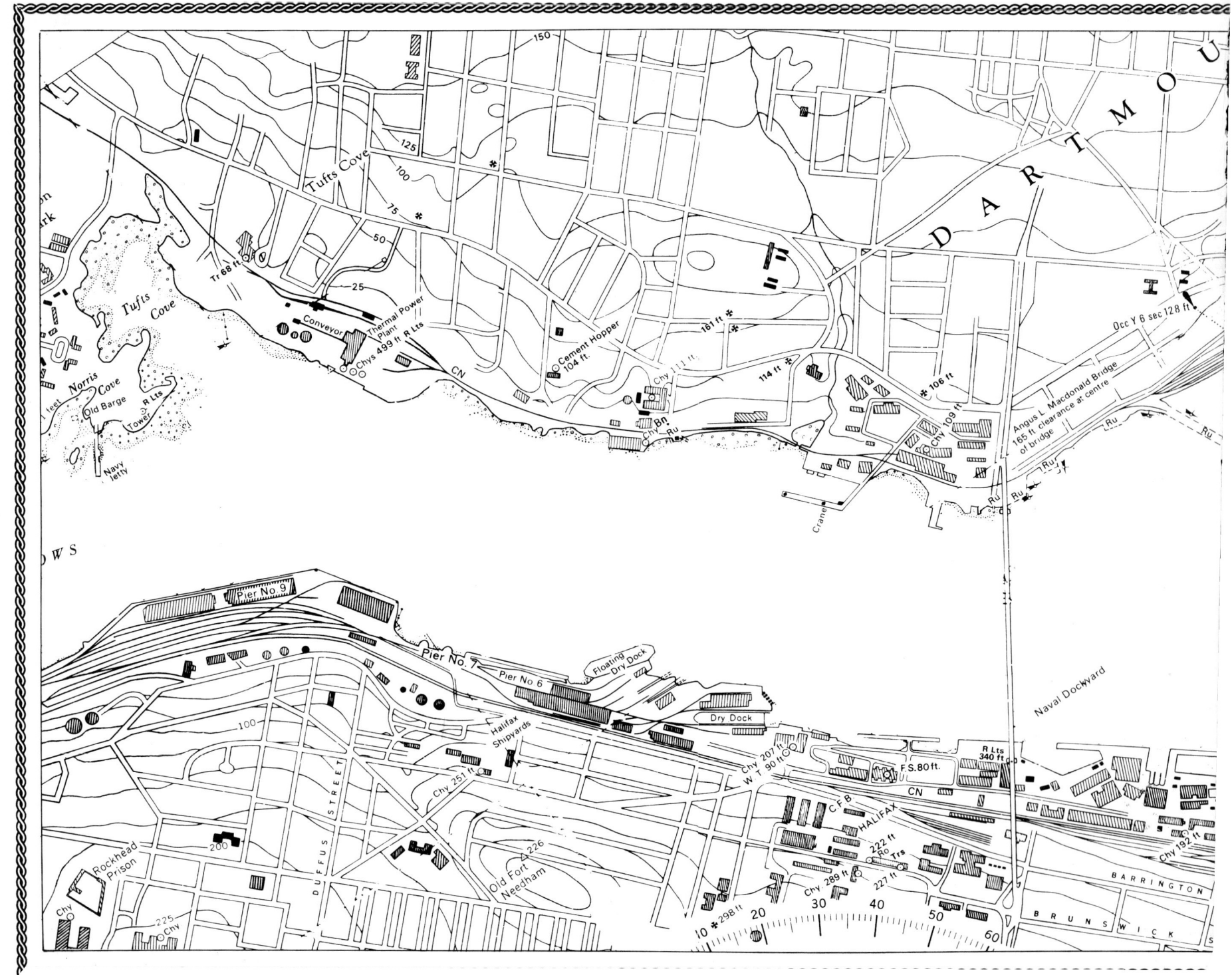